KABBALAH as LITERATURE

KABBALAH
as
LITERATURE

THE REVOLUTION OF
INTERPRETATION

GILAD ELBOM

FORTRESS PRESS
Minneapolis

KABBALAH AS LITERATURE
The Revolution of Interpretation

All translations from Hebrew and Aramaic, including the Hebrew Bible, are the author's.

29 28 27 26 25 24   1 2 3 4 5 6 7 8 9

Library of Congress Cataloging-in-Publication Data

Names: Elbom, Gilad, author.
Title: Kabbalah as literature : the revolution of interpretation / Gilad Elbom.
Description: Minneapolis, MN : Fortress Press, [2024] | Includes bibliographical references and index.
Identifiers: LCCN 2024000093 (print) | LCCN 2024000094 (ebook) | ISBN 9781506494883 (hardback) | ISBN 9781506494890 (ebook)
Subjects: LCSH: Cabala--History.
Classification: LCC BM526 .E438 2024 (print) | LCC BM526 (ebook) | DDC 296.1/6--dc23/eng/20240108
LC record available at https://lccn.loc.gov/2024000093
LC ebook record available at https://lccn.loc.gov/2024000094

Cover design: Laurie Ingram Art + Design.com
Cover image: Tzimtzum, watercolor painting by Emily Elbom

Print ISBN: 978-1-5064-9488-3
eBook ISBN: 978-1-5064-9489-0

CONTENTS

When I tell my religious friends that I am studying the Kabbalah, they often say, "On your own? Without a rabbi?" When I tell my secular friends that I am studying the Kabbalah, they often say, "Isn't it dangerous? Aren't you afraid of losing your mind?" When I tell my academic friends that I am studying the Kabbalah, they often say, "Ah, yes. Gershom Scholem. I've always wanted to read him." The truth is that I am not afraid. The human capacity to produce and understand infinitely multilayered texts means that the Kabbalah can be studied with or without an experienced rabbi, with or without the help of academic research, and, most decidedly, without fear. In other words, I do not feel the need to exchange the inherent ambiguities of the Kabbalah for the authority of an erudite explicator. In fact, it is precisely the ambiguities, uncertainties, and polyphonies of the Kabbalah that I find appealing: the ability to speak in question marks rather than exclamation points.

Ultimately, the responses of my friends reveal a mixture of reverence and suspicion that seems to obfuscate the fact that the Kabbalah is a collection of literary texts. In many cases, the Kabbalah is treated as paranormal territory: a formidable body of knowledge that can be accessed only with the assistance of a professional guide. This apprehensive outlook is highly reminiscent of a familiar, typically masculine, essentially colonialist narrative. Just as nature, according to this narrative, cannot be explored without a hatchet, a gun, or a camera, so does the Kabbalah remain impenetrable without an ordained expert who mediates between the reader and the raw material. Those who take it upon themselves to uncover the so-called mysteries of the Kabbalah tend to tackle the task in the same way that self-important adventurers might approach Africa, Arabia, India, or China: as an exotic continent, beautiful and bewitching, uncharted and untamed, seductive yet ominous, full of ancient secrets that will either grant curious visitors eternal wisdom or, if they are not careful, lead them to the brink of insanity.

From a psychoanalytic perspective, this view of the Kabbalah could be seen as a typical case of what Jung calls anima possession: an engulfing fascination with a woman, imaginary or real, on whom a man might project his own feminine side. More specifically, it could be argued that the Kabbalah reflects many of the repressed qualities that men are incapable of integrating into their conscious selves. If this is true, it is no wonder that the Kabbalah is commonly considered magical, illogical, dreamlike, erotic, capricious, potentially malicious, and altogether representative of a heightened awareness that is intuitive rather than scientific, associative rather than systematic, supernatural rather than rational. In this context, Gershom Scholem, the quintessential European scholar, is perceived as a modern hero. Armed with a twentieth-century academic education, he conquers the Kabbalah, domesticates it, and presents it to civilized audiences in the form of an intellectual discipline, which he labels *Jewish mysticism*. His successors, who promote this new discipline as the proper key to an otherwise restricted area, continue to control the ways in which the Kabbalah is displayed to the public. Their mission, it seems, is to repackage the Kabbalah in safer, more familiar terms and prevent it, so to speak, from betraying its allegedly wild roots.

This book offers a different approach. My own initial contact with the Kabbalah was entirely unmediated. I was at a bookstore in the city of Bnei Brak, east of Tel Aviv, searching for new editions of old midrashic texts: creative commentaries on biblical literature, often in the form of highly imaginative narrative expansions. I had visited several other stores earlier that day and, having bought two or three books at each of them, decided that this one would mark the end of my shopping spree. I was looking for one more book to buy. I felt that it would be a personal failure, not to mention an insult to the shopkeeper, if I left this last store empty-handed: a feeling with which many book lovers are probably familiar. Finally, having discovered nothing that excited me, I settled for a copy of Tikkunei Zohar. I had not read the Zohar itself, the quintessential Kabbalah book, nor had I heard of Tikkunei Zohar, its more daring companion. I was simply attracted to its bilingual design. Each page was split into two columns: the original Aramaic facing a Hebrew translation. I thought it would be a good opportunity to practice my Aramaic.

When I took it home, back to Oregon, and started reading it, the floodgates of the hermeneutical heavens opened. Never had I encountered such an innovative, virtuosic, delightfully experimental text: a masterpiece of avant-garde biblical interpretation. Impressed with the far-reaching literary, theological, and psychological vision of this thirteenth-century text, I bought other editions, some with elaborate commentaries by subsequent kabbalistic writers. When I realized that many of those commentaries were based on the sixteenth-century school of Isaac Luria, I bought the multivolume Lurianic corpus. The crystalline prose and revolutionary insights of Hayyim Vital, the principal articulator of Lurianic thought, were nothing short of eye-opening. Once again, the remarkable ingenuity of the Lurianic corpus encouraged me to seek similar texts. I spent the next few years reading equally inspiring kabbalistic thinkers, from the seventeenth century to the twentieth, most notably Moses Hayyim Luzzatto, Nachman of Breslov, Yehuda Fetaya, Abraham Isaac Kook, and Yehuda Ashlag. It was only later that I began to consult scholarly publications.

This book is an attempt to examine these seminal kabbalistic texts without exoticizing them, mystifying them, treating them as artifacts of the occult, or replacing them with secondary sources. Readers are invited, therefore, to suspend preconceived notions about the Kabbalah and observe the sophisticated interplay of its literary components: characters, settings, scenes, points of view, sequences of events, stylistic choices, and other devices that contribute to courageous retellings of biblical stories. Common to all these retellings is the desire to challenge existing narratives of power and domination. Gender hierarchies, personal identities, social interaction, human history, the structure of the divinity, and other key concepts are reimagined in unique, poetic, perfectly sensible ways. It is lamentable that kabbalistic literature, consisting of intricate linguistic exercises that demand considerable intellectual effort, is often reduced—or condescendingly elevated—to the realm of the nonverbal, the otherworldly, the inexpressible, or the unknowable. This book strives to rectify this anomaly.

All translations and paraphrases of Hebrew and Aramaic sources— biblical, rabbinic, and kabbalistic—are my own. In many cases, I felt that existing translations failed to capture the linguistic nuances of the text. In other cases, I was unsatisfied with the tendency of English renditions to rely too heavily on transliterations of difficult terms rather than aspire to arrive at accurate translations. Important kabbalistic texts from the twentieth and twenty-first centuries that have not been translated elsewhere are also represented here. I hope this book sheds light on crucial vessels, old and new.

ACKNOWLEDGMENTS ·

This book benefited greatly from the wisdom of my regular study partners: Chris Morrissey, with whom I have been studying semiotics, philosophy, and psychology; Rob Vanhoff, with whom I have been studying the Zohar and Tikkunei Zohar; Noam Krendel, with whom I have been studying Luria and Ashlag, especially the *Tree of Life* and the *Preamble to the Wisdom of the Kabbalah*; Moshe Rachmuth, with whom I have been studying biblical and rabbinic literature; Nina Henrichs-Tarasenkova, with whom I have been studying the New Testament and apocryphal literature; Brian Walter, who has read every word of the manuscript with meticulous scrutiny and scrupulous care; Stuart Stelzer, whose Christian perspective has enriched this book; and Chris Wells, whose profound understanding of literature and theology has been inspiring.

Numerous conversations with Sophie Ell, Giosuè Ghisalberti, Oz Shelach, Nirit Kurman, Lauryn Stanfield, and Sherrie Hoffmann have also contributed to the shaping of this book.

Special thanks to Carey Newman, executive editor of Fortress Press, whose faith in this project has served as a navigational beacon.

A thousand thanks to my wife, Emily Elbom, who has provided invaluable feedback at every stage of the writing process. Her insights on form and content broadened the scope of this book, sharpened its focus, and deepened its engagement with kabbalistic thought.

Excerpts from the first chapter were presented at the Pacific Northwest regional conferences of the American Academy of Religion and Society of Biblical Literature in 2022 and 2023. I am grateful to the members of the Hebrew Bible Research Group on Dress and the Theology and Philosophy of Religion Section for their comments and support.

ACKNOWLEDGMENTS

This book benefited greatly from the wisdom of my regular study partners: Chris Morrissey, with whom I have been studying semiotics, philosophy and psychology; Rob VanAcre, with whom I have been studying the Zohar and Tikkunei Zohar; Noam Kandel, with whom I have been studying Lurianic and Ashlag, especially the Tree of Life and the Preamble to the Rabow of the Arba'ah ha Shoshe Rachmuch, with whom I have been studying biblical and rabbinic literature; Nina Heendla Timascheova, with whom I have been studying the New Testament and apocryphal literature; Brian Walter, who has read every word of the manuscript with meticulous scrutiny and scrupulous care; Sean Stoker, whose Christian perspective has enriched this book; and Chris Wells, whose profound understanding of literature and theology has been inspiring.

Numerous conversations with Sophie Ell, Gisele Chiaiberti, Oz Sbelach, Nili Kurman, Lauryn Stanfield, and Sherrie Hoffmann have also contributed to the shaping of this book.

Special thanks to Carey Newman, executive editor of Fortress Press, whose faith in this project has served as a navigational beacon. A thousand thanks to my wife, Emily Elliott, who has provided invaluable feedback at every stage of the writing process. Her insights on form and content broadened the scope of this book, sharpened its focus, and deepened its engagement with kabbalistic thought.

Excerpts from the first chapter were presented at the Pacific Northwest regional conferences of the American Academy of Religion and Society of Biblical Literature in 2022 and 2023. I am grateful to the members of the Hebrew Bible Research Group on Dirt and the Theology and Philosophy of Religion Section for their comments and support.

The Garments of God

How Multiple Interpretations Cloak the Text

Semiotic Outfits

SOME OF THE most remarkable qualities of kabbalistic literature are the radical creativity, elegant ease, and surprising confidence with which it appropriates and rewrites biblical texts. As a hermeneutical platform, the Kabbalah employs an elaborate network of interrelated images, often referred to as symbols, designed to offer groundbreaking interpretations of familiar narratives. While it might be tempting to begin with a systematic review of kabbalistic symbols, two central concepts could serve as points of entry into the literary mechanisms, thematic concerns, and theological innovations of the Kabbalah: clothing, especially in its metaphorical sense, and the heavenly queen, also known as the Shekhinah. It would be interesting to examine these concepts in the context of an apocryphal narrative to which neither the rabbinic tradition nor kabbalistic thought has paid much attention: the book of Judith.

An interplay of narrative possibilities, the book of Judith tells the story of an attractive widow who, at some point, decides to replace her plain attire with eye-catching clothes. When she goes out to meet a famously dangerous man who holds a high position in the global administration of a voracious empire, the narrative becomes highly complicated. One possibility is that Judith, fascinated by the political and sexual appetite for which the man is notorious, wishes to end her period of mourning and explore the prospects of an erotic adventure with an intriguing, quintessentially virile, so-called larger-than-life bedfellow. Another possibility is that she is motivated primarily by self-preservation. Since the man, in his capacity as the commander of a large army, is about to attack her country, she hopes to entice him into sparing her life. Along these lines, it is also possible that she intends to help his military campaign. If the information she holds about her home country is deemed valuable by the man and his war machine, he might treat her as a strategic asset and guarantee her personal safety.

Yet another possibility is that she is dressed to kill. Rather than look after her own interests, she intends to serve her country and seduce the man in order to assassinate him. This, of course, would be a great personal risk, since she could very well be exposed as a spy. Even if her plot proved successful and she managed to eliminate the man, there is no guarantee that the enemy would abandon the plan to launch a military offensive against her people. Needless to say, there is also the possibility that she is a double agent. In that case, she is likely to present a cover story to her own people, playing the role of a daring operative whose mission is to remove an immediate national threat. She would ask to be accompanied by a personal assistant of her choosing: a trustworthy deputy who would help her accomplish the task. When she managed to establish her credibility as a self-sacrificing patriot and convince her people to allow her to embark on this undertaking, she would betray her country and offer her services to the enemy. And if her people are smart enough to suspect her, would they try to recruit her personal assistant as a counterintelligence agent?

In semiotic terms, her initial change of clothes is a sign: a vehicle that represents an object. In this case, the object is one of the above-mentioned narrative possibilities. Depending on the interpretive viewpoint that defines the relation between the signifying vehicle and its signified object, the narrative changes, sometimes drastically. In other words, the interpretive viewpoint allows signs and meanings to enter into dynamic relations. These relations continue to evolve and change as additional viewpoints enter the system. For example, the fact that Judith announces her plan to save the nation but might defect and help the enemy produces two narratives. Narrative A, originally the object represented by the signifying change of clothes, becomes itself a signifying element: a cover story whose signified object is narrative B. The fact that the reader is aware of the difference between narrative A and narrative B is a new interpretive viewpoint that produces narrative C. The fact that Holofernes, the commander of the army, is unaware of narrative C—the fact that he is oblivious to the tension between narrative A and narrative B—produces narrative D: the story of his failure to decode a sign and protect himself from the plot against his life. The idea of endless sign action—or infinite semiosis—is crucial to the continuous production of additional narratives. When the interplay of possibilities at the heart of the Judith narrative is analyzed in a scholarly setting, it becomes a new sign: a signifier that produces narrative E. When such an analysis, which could be called a metanarrative, assumes the form of an intertextual study, it becomes narrative F: a written documentation of a multifaceted attempt to grapple with the inherent complexity of a sign system. When such a study is quoted by a new one and examined, for example, in a different context—philosophical, theological, psychological—it becomes narrative G. And so on, *ad infinitum*.

In kabbalistic terms, these narrative possibilities are often called garments.[1] Each garment is a layer of interpretation that exposes the richness of the text and expands its meaning. In fact, the letters of the Hebrew alphabet are considered garments. They cloak the ineffable divinity and translate its impenetrable essence into human terms. The first text that the Hebrew alphabet produces is the four-letter divine name: the Tetragrammaton. And soon after, long before creation, the Hebrew letters produce another text: the Torah, the divine wisdom.[2] The vast industry of Jewish textuality—past, present, and future, including the Hebrew Bible and all its rabbinic commentaries, interpretations, and expansions—is perceived as a dress factory that clothes the divine wisdom in accessible narratives. God, according to this view, is experienced as a collection of textual relations.

Against the idea of authorial intent, this view of God promotes a multiplicity of readings as an inescapable feature of the biblical text. Just as a hammer breaks a rock into many pieces, so does this type of hermeneutics extract many interpretations from a single verse.[3] More specifically, this hermeneutics, commonly exercised by the Kabbalah, identifies four interdependent levels of meaning: contextual, allegorical, correlative, and anagogical. Another biblical episode that tells the story of a Jewish woman who, uninvited, approaches a powerful man in order to save her people could serve as a case study. The first level of interpretation, also referred to as plain or literal, would treat the dramatic encounter between Esther and the Persian king, dangerously initiated by the former, as a narrative-changing moment that communicates courage and commitment.[4] The second level of interpretation, also known as symbolic or metaphorical, would treat this scene as the timeless story of the everlasting bond between the Jewish nation and the king of kings.

In this case, Esther would be a signifier that stands for Israel, while Ahasuerus, perhaps surprisingly, would signify the Hebrew God.

The third level of interpretation, which often relies on numerological calculations and morphological parallels, would note, for example, the fact that the preposition *opposite* or *against*, which occurs twice in the opening verse that introduces this scene, is an acronym of the opening words of a common Jewish prayer: "The soul of every living thing."[5] In addition, the numerical value of this Hebrew preposition is seventy-eight, which equals three times twenty-six: the numerical value of the four-letter divine name.[6] These textual features, according to this level of interpretation, capture the essence of the biblical scene. Just as Esther approaches the king with a special request, so do the souls of the people approach God with daily supplications.

Uniquely kabbalistic, the fourth layer of interpretation attempts to ascend to the highest level of understanding. Esther and the king, according to this reading, are the male and female aspects of the divinity. In their capacity as the younger divine configurations in the supernal world of emanation, they are initially, unlike the other configurations, incomplete. Each of the divine configurations ultimately consists of ten parts, also known as ten emanations, ten attributes, ten measurements, or ten internal spheres: crown, wisdom, understanding, mercy, might, beauty, endurance, glory, foundation, and royalty.[7] The world of emanation itself, like the other supernal worlds, consists of ten larger spheres. The younger female divine configuration initially consists of one internal sphere, while the younger male divine configuration initially consists of six. The former—the heavenly queen, the Shekhinah, the sphere of royalty—is the lowest element in the world of emanation. She must approach her male counterpart, the penultimate element in the world of emanation, in order to receive her missing parts and become whole. Like the diminished moon, she has no light of her own.[8] Her tenth and last internal sphere—the royalty of royalty—is hidden in the head of Ancient of Days, the highest divine configuration, who dwells above the world of emanation. When she receives her hidden lights, which are considered her special garments, and acquires her last internal sphere, she rises to the top and shines as brightly as the sun.[9] This new narrative continues to absorb additional texts, revealing and enhancing the generative essence of biblical literature. A rejected rock that becomes a chief cornerstone, Esther is restored to a state of greatness and can now command Mordechai.[10] Now she represents the wife who surpasses her husband: the noble female who, in the world to come, will be the crown above the male.[11]

The ability of this hermeneutical system to suggest hitherto unrealized combinations of literary components produces new successions of imaginative textual expansions. Paradoxically, the harmonizing of disparate constituents is achieved through a true acknowledgment of clashing perspectives. Incorporating fresh, seemingly unrelated, often surprising elements, a vast network of continuous sign relations allows characters, events, images, points of view, and other literary devices to acquire advanced meanings. Some scholars refer to the dialogical nature of these hermeneutical principles in terms of semiotic complementarity, emphasizing the idea that conflict, contestation, and conversation are the building blocks of exegesis, and that a totality of textual potentialities is always greater than the sum of interpretive actualities.[12] Interpretation itself, according to this approach, is a complex sign that testifies to the ever-growing richness of narrative possibilities.

Other scholars discuss the tendency to impose a monolithic order on the polyphonic collage of biblical literature in sociopolitical terms.[13] Foreign to biblical literature, certitude—the notion of coherence, consistency, and closure—serves imperial regimes, capitalist ideologies, patriarchal structures, and other dominant powers. The critique of such powers is based on the observation that the God of the Hebrew Bible displays a wide range of emotional possibilities, as do the text and the self. These possibilities, which often manifest as a spectrum of extremities or a cacophony of claims, facilitate freedom, depth, vitality, flexibility, and transformation. Inescapably ambiguous, the Bible promotes an inexhaustible growth of interpretive avenues. In contrast, monopolistic systems flatten God and reduce the Bible to a single, unalterable, final truth. By doing so, they mask tension, silence alternatives, and suppress change.

The Life-Giving Queen

As its own system of intersecting narratives, the Kabbalah emphasizes, again and again, the centrality of the heavenly queen: the female aspect of the divinity. In keeping with the habiliment metaphor, the daily supplications with which the people approach the divinity are also considered garments. They contribute to the rectification of the Shekhinah, cloaking and adorning her. In addition, each of the divine configurations in the world of emanation cloaks the one directly below it. For example, while the head of Ancient of Days, which consists of his top three internal spheres, remains above the world of emanation, his body, consisting of his seven lower internal spheres, cloaks—that is, indwells or suffuses—the prime configuration in the world of emanation.[14] The latter, known as the patient one, cloaks the intermediate male and female configurations, also known as Father and Mother, who, in turn, cloak the younger male configuration, also known as the impatient one.[15] Usually identified with the traditional Hebrew deity of biblical and rabbinic literature, the younger male configuration cloaks his female counterpart: the heavenly queen, the Shekhinah.

Designated as female divine configurations, Mother and the Shekhinah correspond to the female divine attributes in the overarching ten-sphere structure: understanding and royalty. When royalty is in its usual place, at the bottom of the structure, she allows the lights of holiness to spread throughout the world of emanation. In this state, the four-letter divine name is complete. When royalty rises, as she sometimes does, and occupies the place of understanding, she leaves the lower half of the structure in the dark: a temporary void which the forces of impurity are likely to exploit.[16] In this state, the divine name is missing its last two letters.[17] Applied to the book of Esther, the lamentable nature of this situation is marked by the fact that Mordechai rends his clothes, while its rectification is signified by the royal robes that Mordechai wears when he is honored by the king.[18] The return of royalty to her usual spot repairs the supernal worlds and the physical realm, replaces darkness with light, reintroduces holiness into creation, and reveals the unity of the divine name.[19] A typically imaginative passage from Tikkunei Zohar, one of the quintessential texts of late medieval Kabbalah, envisions Esther, clad in priestly vestments, as the heavenly queen:[20]

> The Shekhinah is called the Day of Atonement. When she adorns herself with beautiful clothes and appears before God, she is called his rosette, his turban, his sash.[21] These clothes are vestments of atonement: four white vestments from the right

side and four golden vestments from the left.[22] It was then, when she adorned herself with these vestments of atonement, that it was said about her, "Esther wore royalty."[23] It was in these clothes that she entered the palace and appeared before the king, standing in the inner court.[24] It was in these clothes that she won his grace.[25] This moment marks the fulfillment of the following words of God: "I will look at her and remember the eternal covenant."[26] And then, immediately, God hears, forgives, listens, and takes action without delay.[27] She is also called the Feast of Lots,[28] named so after the Day of Atonement.[29] In the future, we will delight in that holiday, transforming it from pain to pleasure. While it is now forbidden to wear sandals on that day, which signifies the Shekhinah, in the future it will be said about her, "How beautiful are your feet in sandals, noble lady."[30] Delight, joy, and many good things will be her lot. This will happen soon, in the age of salvation.

Represented by Esther, the heavenly queen forms an intimate connection with the divine king in the world of emanation in order to save the Jewish nation from its human tormentors in the physical realm. What allows her to accomplish this task is the ability to harmonize two divine attributes: judgment and mercy. Her special garments come from both sides: the left and the right. The left side signifies judgment, while the right side stands for mercy.[31] This duality translates into the two alternating positions that the Shekhinah occupies in the world of emanation.[32] The primary position is marked by complete equality with her male counterpart. Her stature is identical to his, and they wear the same crown. In this position, they are both considered great lights: a return to an early stage of creation in which the size of the sun was equal to that of the moon, before the latter was diminished and designated as a lesser light.[33] In this position, the Shekhinah, normally the lowest element in the world of emanation, rises to a higher level and reaches the divine attribute of understanding, which serves as the crown that she shares with her male counterpart.

Accentuating the agility of the Shekhinah, this adventurous interpretation depicts her as a vital constituent that, despite its lowly status, can embody multiple divine attributes. The lights that emanate from the right side of understanding are lights of mercy. The lights that emanate

from the left side of understanding are lights of wisdom. Devoid of
mercy, the left lights are the ones that the Shekhinah receives. And since
wisdom cannot illuminate the lower elements without mercy, the lights
inside the Shekhinah freeze and turn into darkness. In that sense, she
resembles the moon. In order to illuminate the divine spheres below, she
must be diminished. She agrees to surrender her elevated position and
descend to her regular spot at the bottom of the world of emanation.
In that position, she receives her lights not directly from the sphere of
understanding but through her male counterpart, who is now above her.
And since her male counterpart is positioned in the middle, between
left and right, the wisdom that he gives her is mixed with mercy, which
allows her to shine.

The advantage of the primary position, according to this interpretation, is that the Shekhinah—the female sphere of royalty—receives
unmediated wisdom independently of her male counterpart, directly
from the other female sphere: understanding. The disadvantage is that
the lack of mercy prevents her from relaying the divine light that sustains the rest of creation. Dressed in white, she benefits from the pure
mercy that her male counterpart receives but cannot contain it on her
own or use it to assist others. When she descends to her lower position
and receives a mixture of wisdom and mercy, she is a queen dressed in
gold.[34] In that state, she receives mercy-infused wisdom in seven separate receptacles: seven vessels that serve as her maids. Representing her
lower internal spheres, these seven vessels are the virgin companions
who follow her.[35] It is then that she is able to help her dependents in the
physical realm, overturning harsh sentences, changing condemnation
into compassion, transforming affliction into benediction. After all,
given the inevitable transgressions of humanity, a constant stream of
mercy is necessary to sustain life on earth.

This elaborate narrative, as innovative as it may seem, could be
understood as an advanced development of rabbinic commentaries that
present Esther as a divine agent. Some of these commentaries note the
omission of the noun *robes*, *garments*, or *apparel* when Esther appears
before the king. According to the Talmud, when Esther wears royalty,
she is cloaked in a holy spirit.[36] In a similar manner, a holy spirit cloaks
Gideon when he prepares for the battle against the Midianites.[37] The
same spirit cloaks Amasai when he professes his loyalty to King David.[38]
It also cloaks Zechariah the priest when he chastises the wicked king

of Judah.[39] Naturally, these instances suggest that the royal robes that Esther wears are not necessarily literal. Idiomatically, Esther wears royalty in the sense that she acts like a responsible representative of the Jewish nation. More specifically, she assumes the role of a legitimate monarch, replacing the traditional image of a king.

From Object to Agent

In the context of an imaginative shift from male-dominated royal dynasties to a more inclusive notion of governance, Judith could be interpreted as an image of the Shekhinah. Advocating a more inclusive vision, the book of Judith is largely concerned with the exoneration of denigrated elements, among them the tribe of Simeon. While major rabbinic voices claim that all the tribes of Israel are represented in the book of Judges,[40] a different tradition suggests that judges and kings came from every tribe except Simeon.[41] Simeon, according to this tradition, is, first and foremost, a mass murderer. Unable to quench a vindictive thirst for blood, he plays an active role in the planning and execution of the despicable massacre in Shechem, for which he is castigated by his father.[42] What further paints his tribe in a disgraceful light, according to this rabbinic tradition, is the fact that the quintessential fornicator—Zimri, son of Salu—is identified as a Simeonite.[43] In a manner similar to the harsh words with which Jacob condemns Simeon, Moses excludes the tribe of Simeon from the blessings that he bestows on the children of Israel.[44]

Promoting biblical revisionism, the book of Judith offers a resounding counterargument to the vilification of Simeon. The title character is a Simeonite judge: a national savior, exceptionally charismatic, whose eloquence, ingenuity, and bravery vindicate her disparaged ancestor. Proud of her tribal identity, she presents the attack on Shechem as a heroic act rather than a crime.[45] Echoing similar texts, she praises the genuine fury with which Simeon responds to the rape of his sister, contextualizes his retaliation as divinely sanctioned justice, and invokes his glorious legacy as inspiration for her own valor.[46]

In her capacity as an intertextually constructed protagonist designed to challenge the canon and rectify gender imbalance, Judith is portrayed as a woman whose prophetic powers and poetic skills match those of Deborah, while her killer instinct and captivating ability to embody grace under pressure announce her as a more sophisticated, more memorable, more perfect version of Yael. In that sense, she emerges as a unique successor to a long line of judges, kings, and prophets. Most significantly, the book of Judith proposes the unspoken idea of a queen. Considering the fact that the tribe of Simeon has been historically embedded in Judah, a geopolitical situation that limited its independence, the book of Judith could be arguing that the concept of a Simeonite female monarch, as controversial as it may seem, is a perfectly legitimate possibility.

A condensed version of the Judith story, published for the first time in the nineteenth century, wrestles more directly with lust and deception as attributes that characterize the male-manufactured image of woman and the slandered tribe of Simeon.[47] Remarkably economical yet quite complex, this version opens with a ferocious king, ruler of many nations and commander of a great army, who approaches Jerusalem, threatening to destroy it. A young woman, daughter of a family of prophets, is determined to risk her life and assassinate the king in an attempt to save the city. The first obstacle she encounters, however, comes from her own people. When she asks the guards to open the gate and let her out of the besieged Jerusalem, they doubt her sincerity, suspecting that she may have fallen in love with one of the foreign cavalry officers, whom she intends to marry, or that she might be plotting to collaborate with the enemy and help the king capture the city. Although this version refrains from naming any of the characters, it could be argued that it is her tribal affiliation, not merely the stereotypical notion of the wanton and duplicitous woman, that causes the guards to imagine conceivable scenarios in which her uninhibited animalism and potentially treacherous tendencies could lead to a national disaster. Finally, when she swears that she hopes for a miracle from God that would help her kill the king, the guards allow her to leave the city.

Accompanied by her maid, she descends to the enemy camp and introduces herself to the king. She explains that upon hearing from her father that the king is destined to win the war, she came to ask that he spare her life and help her family escape from the city. Impressed by her striking beauty, the king promises to grant her wish and expresses his desire to take her as his wife. She accepts his proposal but claims that she is menstruating. She asks to be permitted to bathe in a spring of water outside the camp before returning to his tent, at which point he could do with her as he pleased. Complying with her request, the king orders his soldiers not to accost her when she ventures outside the confines of the camp. Later that night, after a banquet marked by excessive drinking, she decapitates the inebriated king and exits the camp unquestioned and unharmed.

According to this version, she is fully aware of the sexual price that the king expects her to pay. Despite the credulous nature of the king, his lewd intentions are made immediately clear. Whether or not she manages to avoid his bedchamber, the primary function of the lie that she tells him is to secure her safe departure from his compound on that very same night. Contrary to the parallel episode in the book of Judith, nighttime ablution is neither a candid part of her daily routine nor a characterization device that establishes her purity or piety. In this alternative narrative, her cleansing ritual is a key element in a clever story that she concocts to fool the enemy. Unlike her double in the more familiar version of the story, the Judith of this narrative cannot afford to spend three days with the king and his soldiers, gradually winning their trust, while the people in the beleaguered city are dying of starvation.[48] Rather than a cautious infiltrator who slowly numbs the enemy, Judith is reimagined as a resolute, resourceful, rapid-fire strategist who wastes no time, knowing that she must, quite literally, go for the throat.

When she returns to the city and knocks on the gate, informing the guards that she has managed to kill the dreadful king, they refuse to believe her. Once again, the reputation of her tribe, or perhaps a common gender stereotype, seems to render her unreliable. At this point, what serves as a long exposition in the traditional book of Judith becomes a swift and effective flashback in this version.[49] The fast pace of this alternative narrative mirrors the quick thinking of the main character, who suggests that the severed head that she is carrying in her bag be shown to a former minister who used to be employed in the service of the king. Following a failed attempt to dissuade the king from waging war on a nation loved and protected by its deity, the defrocked minister was bound to the city gate as a form of punishment. The guards agree to her proposition. When they show the head of the dead king to the former minister, he recognizes it, praises the God of Israel, and announces that Jerusalem has been saved.

This climactic moment illuminates the parallel scene in the book of Judith, according to which the Ammonite chief who advises Holofernes not to launch a military campaign against the Israelites faints at the sight of the head of his former commander.[50] Without the skepticism of the Hebrew guards, the dramatic reaction to the severed head reveals nothing about the heroine. The imaginative retelling of this scene, devised to establish the absolute dependability of a young woman suspected of treason, communicates the implied assertion that anti-Simeonite accusations, as well as male-centered perspectives, are unjust and outmoded.

Other interpretations of the Judith narrative highlight the ambiguity of the text. The suspenseful nature of the story stems from the possibility that it is not entirely clear, not even to Judith herself, whether she is going to help Holofernes capture the city and save herself or kill him and save her people.[51] She enters his encampment, according to this reading, without a preconceived course of action and decides to decapitate him only when he makes it clear that he intends to possess her sexually, with or without her consent. It is then that killing him becomes morally justified, both as a personal act of self-defense and as a national mission to rescue Israel. In symbolic terms, what Holofernes intends to do to Judith is a synecdoche of what Nebuchadnezzar intends to do to the Jews. In that sense, Holofernes seals his own fate when he declares that allowing Judith to leave the camp undefiled would be a blemish on his virility.[52] Despite the valuable information that he receives from Judith about the potential weakness of her people, Holofernes is unable to stay focused on his professional duties.[53] Not content with the promise of accomplishing his military task, he devises a rapacious plot to satisfy his own hunger, his own needs, his own ego. At this point, to employ a predictable pun, he loses his head.

From a comparative perspective, Judith corresponds with other biblical widows who remove, rather ostensibly, common clothes that indicate grief, substituting them for more adventurous garments that foreshadow personal and political triumphs. Divesting herself of the predictable role of a pious, patient, passive relict, Tamar replaces her mourning attire with clothes that identify her as a self-employed sex worker. So effective is her new costume that her own father-in-law fails to recognize her.[54] Instructed by Naomi, Ruth achieves the same effect with a similar makeover.[55] Designed to communicate her availability and entice a potential husband, her new look heralds a new status, a new beginning, and a new life. In terms of narrative development, however, none of these women know that the decision to display such a daring sense of fashion will ultimately result in the birth of the Davidic dynasty and signal a turning point in the history of the Hebrew nation. Judith, on the other hand, is highly aware of the far-reaching implications that her wardrobe change could carry. On a personal level, the dramatic contrast between the sackcloth that marks her everyday appearance and the attractive gown, shoes, tiara, necklaces, bracelets, rings, earrings, and other jewelry that she wears in preparation for her mission behind enemy lines signifies, somewhat paradoxically, a courageous transformation from object to agent.[56]

Equally important is the possibility that this extraordinary metamorphosis, enhanced by the anointing of her body, suggests a coronation scene. In that sense, the book of Judith offers a more ambitious version of the biblical Esther. Clad in royal apparel, Esther secures her position as the Jewish wife of the Persian king.[57] In contrast, the Esther of the Talmud and the Kabbalah, like Judith, is clothed in both physical and metaphorical raiment. Expressing a yearning for liberation from imperial powers and anticipating the reinstitution of political independence, the ceremonial beautification of Judith is a scene that casts her in a messianic role and imagines her as the sovereign queen of the Jewish people: an earthly version of the Shekhinah.

Following the destruction of the temple in Jerusalem, the Shekhinah leaves the comfort of her palace and accompanies the Jewish nation in exile, dejected and begrimed. With the help of prayer, Torah study, the keeping of the commandments, and the good deeds that righteous people perform, she is bound to return to her heavenly palace and reunite with her divine lover: the Hebrew God. In order to ensure that she finds favor in the eyes of her male counterpart and arouses him to shower her with his sweet bounty, she must be majestically clothed and ornamented before she enters the royal bedchamber in the world of emanation. Once she couples with her divine lover, she can transmit the bounty that he bestows on her to the physical realm below. In kabbalistic terms, this intimate act sweetens strict verdicts and guarantees unconditional forgiveness. The well-known Hebrew term that denotes the preparation of the Shekhinah for this intimate reunion with God is *tikkun*. The literal meaning of the word is *rectification* or *repair*. More specifically, especially in its plural form, it signifies the regal garments and ornaments into which the good deeds of humanity translate. The capacious framework of kabbalistic literature extends a theological invitation to Esther and Judith, encouraging them to join this narrative. Judith, who represents the lowliest, most humiliated tribe of Israel, ultimately rises to a royal status. Like the kabbalistic Esther, she serves as a go-between that connects the physical realm with the supernal worlds: a celestial shuttle that guarantees the continuous exchange of human righteousness, which she submits above, and divine mercy, which she distributes below.

The Evil Ego

The centrality of late medieval Kabbalah notwithstanding, it is the sixteenth-century Lurianic worldview that undeniably dominates the fourth level of interpretation, often at the expense of other schools. The differences and similarities between the world according to Isaac Luria and the kabbalistic platform of his great predecessor, Moses Cordovero, are frequently debated by modern scholars of sixteenth-century Jewish thought. Having acquired the status of uncontested holiness, the Kabbalah of Isaac Luria serves, unlike that of Cordovero, as a universal prism through which all biblical, rabbinic, and other kabbalistic texts are inspected and interpreted. A common claim among Kabbalah scholars is that the writings of Cordovero are based on philosophical investigations and analytical abstractions, while the Lurianic corpus is vividly imaginative.[58] Against this claim, some suggest that the answers that Cordovero proposes, despite the theoretical nature of the theological questions that he addresses, do belong, in admittedly subtle ways, to the realm of the imagination.[59] Other scholars argue that the ascendency of Lurianic Kabbalah can be attributed to the fact that it ultimately revolves around evil, exile, and redemption, concepts that have always occupied Jewish thought and that were particularly popular after the expulsion of the Jews from Spain and Portugal in the late fifteenth century.[60]

In a sense, the tension between the academic and the literary is intrinsic to most kabbalistic texts. Just as rabbinic literature oscillates between halakhah and aggadah—between legalistic debates and narrative expansions—so does the Kabbalah alternate between logical assertions and playful storytelling, often in the same text. Lurianic Kabbalah, however, does seem to anticipate modernist and postmodern narrative strategies, most notably the declining importance of external action and the growing interest in internal processes. With his innovative prose and broad stylistic range, Hayyim Vital, prime articulator of the Lurianic corpus, reshaped the Kabbalah as a fascinating interplay of various cosmological components, paying special attention to the ever-changing aspects of the divine system and the multifaceted parts of the human soul. The emphasis that Vital placed on the nuances of psychological mechanisms could be construed as an early attempt to advance kabbalistic literature toward what might be described as the modern novel. Particularly noteworthy is his *Book of Visions*, an introspective journey that combines several literary forms, including personal journal entries, detailed dream diaries, and intricate tapestries of thoughts, emotions, fantasies, and aspirations. Notions of constancy, security, familiarity, and control are replaced with a sense of anxiety, impermanence, alienation, and ambivalence.

Throughout the *Book of Visions*, scathing verbal attacks are launched against the designated villain: an eminent member of the Jewish congregation in Damascus who scorns the prophetic and messianic consciousness of the narrator. The required presence of a monstrous opponent, whom the narrator accuses of jealousy, arrogance, and sexual depravity, could be understood as a classic case of an alter ego: a doppelgänger who externalizes the repressed desires of the narrator himself and serves as a reflection of his self-tormented psyche.[61] Torn between self-aggrandizement and self-flagellation, Vital despises his nemesis, perhaps as an extension of his own violent tendencies, impure urges, and other self-confessed weaknesses.

Applied to biblical literature, these principles could reveal Holofernes as the quintessential alter ego. In addition to his role as an evil entity that threatens to destroy the nation from without, he stands for unrestrained desires that destabilize the individual from within. Metaphorically speaking, Judith cloaks Holofernes and acknowledges the fact that he dwells inside her. Her descent from the top of a fortified hill to the enemy camp below is a journey into her own unconscious. Like the sphere of royalty in the world of emanation, she is willing to occupy a lower position in order to confront her own imperfections and serve a social cause. Like the moon, she agrees to relinquish her own light for the sake of collective illumination. Having cleansed herself of pride, she promotes an ethics of humility as a necessary step toward her own rectification and the repair of the world.

The same reading can be applied to other biblical narratives. On a literal level, Abraham is instructed to kill his son.[62] On a deeper level, he is asked to sacrifice what he loves the most: his own ego. Translated into the language of Ashlagian Kabbalah, a twentieth-century platform that identifies altruism as the most important divine attribute, Abraham is a typical vessel that must develop the ability to receive the divine blessing in order to share it with others. In that sense, Isaac is an extension of the narcissistic consciousness of his father. Similarly, Holofernes is an embodiment of the comfort and prestige that Judith must sacrifice when she assumes the responsibilities of a civil servant. Not unlike Esther, she enjoys the status of a venerated woman who lives in splendid isolation, largely removed from the needs of the people. At some point, she realizes that she must risk her precious position in order to help those who depend on her. Esther, following a passionate plea from Mordechai, comes to the same conclusion.[63] In theological terms, the willingness to curb self-serving inclinations in order to provide for others is the epitome of godlike behavior.

This kind of imaginative exegesis is premised on an open-ended exploration of narrative strategies and meaning-making mechanisms. It treats biblical literature, particularly when juxtaposed with rabbinic interpretation, kabbalistic commentary, contemporary scholarship, and other hermeneutical endeavors, as a self-reflexive collection of narratives that investigates its own complexity, embraces uncertainty, promotes recursive reflection, invites a constant revision of previous readings, calls into question the notion of an agreed-upon meaning, and emphasizes the communal nature of engagement with the text. Rather than copyrighted arguments that establish the authority or expertise of individuals, new readings contribute to an ongoing collaborative project whose goal is to illuminate the text from as many perspectives as possible and resist the notion of a definitive interpretation.

The interpretive perspective that some of these medieval, sixteenth-century, and twentieth-century kabbalistic texts adopt could be described as prototypically feminist. The kabbalistic divinity is no longer a male deity who single-handedly rules the world and saves humanity. Unlike the God of biblical poetry, the kabbalistic divinity is not a superhero who wears justice, zeal, vengeance, majesty, strength, splendor, courage, glory, or other divine attributes.[64] Appropriated by the Kabbalah and converted into interactive spheres, the divine attributes are dynamic qualities shared by all the elements of a collaborative system. In kabbalistic terms, the system as a whole is known as the divinity: a grammatically feminine Hebrew noun.[65] The particular element of the divinity to which such names as God, the Most High, or the Holy One Blessed Be He refer—common masculine appellations in biblical and rabbinic literature—becomes the younger male divine configuration of kabbalistic theology: an interdependent component that forms a close partnership with his female companion, receives sustenance and guidance from the older divine configurations, both male and female, and relies on humanity for the completion of the divine plan. Just as the Kabbalah offers a radical revision of the stereotypically gender-coded characteristics of God, so do modern scholars challenge privileged readings that serve patriarchal ideologies. New roles are assigned to major and minor female characters, among them the monstrous, the scandalous, the stigmatized, the victimized, the overlooked, the underappreciated, the nameless, and the disembodied. Notable examples include Potiphar's wife, Samson's wife, Abimelech's killer, Jephthah's daughter, the concubine at Gibeah, the wicked woman of Proverbs, the seven-headed whore of Revelation, the women who accompany Jesus, the feminine manifestation of wisdom, also known as Sophia, and Gomer, daughter of Diblaim, the harlot who marries Hosea.[66] Common to the Kabbalah and feminist scholarship is the attempt to question popular perspectives that treat biblical stories as historically accurate, culturally valid, enduringly true, or indisputably realistic.

Considering its literary and theological sophistication, it could be argued that the Kabbalah calls itself the true wisdom (חוכמת האמת) not because it promotes its unique version of the human–divine story as an optimal narrative but precisely because it rejects such an idea. What makes the Kabbalah true is its capacity to examine the potential complexity of every textual component while refraining from suggesting a best option. Every letter of the Hebrew Bible is treated as an elastic unit that carries multiple meanings. Every textual element comes with built-in shifting roles that future readings will continue to reveal. A

biblical character, therefore, is not a mimetic representation of a historical or mythological figure. A biblical character—like any other literary
device, and like the divinity itself—is a meeting point of relational definitions and interchangeable functions.

The Dead Kings of Edom

The multilayered hermeneutical model that the Kabbalah proposes,
with its emphasis on endless creativity, is premised on the idea that the
biblical text must be reimagined and reinvented. To reduce inexhaust-
ibly complex literature to its plain sense is to deprive it of its generative
power. Essential yet insufficient, the plain sense is an outer shell that
obscures the splendor of the text. The role of the reader is to undress
the text in order to reveal its true garments: the inner, more sophisticated, more beautiful layers that cloak it, adorn it, and accentuate its
essence. Only through an interplay of interpretive possibilities can the
true meaning of the text be grasped.

Translated into self-referential terms, Psalm 45, for example, tells
the story of hermeneutics itself. Allegorically speaking, the queen is
the Torah, while the king is the dedicated scholar. A reading that transcends the literal adorns both of them, exposing the depth, wisdom,
and beauty of the text. More advanced levels of interpretation will suggest additional possibilities, expand this textual system, and enhance
its theological scope. Along these lines, the king can be viewed as the
younger male divine configuration in the supernal world of emanation: *Zeir Anpin*. An emblem of judicial power, he is often presented
as a ruler and warrior. In need of wise counsel, he must be cloaked
by the older male divine configuration: *Arikh Anpin*. Characterized
by endless patience, the latter softens the harsh nature of the former
through three vertical channels. The right channel represents mercy.
The left one stands for might. The middle one, which leads directly
to the younger configuration, reconciles the other two and produces
compassion. According to kabbalistic readings of the text, the three
types of perfume that adorn the king—myrrh, aloes, and cassia—refer
to these three channels.[67]

Openly uncomfortable with data-driven passages that threaten
to render biblical literature tedious, insipid, or otherwise uninspired,

kabbalistic literature often takes it upon itself to offer the kind of creative interpretation that attempts to convert even the most pallid portions of sacred texts into crucial scenes in the story of creation, the divinity, and humanity. Another notable example is the curious list of the eight kings of Edom, appropriated by kabbalistic cosmology and translated into pivotal elements in the early stages of creation.[68] According to Lurianic Kabbalah, the first seven kings represent the broken vessels in the primordial structure of *Adam Kadmon*.[69] Unable to sustain the divine light that issues from various openings in this primordial structure, the vessels shatter. The eighth and last king, the only one whose death is not recorded in the biblical text, signifies a process of repair. Equally important is the fact that he is the only king whose wife is mentioned. Standing for cooperation, stability, and female–male unity—rather than the egocentric chaos that allows the breaking of the vessels—the eighth king represents the final cluster of emanations that issues from the primordial structure. In its capacity as a corrective force, this cluster of emanations collects the pieces of the broken vessels, joins them together, restores them to their proper places, and facilitates the beginning of time and the birth of the first supernal world: the world of emanation. Once completed, the world of emanation hosts the divine configurations that govern the lower worlds: the world of creation, the world of formation, and the world of action.

The temporary collapse of the divine system—the breaking of the vessels—foreshadows subsequent catastrophes in the supernal worlds and the physical realm. Most immediately, the dead kings of Edom anticipate the sparks of divine light that fail to be incorporated into the world of emanation and sink to the lower worlds, where they are tainted by impurities. As key components in adjacent narratives, the dead kings of Edom point to the future souls of humanity, originally contained within the prelapsarian Adam.[70] When Adam sins and eats from the forbidden tree, the unborn souls fall from their lofty quarry in the world of creation to the lower worlds, where they roam in their disembodied state, unprotected from evil forces. The forbidden tree in the garden of Eden, associated with the knowledge of good and bad, foreshadows the current condition of the sparks and the souls: a lamentable mixture of the inherent good and the residual bad. Contrasted with spiritual pursuits and altruistic tendencies, the evil forces manifest themselves primarily as materialistic concerns and selfish desires.

Perhaps surprisingly, the dead kings of Edom also stand for the people of Israel. With the destruction of Jerusalem, the people of Israel are forced into a long and bitter exile, often marked by oppression and humiliation at the hands of the nations of the world. In this context, the dead kings of Edom also serve as a metaphor for the Shekhinah, who joins the dispossessed in exile. The role of the Hebrew nation is to keep her company, build her a shelter, and adorn her in preparation for a glorious return to her divine lover. Translated into universal terms, the task of humanity, according to the kabbalistic worldview, is to sift through the physical realm, extract the holy sparks, separate them from the slag or dross that dims their light, and elevate them to the upper worlds. This is achieved through the keeping of the commandments, acts of loving-kindness, and daily Torah study, with special attention to the Kabbalah itself. Neglecting to study the Kabbalah means that the Shekhinah dwells in the gutter, the world regresses to chaos, and the dead kings of Edom are held captive by the serpent.

In psychological terms, the serpent stands for the inability to resist self-centered impulses: the inclination to satisfy narcissistic needs at the expense of social causes, collective action, or care for others. Nothing could be further from the divine mind than the childish urge to prioritize the self. The kings of Edom die, the vessels break, the world is destroyed, the Shekhinah is forlorn, and the serpent prevails when demanding infants fail to develop into thoughtful adults. Evil, therefore, is not an alien monster but the unbridled ego. The ultimate goal is not to eliminate evil but to transform it into the kind of maturity that presupposes a strong sense of personal responsibility. Along these lines, Eve is not to blame for the mistake that her husband makes. Adam alone is responsible for his sin. In fact, the greatest sin that Adam commits is blaming Eve. Adam is blessed with the most wonderful gift in the world—a loving human companion to alleviate his loneliness—yet he repays God with sheer ungratefulness, denigrating his female companion rather than acknowledging his own transgression.[71]

So grave is the error that Adam commits, and so serious are its consequences, that repairing the damage becomes an overwhelming task. Even the most diligent keepers of the commandments would not be able to restore the world to its paradisiacal state. The workload, therefore, must be shared by all of humanity and spread across six thousand years. This ongoing collective effort introduces the concept of reincarnation:

the transmigration of souls. Different individuals are placed in charge of refining and elevating different sparks, and those who are unable to finish their assigned portion—that is, those who fail to perform all six hundred and thirteen commandments, or those who break some of the commandments and derail the project—are reincarnated in future generations, again and again, until each soul completes its designated path.

The kabbalistic narrative of imperfection and rectification describes several occasions on which this massive reconstruction project seemed to have approached its conclusion, only to be delayed by major setbacks. Noah, the most righteous man of his generation, who had only seven commandments to follow, was the hope of humanity, yet he failed to save most of the population from the deadly flood. In addition, he could not resist the temptation to drink to the point of embarrassing intoxication, a moment of human weakness that hindered the rectification process and caused a great deal of agony to his sons, his future descendants, and the rest of the world. Similarly, the people were on the verge of utter holiness at Mount Sinai, yet the temptation to create the golden calf as a poor substitute for God and the Torah—the urge to replace spiritual content with material objects—was another replication of the structural frailty signified by the dead kings of Edom and prefigured by the shattered vessels, the degraded sparks, and the fallen souls. In other words, a greater degree of awareness—or the gradual growth of the human soul—redeems the dead kings of Edom, rejects unholy forces, and elevates the sparks to the supernal worlds. The history of creation, according to this narrative, is a constant interplay of damage and repair, regression and progression, small-mindedness and expanded consciousness.

The rejection of unholy forces—sifting the good from the bad—is considered an awakening below that merits abundance from above.[72] The purpose is to arouse the divine configurations in the world of emanation to bestow their bounty on the lower worlds. The distillation, clarification, or purification of the dead kings—that is, the refinement of the holy sparks—is the spiritual equivalent of a meteorological phenomenon: mist that rises from the land and triggers rain that falls from the sky.[73] In kabbalistic terms, the mist—which represents repentance, prayer, daily Torah study, and other good deeds—is referred to as feminine water. Just as the female beautifies herself to arouse the male into showering her with the kind of intimate attention that will produce new

life, so does humanity appeal to God in order to receive divine succor.
In exile, however, the Shekhinah cannot beautify herself. Without the
daily work of commandment-keeping devotees, she is helpless. It is the
duty of humanity, therefore, to adorn her, rectify her downcast state,
and ensure a joyful reunion with her spouse: the younger male configuration in the world of emanation, the divine king that replaces the
mortal kings of Edom. Once again, the regular coupling of God and
the Shekhinah, which bestows goodness upon the earth and guarantees its continuous existence, would not be possible without humanity.
Mutually dependent, humanity and the divinity rely on each other for
the daily maintenance of their inherently fragile structures.

Textual Actualization

One of the most important concepts in kabbalistic theology is the five-
part structure of the human soul. The lowest part of the soul is the
lifeblood: the basic quality that animates the body.[74] Those who follow
the commandments, labor in the Torah, and practice altruism hope
to acquire the next part of the soul: the spirit.[75] Those who excel in
such tasks hope to obtain the next part: the soul itself.[76] The highest
levels—the inner and the innermost parts of the soul—are granted to
the righteous almost automatically when they complete the correction
of the third part.[77] Salvation, the coming of the messiah, and the ingath-
ering of the exiles will concur with the comprehensive rectification of
every soul and the successful disentanglement of the holy sparks from
the contaminants in which they are mired. At that time, the physical
realm—the world of action, where humanity dwells—will ascend to the
world of formation, where the angels reside. This ascension will mark
the final stages of the cyclical cosmology that the Kabbalah constructs:
the trajectory of the universe from deficiency to perfection. Mutually
inclusive, the world of action and the world of formation will ascend
to the world of creation, where the repository of the souls is located.
The separate constituents of creation will be gradually reincorporated
as humanity returns to its divine origin.

The next stage, the ascent to the world of emanation, will mark the
end of six thousand years of creation. A new era will begin with the seventh millennium and the reintegration of creation into the primordial

structure. More specifically, the seventh millennium will be spent in the metaphorical mouth of the primordial structure: the phase that precedes the death of the Edomite kings, in which the divine light is too pure to produce independent vessels. The eighth millennium will be spent in the metaphorical nose of the primordial structure, which represents a higher quality of divine light. The ninth millennium will be spent even higher, in the metaphorical ears of the primordial structure. The tenth millennium will mark the return to the earliest light: the one that issues from the metaphorical hair of the primordial structure. It is possible, according to this kabbalistic narrative, that the next and final stage of the reversed cosmological journey will take humanity even further, to the very core of the divinity: to the purest, indivisible, infinite light that initiates the entire process.

The infinite light initiates the creation process as a pure expression of its own independent will. Similarly, Eve eats from the tree of knowledge because of an immanent desire to do so, represented by the serpent. The same self-generated craving compels Adam to sample the forbidden fruit, and no attempt to recriminate Eve could exculpate him. Both scenes, the creation of the universe and the transgression of Adam and Eve in the garden of Eden, begin with a categorical rejection of a common narrative device: cause and effect. The absolute will of God is entirely spontaneous, as are the complex inner drives that govern human beings. Diverting the focus from external factors to internal forces, the Kabbalah suggests that humanity can certainly introduce positive changes in the upper worlds, but by no means can it influence the original divine wish to create and sustain the physical realm.

In the earliest cosmological stages, the desire to initiate the creation process translates into the willingness of the divinity to impose unprecedented limitations on its own infinite light. A one-time restriction of the all-encompassing light, known as an act of contraction, produces an empty space. Having withdrawn from this space, the divine light enters it again, this time as a single beam, and creates the primordial structure: an early system whose shape anticipates the human form. Growing more complex, the divine light is divided into clusters of emanations that issue from the metaphorical body parts of the primordial structure. Each cluster consists of ten emanations. The ultimate purpose of the divine light is to produce the vessels that will eventually hold it. In human terms, the vessels express the desire of creation to receive and enjoy the bounty of the divinity. Each of the four worlds that follow the primordial structure—emanation, creation, formation, and action—consists of ten spheres that function as pipelines: mazelike channels through which divine bounty is transmitted downward.

Particularly fascinating is the vibrant nature of the ten spheres. While some of them are designated as either male or female, others are gender-fluid. Numerous attempts to capture the essence of these spheres or translate their names into other languages enhance their flexible identities.[78] For example, the third sphere, understanding, is sometimes called intelligence. The fourth sphere, mercy, is sometimes called magnanimity, kindness, or grace. The fifth sphere, might, is sometimes called severity, discipline, or judgment. The sixth sphere, beauty, is sometimes called truth. The seventh sphere, endurance, is sometimes called eternity or victory. The eighth sphere, glory, is sometimes called splendor or praise. The last sphere, royalty, is commonly referred to as monarchy or kingship. It is possible, however, especially considering the distinctly female nature of this sphere, to call it queenship. When the sphere of knowledge is added, it appears as the fourth sphere: the one that connects the top three, which are considered the head, to the bottom seven, which are considered the body. In the case of the Edomite kings, when knowledge is the fourth sphere, the seventh and eighth spheres, endurance and glory, count as a single sphere.

The first cluster of emanations that issues from the primordial structure—the light of the hair—is not accompanied by any vessels, and neither are the next clusters: the light of the ears and the light of the nose. It is only in the next phase—the light of the mouth—that a vessel begins to form. More specifically, it is only then that the light, which grows constantly thicker, allows a certain degree of contact between two of its aspects: the inner light and the surrounding light. This kind of contact—a clash of two forces—engenders the vessels, which also function as the letters of the Hebrew alphabet.[79] Before the letters are revealed, God cannot be known by name. It is through the vessels and the letters that the otherwise unknowable divinity can be studied and experienced. According to this narrative, and contrary to the common association of kabbalistic knowledge with mystical, ecstatic, or nonverbal experience, any attempt to construct a theology outside human language would be meaningless. The alphabet itself, according to this narrative, is the embodiment of God. And since the alphabet is used by no other species on earth, it is the duty of human readers and writers to arrange and rearrange the divine letters in order to guarantee the continuous actualization of God. In kabbalistic terms, those who engage in Torah study—that is, those who are devoted to textual scholarship—build a house for the divine presence: more specifically, a palace for the exiled Shekhinah.

Naturally, the emphasis on human textuality is unapologetically anthropocentric. In semiotic terms, certain signs become more meaningful when examined from certain perspectives. For example, a dark cloud in the sky has always been a sign of precipitation, just as a red glow on the horizon has always been a sign of the rising sun. It was not until the appearance of human beings, however, that these signifier–signified relations could be discussed in emotional terms: sadness, romance, hope, excitement, pensive introspection, the promise of adventure, and so on. Similarly, it was not until the arrival of human beings that these natural phenomena could be addressed from religious perspectives: feminine water below that produces divine opulence above, or the merging of evening and morning as a metaphor for the intimate union of the younger divine configurations in the world of emanation.[80]

Needless to say, the fact that clouds had been producing rain and the earth had been revolving around the sun for millions of years before the appearance of human beings can be interpreted as proof of the existence of God. What the Kabbalah seems to claim, however, is that the idea that God exists outside the text—in the beauty of nature, in the harmony of creation, or in the eternity of time—should be approached with suspicion. God can be seen every time one opens the Bible, every time one reads biblical commentary, every time one engages in biblical scholarship. To circumvent the text and attempt to see God directly, so to speak, is a conceited act that borders on blasphemy. This might be the mortal sin that Abel commits when his offering is accepted. According to kabbalistic literature, Abel, who peeks at the Shekhinah, must be killed by his brother. Moses, a reincarnation of Abel, is careful not to make the same mistake when he encounters the divinity at the burning bush.[81] In theological contexts, it is possible to understand the condemnation of Abel as a statement against the transcendental belief that the divinity can be known or experienced outside intellectual realms.

From Spheres to Configurations

Large parts of kabbalistic literature are devoted to the concept of the vessel: its formation, development, collapse, and recovery. It should come as no surprise, therefore, that the Hebrew term *Kabbalah* denotes reception. Learners of the Kabbalah receive this ancient wisdom from older authorities and transmit it to the next generation. More importantly, the term *Kabbalah* signifies the kind of wisdom that transforms the receiver from a receptacle to a relay: from an empty vessel eager to sustain itself to a more perfect container that retains divine opulence in order to share it with others.

In the early stages of creation, the first vessel that forms is a large receptacle that holds the ten emanations of the light of the mouth. The next cluster of ten emanations—the light of the eyes—is preceded by another act of contraction. In an attempt to increase the density of the light and guarantee the formation of ten individual vessels, the bottom half of the metaphorical body of the primordial structure is emptied. The lights inside rise to the top, where they are kept, in their condensed and intensified form, by a diagonal barrier that stretches from the chest to the back: the equivalent of the diaphragm. When these fortified lights issue from the eyes of the primordial structure, they are accompanied by ten vessels. The vessels come out first, line up outside the lower half of the primordial structure, and await their lights. At the same time, the lights that remain inside the primordial structure break through the diagonal barrier and travel back to the lower half—the abdomen, genitals, legs, and feet—from which they issue to support the lights outside.

Despite the intensity of the light, most of the vessels that are formed at this stage are not strong enough to accept and contain the ten emanations that issue from the eyes of the primordial structure. When these vessels break, it is largely because the humanlike shape of the primordial structure does not include both aspects of humanity—male and female—and is therefore incomplete.[82] In other words, it is the loneliness of the seven Edomite kings—their failure to make contact with female counterparts—that leads to their death. The absence of a female element renders the vessels weak, unstable, and breakable. The fact that only the vessels of the lower spheres shatter means that the top three spheres—crown, wisdom, and understanding—already consist of male and female elements. In addition to the ability to receive and hold the light of the eyes, the vessels of these top spheres are also capable of receiving and holding all the previous lights that issue from the metaphorical openings in the primordial structure. These lights are considered female elements that strengthen the top spheres and further contribute to their stability and durability.[83]

The eighth king represents the next and final cluster of emanations: the light of the forehead. With his wife—Mehetabel, daughter of Matred, daughter of Mezahab—he repairs the shattered vessels.[84] The light of the forehead helps the vessels reunite with their matching spheres and ensures that each divine configuration in the next supernal structure—the world of emanation—consists of male and female elements. It is the final version of the world of emanation, made possible by the wife of the eighth king, that marks the beginning of time. Without her, history itself could not be imagined. Appealing to the third level of interpretation, the Kabbalah notes that the numerical value of her Hebrew name—Mehetabel—is ninety-seven: the same as the numerical value of the Hebrew word that denotes time.[85] The presence of a queen—a biblical character who is acknowledged, named, and placed within the genealogical context of her own family, along with her mother and grandmother—signals divine rectification and heralds the creation of male and female human beings in the physical realm: the world of action.

One of the most crucial junctures in Lurianic cosmology is the development of the divine configurations in the world of emanation. Bound together in a prototype of a vessel, the ten emanations that issue from the mouth of the primordial structure are collectively known as *striped*.[86] Often referred to as its own intermediate world, the mouth is the first of three phases that mark the transition from the primordial structure to the world of emanation. The second phase is the intermediate world that forms when the next cluster of emanations issues from the eyes of the primordial structure. These emanations—ten spheres and ten individual vessels—are collectively known as *speckled*.[87] This phase, which marks the breaking of the vessels, is also known as the world of chaos. The ten spheres that issue from the forehead of the primordial structure and repair the broken vessels are collectively known as *spotted*.[88] This third and final phase is also known as the world of rectification, which then becomes the world of emanation.

When it does, its ten spheres grow and develop into five major configurations. The first sphere—the crown—develops into the prime configuration in the world of emanation. Essentially male, this configuration has an internal female side, whereas the next two spheres—wisdom and understanding—develop into two independent configurations, one male and one female: Father and Mother. In kabbalistic terms, Father and Mother are gestated inside the female side of the prime configuration. When they are fully developed, they give birth, so to speak, to the younger configurations: God and his female companion, the Shekhinah. God, the divine king, is a developed version of the next six spheres, collectively known as beauty, while the Shekhinah, the heavenly queen, is a developed version of the last sphere: royalty. Each of these configurations consists of an active formation of ten internal spheres.

As if to provide an illuminating flashback or belated exposition, Lurianic cosmology also imagines the lives of the Edomite kings before they died. Apparently, their role was to serve Father and Mother. In their capacity as the divine parents that give birth to the younger divine configurations, Father and Mother must be prompted to copulate. Just as the people of Israel are considered the children of the Shekhinah, so are the Edomite kings considered the children of Mother. In other words, if the duty of humanity below is to awake and prepare the heavenly queen for an intimate union with her divine lover, it is likewise the duty of the Edomite kings above to perform this service for Mother. And if the Edomite kings are considered her children, the embryonic stages of their lives must be spent inside her. Their role, therefore, is to guarantee the utmost degree of intimacy between Father and Mother in order to facilitate their own birth. Had they not died, their mission would have been to provide continuous assistance to Father and Mother, ensuring the highest degree of conjugal union: face to face. It is then, when Father and Mother are in a state of expanded consciousness—capable of embracing, kissing, and accommodating each other—that the bounty they bestow on the lower worlds is of the highest quality. When the kings die, Father and Mother must resort to the lowest degree of intimacy: back to back. This means that the death of the Edomite kings—that is, the breaking of the vessels—damages not only the seven lower spheres but also two of the top three: wisdom and understanding, which correspond to Father and Mother. As a result, the damage spreads to the lower worlds. Now they are forced to manage with lesser amounts of bounty.

Specific details in the biblical text, according to the kind of imaginative exegesis that the Kabbalah promotes, reflect the fact that wisdom and understanding—the parental configurations—are impacted by the breaking of the vessels. The four Edomite kings whose fathers are mentioned stand for four configurations: Father, Mother, Old Israel, and Comprehension.[89] Embedded inside Father and Mother, Old Israel and Comprehension are subordinate configurations that participate more directly in the construction of the younger divine configurations: God and the Shekhinah. The fact that the fathers of these four kings are mentioned only once, when the kings are named for the first time, and not when their deaths are reported, means that the damage to the top spheres is partial rather than complete.[90]

The elements of creation—the vessels and the lights, the ten spheres, the five aspects of the human soul, the supernal worlds, the divine configurations—cloak one another in the same way that the various levels of textual interpretation serve as encapsulated garments, dressing one another in layers of new meanings. Those who champion the creative pluralism of biblical interpretation identify the dismissal of such obvious diversity with a masculine yearning for the illusion of mastery, mostly as a coping mechanism in the face of anxiety.[91] More specifically, the decline of religious, economic, and sociopolitical apparatuses that rely on the belief in some unchanging, reassuring, universal truth is experienced as a sense of loss. Petrified adherents of these apparatuses, who equate them with concepts such as mother, home, and nature, respond to their dissolution with pathological empiricism: an obsessive dependency on facts. The result is the treatment of the body, the earth, and human emotions as feminine domains—fickle, unstable, unreliable—from which thinking brains must escape if they wish to examine the data of the world, including biblical texts, from critical, logical, detached, uninvolved, presumably scientific, allegedly objective points of view. When it comes to biblical interpretation, the tension between objectivism and pluralism often takes the form of an open clash between hegemony and perspective, doctrine and context, orthodoxy and innovation, religious absolutes and theological experimentation.

Despair and Repair

In keeping with the principle of capacious hermeneutics, additional textual units, biblical and rabbinic, are recruited to serve as key episodes in the cosmological narrative that the Kabbalah constructs. Originally, the names of the three intermediate worlds that anticipate the world of emanation—the transitional phases marked by the lights that issue from the mouth, eyes, and forehead of the primordial structure—denote the irregular types of goats that Jacob sees in his dream: striped, speckled, and spotted.[92] According to God, these are essentially the doings of Laban. In a surprising hermeneutical maneuver, the manipulative and exploitive Laban, whose Hebrew name means *white*, is treated by this kabbalistic narrative as a representation of the Highest White: the purest, indivisible, infinite light that initiates the creation process.[93] The various stages that ultimately lead to the world of emanation are the doings of this light. Jacob, who represents the world of emanation itself, is the one who directly benefits from these stages, especially the last three.[94]

From a male-centered point of view, biblical literature itself, especially in the so-called age of reason, becomes a feminine entity: an inconsistent, irrational, capricious creature that needs to be conquered, domesticated, and controlled. Like a newly discovered territory, it must be accurately mapped, carefully demarcated, diligently colonized, and systematically divested of its mysterious, exotic, disorderly, self-contradictory, or otherwise frightening features. As a counterargument, the Kabbalah suggests that the text, like humanity and the divinity, is a natural mixture of male and female elements. In fact, every kabbalistic sphere consists of female and male elements. The lights that issue from the eyes of the primordial structure, for example, are considered feminine. They are often referred to by the combined numerical value of a certain spelling of the Hebrew letters of the Tetragrammaton: fifty-two. Similarly, the lights that issue from the forehead of the primordial structure are considered masculine. They are commonly referred to by the combined numerical value of a different spelling of the letters of the Tetragrammaton: forty-five.[95] There is no single spark in the world of emanation, according to the kabbalistic worldview, that does not contain both forty-five and fifty-two: that is, both male and female lights.[96] The divine configuration that resides above the world of emanation—Ancient of Days—also consists of male and female aspects. In charge of translating the finite dimensions of the physical realm into eternal and spiritual terms in the supernal worlds, this divine configuration transforms the commandments that are performed on earth into future rectifications in the mouth, nose, ears, and hair of the primordial structure, for which humanity will be rewarded when it makes its restorative journey back to the early stages of creation.

In many cases, the actions, motives, and technical details of elements in kabbalistic literature are presented in emotional terms. When the vessels break, they fall from the world of emanation to the world of creation. Worried about their vessels, the lights of the eyes rush to support them, give them hope, and guarantee that they do not perish. In an attempt to illuminate their vessels from afar, the lights descend to the bottom of the world of emanation. The rule, according to kabbalistic cosmology, is that as long as the distance between a light and its vessel does not exceed the length of three spheres, illumination from afar is possible. For example, when the first vessel breaks—the vessel of knowledge—it falls to the world of creation, where it occupies the spot reserved for its sphere: the fourth sphere. Its light hurries to the very bottom of the world of emanation and occupies the spot normally reserved for the last sphere: royalty. The distance between the royalty of emanation and the knowledge of creation is three spheres—crown, wisdom, and understanding—and the light of knowledge keeps its vessel alive. At some point, the vessel of the crown in the world of emanation, which does not break, expands from above and absorbs the light of knowledge. The light of knowledge accepts the invitation and climbs back, returning to its original place. Its vessel, helpless without illumination, loses hope and sinks to the bottom of the world of creation.

A similar thing happens to the next vessel: the vessel of mercy. When it meets the light of the eyes, it shatters and falls to the world of creation, where it occupies the spot above knowledge: understanding. Its light hurries to the bottom of the world of emanation and occupies the penultimate spot: foundation. Once again, the distance between the light and its vessel is three spheres: the royalty of emanation plus the crown and wisdom of creation. At some point, however, the vessel of wisdom in the world of emanation, which also stays intact, expands from above, like the vessel of the crown, and absorbs the light of mercy. And when it does, the vessel of mercy collapses and sinks to a lower spot in the world of creation. A similar thing happens to the vessel of might when its light climbs back to join the unbroken, now expanded vessel of the third sphere in the world of emanation: understanding.[97]

As if the initial shattering is not devastating enough, the second breakdown of the vessels introduces, from a human point of view, the problem of despair, especially in the face of crisis, failure, inequity, injustice, evil forces, trying circumstances, suffering, death, and the fundamental imperfection of creation. The negative aspects of the physical realm are perceived as inevitable extensions of the inherent weakness of the supernal worlds. Solutions to this problem are often suggested in the form of multilayered narratives. For example, a human being who commits a transgression creates an accuser: a personal prosecutor, also known as an angel of destruction.[98] This prosecutor stands before God and proclaims: "So and so made me." Like any living creature, this prosecutor, whose reality cannot be ignored or denied, must be supported and sustained. In spite of the fact that it is the duty of sinners to support their personal prosecutors, God agrees to perform this thankless task. This is how some kabbalistic commentators, including the allegedly theoretical Cordovero, interpret the conversation between Cain and God after the killing of Abel.[99] Contrary to common translations, Cain does not complain that his punishment is too great to bear.[100] Rather than a declarative statement that allows him to protest the severity of his sentence, he uses an interrogative clause that communicates a rhetorical question: "Is my sin too great to be forgiven?" Cain, who promises to repent, asks God to do him a favor and provide for his personal prosecutor until he serves his sentence. Upon the completion of his atonement, when he has paid his debt, his prosecutor will cease to exist.

This interpretation raises interesting theological questions. What happens to personal prosecutors once sinners atone for their transgressions? For example, if Pharaoh, Sennacherib, Haman, and other foreign tyrants are prosecutors commissioned by God to oppress Israel until the nation repents, why should they be punished once their job is done, and their services are no longer required? The answer, according to the Kabbalah, is that the oppressors of Israel function like the scapegoat that carries the sins of the nation.[101] The scapegoat represents the so-called other side: the forces of impurity.[102] God grants Samael, the evil angel in charge of the other side, a letter of appointment that authorizes him to claim the debts of criminals and castigate them until their sins are scoured, often by torture or death. In other words, Samael, who operates what could be called a collection agency, buys the transgressions of the wicked from the original creditor: God. When the wicked have repented, God demands that Samael return the acquired debt and pay for the transgressions that he now owns, usually with the same currency: torture or death.

Evil, therefore, does not exist independently. Appointed by the divinity, cruel oppressors are temporary representatives with limited power. When old ones complete their mission and retire, they are replaced by new representatives, who inherit both the transgressions of Israel and the letter of appointment that allows them to oppress the nation in an attempt to encourage it to repent for its remaining sins. With the generational dwindling of the sins of the people, evil is diminished, little by little, until it disappears completely, like the biblical scapegoat that wanders into the wilderness, never to be seen again. In rabbinic terms, evil must cease to exist, like the rock, tree, sword, or rope that must be buried in the ground once it has been used in cases of court-mandated executions by stoning, burning, beheading, or strangulation.[103]

The biblical story of the giant statue that Nebuchadnezzar sees in his dream is another narrative that exemplifies this process.[104] Made of gold, the head of the statue represents Nebuchadnezzar himself: the Babylonian Empire. Made of silver, the chest and arms represent the Persian Empire. Made of bronze, the belly and thighs represent the Greek Empire. Made of iron, the legs represent the Roman Empire. Made of a mixture of iron and clay, the feet and toes represent the waning and crumbling of the Roman Empire. The historical chain of pain and humiliation that the nations of the world inflict on Israel weakens and becomes more fragile with the advancement toward atonement and the approaching salvation. Based on the battlefield vision of Zechariah and the kabbalistic interpretation of worldwide judgment as the day in which God will hold accountable those who have oppressed Israel, the demise of the terrifying statue is imagined as the disappearance of evil.[105] Having disintegrated and collapsed, the statue will be resurrected by God and ground to dust.[106]

According to these visions, God is determined to punish the enemies of Israel and avenge gentile evil even when it no longer exists. According to other visions, especially the universal peace that Isaiah predicts, the gentiles will be happily accepted into the divine system.[107] These coexisting approaches embody not only the difference between ethnocentrism and universalism but the tension between the desire to eliminate a monstrous entity and the dependency on such an entity as a necessary tool for self-determination. Hayyim Vital, for example, wishes for the downfall of his sworn enemy but, at the same time, revives

him as a despicable literary character and subjects him to textual vengeance. Obsessed with his legendary nemesis, Vital seems to suggest
that without the presence of a constant challenge, it would be hard for
him to shape his own identity as a persecuted messiah.

One of the implications of kabbalistic narratives that acknowledge
the inherent imperfection of creation is a permanent sense of anxiety.
Those who live by such narratives believe that every infringement of the
law, even the smallest one, and even if committed accidentally, vandal-
izes the supernal worlds, obstructs the rectification process, prolongs
the exile, and delays the coming of the messiah. On the other hand, it
is, after all, a collective human effort. There is no need, therefore, to
worry about the inability to observe every commandment. Previous
generations have already fulfilled, collectively, large parts of the law.
Human souls transmigrate from one generation to another and travel
through history toward a future point at which every person will have
kept every possible commandment. When this goal is achieved, the
elements of creation will finally be complete: the human self, the divine
plan, and the divinity itself.

CHAPTER 2

The Blueprint of the Universe

How the Text Became Flesh

The Wise and the Restless

A YOUNG MAN lives with his father on a beautiful and prosperous estate. Servants are at his beck and call. High-quality food is cooked to his exact specifications. All imaginable conveniences are at his disposal. Despite the luxury of this modern paradise, he grows increasingly restless. Unlike his brother, he feels suffocated. The serpent senses his impatience and tempts him to leave home. The young man approaches his father and demands his share of the inheritance, then packs a suitcase and embarks on a wild journey, squandering all his money on women and alcohol. Now he is destitute and lonely. On the brink of starvation, he finds employment as a swineherd. Feeding the pigs, he notices that they are, in fact, eating better than him. It is then that he decides to return to his father and beg for forgiveness. Much to the chagrin of his brother, his father accepts him with open arms and prepares a fancy banquet in his honor. His brother, a complaisant type who seems to be content with a quiet life at home, protests the idea of celebrating his ungrateful sibling, suggesting that people who make rash decisions should bear the consequences of their actions. His father, neither judgmental nor reproachful, explains that what this situation requires is compassion, not condemnation.

At the conclusion of this narrative, readers are left with the question of interpretation, especially if it is presented as a parable.[1] Who are the main characters? A forgiving father and a prodigal son? God and Israel? The divinity and humanity? Would it be possible to advance to the next hermeneutical level and read this parable as a story about two aspects of the divinity itself? Would it be possible to offer a kabbalistic interpretation?

The kabbalistic perception of the divinity relies on constant friction between two opposing forces: the willingness to be enlightened by a higher source of wisdom and the tendency to reject supervision from above. Following the unprecedented restriction of the pure, indivisible, infinite light, the transition from ten separate attributes in the primordial structure of creation to the five interconnected configurations that constitute the supernal world of emanation is often marked by tension between an older, patient, forgiving deity and the younger, quick-to-anger, impulsive aspect of the divine system. Two divisions, horizontal and vertical, express this tension. Accentuating the interplay of thought and action, the horizontal division distinguishes between the head, represented by the top three spheres, and the body, represented by the lower seven spheres. The vertical division accentuates the tension between clemency and condemnation, represented by the second and third spheres: mercy and might. Mercy, the power to pardon, is on the right. Might, the authority to convict, is on the left. Mercy comes with thought. Might is an expression of action.

Lurianic Kabbalah, in a manner similar to Jesus, translates these divisions into literary characters. Representing mercy, the prime divine configuration is modeled after the apocalyptic figure of the quintessential wise ruler in the book of Daniel.[2] His clothes are snow-white, his hair is like pure wool, and he looks before he leaps. Representing might, the younger male divine configuration is modeled after the quintessential image of the passionate male lover in the Song of Songs.[3] His hair is raven-black, his physique is impressive, and he shoots from the hip. The original name of the apocalyptic ruler in the book of Daniel is Ancient of Days. The literary theology of the Kabbalah often appropriates this appellation and uses it to designate the divine configuration that surpasses the prime one: the one whose head remains above the world of emanation. The biblical description of the wise ruler, however, is used by the Kabbalah to characterize the prime divine configuration in charge of the world of emanation. Signifying patience, abundant radiance, a large countenance, or a magnanimous persona, the Aramaic name of this divine configuration is *Arikh Anpin*. Signifying impatience, limited radiance, a small countenance, or a parsimonious persona, the Aramaic name of the younger divine configuration is *Zeir Anpin*. Commonly referred to by their acronyms, AA and ZA play the roles of mentor and protégé. In order to achieve a higher degree of composure, the hot-blooded ZA must be enlightened by the emotionally balanced AA.

Many biblical verses are reinterpreted by the Kabbalah, often in unexpected ways, to convey the nature of this relationship. For example, when God descends in a cloud and appears to Moses on top of Mount Sinai, proclaiming the thirteen attributes of divine mercy, it is a complex God that includes both a younger side and an older side.[4] Altering the syntactic structure of this famous episode, the kabbalistic level of interpretation treats the first occurrence of the divine name as the subject of the sentence, the second one as the vocative that introduces the direct speech. According to this interpretation, God says, "God, a merciful and compassionate God, patient and charitable." In other words, ZA, the younger Lord, calls to AA, asking to be guided by the wisdom of the higher Lord and benefit from his equanimity. Elsewhere in kabbalistic writings, the thirteen attributes of mercy that the Bible lists in Exodus are understood as a reference to ZA, whereas a similar list that appears in Micah is interpreted as a description of AA.[5] Despite the rabbinic tradition according to which Moses, unlike Micah, received these attributes directly from the mouth of God,[6] the list that the prophet provides is a manifestation of superior, absolute, everlasting mercy. Late medieval kabbalistic thinkers refer to these attributes as the actions of the crown.[7] Christian thinkers refer to them as the roots of divine mercy: Misericordia. In kabbalistic terms, Misericordia, identified by Thomas Aquinas as the greatest virtue,[8] originates from the highest of the ten spheres: the crown.

Without AA's supervision and illumination, ZA would have condemned all of humanity. The braking system that restrains ZA grants amnesty to those who commit transgressions—the vast majority of humanity—and guarantees the continued existence of the physical realm. AA's job, therefore, is to keep a constant watch on ZA. According to the Zohar, AA's eyes have neither eyebrows nor eyelids. They are always open, like the eyes of fish.[9] In this context, other biblical verses undergo kabbalistic transformations. For example, the God who watches over Israel, the one who never sleeps and never slumbers, is AA.[10] Israel, according to this new interpretation, is ZA, who must remain under the perpetual vigilance of AA. AA's mission is to ensure that ZA enjoys a good balance of left and right: that his judgmental side is softened by a graceful side. This means that AA has only one side: the right side.[11] He is all mercy. And if he has only one side, he must have only one eye. According to the Zohar, when the Bible uses the singular noun *eye*—for example, "the eye of the Lord is on his followers"—the reference is to AA.[12] When the Bible uses the plural form *eyes*—for example, "the eyes of the Lord scan the earth"—the reference is to ZA.[13] In theological terms, human–divine relations are perceived as the desire to narrow the gap between left and right, between the bottom and the top, between the world of action and the world of emanation. In social terms, one of the most explicit expressions of this concept is the importance of watching over the unfortunate.[14] Since humanity is commanded to emulate the uppermost eye, turning a blind eye to the plight of the poor is ungodly behavior. The goal is to imitate not ZA, the traditional God of biblical and rabbinic literature, but the supernal crown: AA.

In similar ways, AA's nose represents the emotional stability that mitigates ZA's fiery temper. Like the eye of ultimate kindness, the nose is an aperture that allows the supernal crown to breathe life into the proverbial nostrils of the lower spheres.[15] Every person is obligated, therefore, to be as long-suffering as AA, avoid the fuming of the nose that signifies anger, and exercise extreme patience, even with those who are clearly indecent.[16] AA's ears and mouth further portray the world of emanation as a network of pathways through which divine wisdom flows from the older configuration to the younger one. AA's forehead, also known as the will of all wills,[17] is another important part. A window to the brain, it reveals the contents of the so-called divine skull: the wisdom of the upper spheres. In other words, it reflects the innermost divine intentions. Its role is to sweeten harsh judgments and eliminate divine wrath. The afternoon Sabbath prayer is considered an hour of mercy: the time in which the will of all wills is revealed, the time in which AA's positive influence on ZA reaches its peak, the time in which prayers are heard, sins are pardoned, and sentences are commuted.[18]

In kabbalistic terms, the prodigal son and his father stand for ZA and AA, while the obedient brother could be understood as another version of the prodigal son himself. More specifically, if the prodigal son represents the foolhardy nature of the younger divine configuration, his brother demonstrates the judgmental tendencies of the same configuration. Along these lines, AA could be perceived as a predictable, dependable, rather static figure, while ZA could be appreciated as an adaptable character who oscillates between passion and prudence, independence and subordination, recklessness and reason. At the same time, AA's inexhaustible inner resources endow him with more depth, whereas ZA's impetuous inclinations render him somewhat superficial. Leaning toward strict justice, ZA tends to adhere to the letter of the law. In that sense, he represents a literal approach to the text: a partial understanding based on limited imagination. AA, on the other hand, stands for anagogical hermeneutics: more ambitious readings that reach beyond the obvious, beyond the elementary level of interpretation. To be like AA is to probe the infinite complexity of the divine mind and enjoy the true freedom that comes with creative thinking. In psychological terms, the tension between AA and ZA is a reflection of an archetypal human conflict: the inevitable clash between the need to benefit from the experience of an accomplished role model and the desire to establish a self-differentiated identity, often through the symbolic elimination of an influential precursor.

Defenders of Humanity

The drama of AA and ZA is one of several intersecting plots that involve the divine configurations. The other characters in the world of emanation are the intermediate configurations—Father and Mother, the so-called middle generation—and the Shekhinah: the sphere of royalty, the heavenly queen who accompanies, supports, and completes ZA. The duality of the biblical epithet throughout the second creation narrative in Genesis—the Lord God—is interpreted by the Kabbalah as a reference to Father and Mother.[19] At some point, Father and Mother breathe life into a new divine being: ZA, the younger male configuration. In the Hebrew of rabbinic literature, he is referred to as the Holy One Blessed Be He; or, less literally, the Blessed Holy One.[20] In the Aramaic of the Zohar, he is called the Blessed Holiness.[21] In any case, it soon becomes clear that he cannot function without a female companion. Father and Mother, therefore, put him to sleep and create another divine being: the Shekhinah. In the Aramaic of the Zohar, she is often referred to as the Matron.[22]

This innovative retelling of the second creation narrative is set not in the garden of Eden but in the world of emanation: the first of three supernal worlds. Chronologically, the birth of the younger divine configurations takes place long before the appearance of humankind,

which occurs only after the shaping of the physical realm: the world
of action. In fact, it is the younger divine configurations—the Blessed
Holiness and his Shekhinah—who announce their intention to create
a human being.[23] The angels, however, are not excited about the idea.
Like children who resent the thought of sharing a private world with
a new sibling, they cite a powerful line of biblical poetry in support of
their objection, arguing that mortals cannot dwell in a lofty place.[24] Not
surprisingly, the original meaning of this aphorism is quite different.
What the psalter means to say, at least according to the first, contextual,
most immediate level of interpretation, is that when wealthy mortals
depart from this world, they rest in their graves, not in their riches.
Conversant with advanced modes of rabbinic and kabbalistic hermeneutics, the angels offer an alternative reading of this verse. Infuriated
by the attempt to promote an exclusive agenda and disparage humanity,
the Blessed Holiness points an accusing finger at the jealous angels,
burns them on the spot, and replaces them with a new group of angels.
When he reveals the plan to create a human being to the new angels,
they respond with another biblical reference, asking for more information about humanity.[25] As in the case of the other quotation, the
plain meaning of this biblical reference is different. More specifically,
it is a rhetorical question that belittles mortals. In some of the rabbinic
versions of the story, the angels use the same quotation in its original
sense, wondering why God would want to bother with the creation of
such a worthless thing as a human being.[26] In the rabbinic imagination,
this is the exact verse that the angels quote when Moses ascends to the
heavenly palace to receive the Torah, demanding to know why God
would want to give this most precious of texts to mere flesh and blood.[27]
In the kabbalistic retelling of the story, the angels, once again, subject a
biblical passage to a new interpretation, using it to ask for clarifications
about the nature of humanity. In response to their request, the Blessed
Holiness describes the proposed human being as smarter than the angels
themselves.[28]

Most of the angels are happy to hear that. Actually, what they are
curious about is whether they would gain something from the creation
of humanity.[29] The Blessed Holiness assures them that they would. The
role of humanity, over a period of six thousand years, would be to lift
the holy sparks from the bottom of the world of action to the top of
the world of emanation. At the end of the process, the entire world of

action will be reincorporated into the world of formation, which will be reincorporated into the world of creation, which will be reincorporated into the world emanation. In other words, humanity itself will rise to the very top, bringing all the lower worlds closer to the oneness of the infinite light. The angels, who reside in the world of formation, will eventually be propelled to an elevated position.

Two angels, however, are unhappy with this proposition. Their names are Aza and Azael. Distinguished from the rest of the angels, they can trace their superior position to the death of the Edomite kings: the cataclysmic event that marks the breaking of the vessels. While all the other angels come from the seven lower spheres, which fall to the world of creation when the vessels shatter, Aza and Azael come from the higher spheres of wisdom and understanding, which, although partially damaged, remain in the world of emanation. As angels who enjoy a better pedigree, a relatively stable status, and a more balanced internal structure, Aza and Azael suspect that the creation of humanity is bound to affect them negatively. Possessed with the power to foresee the future, and having largely recovered from the trauma of the dead kings, they know that Adam and Eve would eat from the forbidden tree in the garden of Eden. They also know that this fateful transgression would result in their own regression to a partially damaged state.[30] Even the willingness of humanity to repent, refine the tainted sparks, and rectify creation would not help Aza and Azael, who would be forced to wait for the complete rectification of the physical realm and the supernal worlds before the damage to their own structure is repaired and their senior status is restored.

According to other kabbalistic versions of the story, it is the Shekhinah who suggests to her male counterpart the idea of a human being.[31] Aza and Azael, who oppose it, try to dissuade the Blessed Holiness from listening to his heavenly queen. Referring to Adam and Eve, the two angels inform the Blessed Holiness that this future human being, the first man on earth, is destined to commit a sin with his woman. Woman, they tell the Blessed Holiness, is the dark side of creation.

While it is obvious that Aza and Azael are trying very hard to malign humanity, it is not entirely clear whether they express misogynistic views. On the one hand, they could be reciting a basic kabbalistic principle: humanity, the whole of creation, and the divinity itself would be incomplete without equal measurements of male and female elements. This is how the Zohar understands the creation narratives of Genesis, in which mutually dependent entities signify the interplay of male and female forces: light and darkness, the heaven and the earth, morning and evening, day and night, the water above the firmament and the water below, the sun and the moon, the six days of creation and the seventh Sabbath day, the river and the garden, and so on. On the other hand, embedded in the defamation of humanity is the suggestion that any female entity is a dubious, dangerous, or sinful force. In response to this accusation, the Shekhinah tells Aza and Azael that the very thing that they so hastily condemn—the female side of creation—will be the cause of their own downfall. What she refers to is the future biblical episode in which the sons of God—in other words, the angels—lust after human daughters.[32] Having exposed the hypocrisy of Aza and Azael, the Shekhinah demotes them, expels them from their holy habitat, and proceeds with the plan to create humanity.

At this point, the text switches to a self-reflexive mode, exposing the frame narrative: an experienced narrator who tells the story of the angels and the Shekhinah to a group of kabbalistic scholars. The scholars, all men, comment on the debate between the angels and the Shekhinah, calling attention to the fact that Aza and Azael are not lying. After all, Adam would indeed sin with Eve. The narrator responds by telling the scholars about the effective retort with which the Shekhinah silences Aza and Azael. You, she says, have been very critical of Adam, much more so than the rest of the heavenly host. If your own behavior had been better than his, your excessive criticism may have been justified. But that is not the case. Adam is destined to sin with one woman, whereas you, the Shekhinah says, will sin with many women. After all, the Bible does use the plural noun, not the singular, when describing the objects of desire that the angels pursue: human daughters. Furthermore, even if Adam sinned, he was quick to repent, return to his divine master, and correct his mistake.

In some alternative versions of the story, it is the male counterpart of the Shekhinah, the Blessed Holiness, who chastises Aza and Azael when they vilify Adam.[33] Had you been in his place, he says to them, you would have done worse. The angels disagree. If we were on earth, they insist, we would behave righteously. Do you really think, the Blessed Holiness asks them, that you could resist the evil urge? We know we can, the angels reply. The Blessed Holiness throws them out of heaven and drops them down on earth, where they become known as the Nephilim.[34] As soon as they find themselves on earth, they are consumed by the evil urge.[35] They take for themselves human women, as many as they can, and lose their holy status. As in the case of Adam and Eve, it is not sexual desire that constitutes sinful behavior but the inclination to satisfy selfish urges rather than acknowledge the needs of others.

This interplay of creative variations serves two purposes. First, it emphasizes the vibrant qualities of the text itself. Rather than a monolithic portrayal of the divinity or an official version of creation, the Zohar offers a tapestry of possibilities, a network of combinations, a plurality of viewpoints. Second, it emphasizes adjustable gender roles. While some scenes shape the divine ruler in the traditional image of a king, others depict a clever queen who knows how to handle even the most difficult members of her cabinet, and even when they resort to aggressive, manipulative, or sanctimonious tactics.

The relations among the divine configurations in the world of emanation are further explored in a parable that equates creation to the construction of a royal palace. In the rabbinic version of the parable, a king who builds a palace cannot do anything without an architect, and an architect cannot do anything without a blueprint. The blueprint is the Torah: the sacred text that has always been in existence. Just as an architect consults a house plan when building the various rooms and hallways of the palace, so does God consult the Torah when creating the world.[36] In the kabbalistic version of the parable, ZA is the king, the Shekhinah is the architect. Unable to make her own decisions, the Shekhinah awaits orders from the king. Unable to translate his own ideas into practical terms, the king is dependent on the Shekhinah for the execution of his vision.[37] In fact, there are two kings and two architects in the world of emanation. The higher king and architect are Father and Mother, who give birth to—or construct—ZA and the Shekhinah. The lower king and architect are ZA and the Shekhinah, who give birth to—or construct—the human souls and the next three worlds: creation, formation, and action. Throughout most of the first creation narrative in Genesis, it is Father who says, and Mother who does. For example, Father says, Let there be light, and Mother creates the light. Father says, Let there be a firmament, and Mother creates the firmament. In other words, the male aspect of the divinity, the voice, imparts the design of creation to the female aspect of the divinity.[38] In her role as master craftswoman, the female aspect of the divinity is in charge of transforming thought into action.[39] The only exception is when the divinity decides to create humanity.[40] This time, it is the Shekhinah who says, "Let us make a human being in our image, after our likeness." This time, it is the female aspect of the divinity that represents thought.

The Life of the Vessel

In the late medieval Kabbalah of the Zohar, thought and action are complementary aspects of the divinity. In the sixteenth-century Kabbalah of Isaac Luria and Hayyim Vital, thought and action can be considered lights and vessels. In the twentieth-century Kabbalah of Yehuda Ashlag, the focus shifts from the light to the vessel: from the divinity to humanity. Creation, according to this branch of the Kabbalah, is the desire to obtain the infinite abundance of the divine light. This desire must be rectified, purified, and properly refined. Ultimately, it must be transformed from a self-serving instinct into the godlike ability to receive in order to give, to acquire in order to share, to absorb as much of the heavenly plenty in order to transmit it to others.[41]

According to Ashlagian Kabbalah, the formation of a vessel that can accept the divine light is a four-stage process. During the first stage, creation is a vessel that lacks self-awareness. It receives sustenance from above without questioning its passive role. Like a newborn baby, it is characterized by a categorical inability to contribute to its own nourishment. It maintains a symbiotic relationship with the light that cloaks it, remaining inactive. During the second stage, the vessel becomes conscious of the fact that it is supported by a higher power. Ashamed of its unequal role in the relationship, it rejects the light. Now it wishes, more than anything else, to resemble its benefactor. Like a slightly older child who insists on being independent, the vessel attempts, prematurely, to establish an autonomous identity. When it realizes that it cannot make it on its own, it moves to the third stage. Now it accepts only a small amount of the divine light, no more than the minimum necessary for its basic needs. This small dose of goodness, however, reminds the vessel of the unlimited amount of divine succor that it enjoyed in the past.

The reduced amount of light, in other words, triggers in the vessel the memory of the copious amount that it relished during the earliest stage of its existence, which, in turn, triggers a deep yearning for more. Now it desires all the light that it can get. This is the fourth stage. By the end of this stage, the vessel reaches the most potent degree of craving. The fourth stage, therefore, is diametrically opposed to the essence of the divinity. While the divinity lacks nothing, wishing only to bestow its goodness on others, the vessel, particularly in its final form, is focused on egocentric needs. Despite the obvious ungodliness of this stage, the burning ambition that it represents is absolutely vital for the formation of a complete vessel. In human terms, a complete vessel is an individual who is eager to enjoy all that the world has to offer. Now the vessel must begin the process of rectification. Now it must learn to impose limitations on its hunger for more and share the divine light with neighboring vessels. Like a human being motivated by love rather than self-gratification, it must cultivate the ability to delight in divinely sanctioned pleasure while focusing on the act of bringing pleasure to others.

The formation of the vessel is a schematic process that serves as a master plan of creation. Anticipating the next episodes in the cosmological narrative, the life cycle of the vessel provides a wiring diagram, so to speak, for numerous structures and events that follow the same pattern: the lights that issue from the metaphorical body of the primordial structure, the letters of the alphabet, the ten spheres, the divine configurations, the supernal worlds and the physical realm, the tension between mercy and judgment, the descent of the human soul from its divine origin to a corporeal domain, and, perhaps most importantly, the psychological growth of every human being. For example, the first sphere, the crown, represents the infinite light: the unchanging wish of a benevolent divinity to bestow its endless goodness on creation. The second sphere, wisdom, represents a passive recipient: a vessel during the first stage of its development, unaware of its complete dependency on the divine light. It also represents the initial separation of the human soul from the infinite light and its subsequent descent to the first supernal world: the world of emanation, where it exists in an embryonic state. The third sphere, understanding, represents the second stage in the development of the vessel: the beginning of self-consciousness, followed by an initial rejection of the light. It also represents the transition of the human soul from the world of emanation to the next supernal world:

the world of creation, where it is now completely separated from the infinite light. At this point, despite its inability to express an intense desire, the soul begins to develop its own sense of volition.

The next six spheres, collectively known as beauty, represent the third stage in the development of the vessel: the willingness to accept a limited amount of light. This cluster of spheres also represents the descent of the soul from the world of creation to the next supernal world: the world of formation, which functions as an active environment that triggers self-awareness. At this point, when the downgraded soul is known as a spirit, it learns to gain a better understanding of itself. This cluster of six spheres also represents ZA: the younger male configuration. Like the vessel and the spirit, ZA must navigate between self-generated decisions and the wise counsel he receives from above. Needless to say, this is a most difficult stage. In human terms, this is the stage during which the youth are confronted with the obvious disadvantages of their daredevil proclivities. At the same time, aware as they may be of the need to embrace more sensible habits, they are afraid that guidance from the older generation would compromise their independence.

The last sphere, royalty, represents the fourth and final stage: a complete, self-governed, self-centered vessel that desires to accept as much of the divine light as possible. At this point, the vessel is entirely separated from the infinite light. The sphere of royalty also represents the final descent of the human soul from the world of formation to the physical realm: the world of action. In this world, the spirit becomes the lifeblood of humanity. The lifeblood—the egocentric desire to satisfy immediate urges—is bestial but necessary. The goal of humanity is to strengthen the soul and prevent the lifeblood from holding the reins. In that sense, the body is not an abject thing whose needs must be denied but an indispensable part of creation that must be acknowledged and celebrated, especially when it is used for the keeping of the commandments and the performance of charitable acts, for the formation of meaningful relations with fellow human beings, and for a genuine expression of deep love. A pleasure-seeking person, therefore, is a complete vessel, shaped in accordance with the divine plan. If divine generosity is endless, the purpose of creation is to serve as an expansive receptacle that aspires to self-actualization. In other words, the fulfillment of emptiness with unbridled pleasure is perfectly compatible with the will of God. Nevertheless, it is only half of the divine plan. Now the vessel must embark on a journey toward altruism.

This pattern becomes evident when biblical stories are examined from the psychological perspectives of Ashlagian Kabbalah. Representing hedonism, the serpent encourages Adam and Eve to focus on themselves. When they eat the eye-pleasing fruit, they express a healthy craving for the pleasures of adulthood. Without this craving, they would not be able to disentangle themselves from an overprotective environment that provides for their material needs but keeps them in a childish state. Similarly, the selfish demands of the prodigal son are healthy expressions of adult aspirations. Without this hedonistic appetite, he would not be able to make his own choices, his own mistakes. Now, like Adam and Eve, he must embark on the second leg of his journey, at the end of which he will return home as a better, more considerate, more conscientious vessel. If the fourth stage of the vessel represents the individual, the infinite light stands for the community. In other words, the journey of the vessel back to its divine origin is a voyage toward social awareness. The sphere of royalty, therefore, while marking the most selfish, most impure, most conceited stage in the development of the vessel, anticipates the end of the journey: the completion of the rectification process.

The primary mechanism that facilitates the rectification of the vessel is a special filter that transforms hedonism into altruism. Known as a screen, it regulates the flow of divine light.[42] If accepted directly, the divine light would flood, overwhelm, and paralyze the vessel. More specifically, it would shame the vessel. The realization that accepting the light for self-serving purposes would be a disgraceful act is the first stage in the rectification of the vessel. In the next stage, the vessel expresses a willingness to accept the light not because it nurtures narcissistic needs but because it can foster true love: love for the collective rather than the individual, for the concept of partnership rather than the self. This is when the screen becomes operational. Acting as a protective device, its initial function is to identify the precise amount of divine light that the vessel can use to benefit others. It then separates this type of light from any excess light that cannot be converted into an altruistic force. The screen blocks the excess light and allows only processed light to diffuse into the vessel.

The processed light that enters the vessel is a mixture of direct light and reflected light. When direct light hits the screen, it must be rejected. The screen determines how much of the direct light can be converted into altruism and turns this portion into reflected light, which contains antidotes against egotism. These antidotes express the willingness of the vessel to rectify itself: to eliminate the discrepancy between its own shape and the divinity that shapes it, between the selfishness of creation and the selflessness of the creator. The reflected light mixes with the direct light, enriches it, and allows it to pass through the screen. When it indwells the vessel, it becomes its inner light, while the excess light becomes surrounding light: light that hovers outside the vessel, waiting to be admitted. This is the third stage in the rectification of the vessel. The fourth and final stage represents the ultimate purpose of the vessel: to absorb all the divine light. And since the divinity does not wish to give humanity a partial gift, a rectified vessel is a vessel that can convert the entirety of the divine light, with no residue, from self-centered desire into love.

This version of the kabbalistic narrative, typically Ashlagian, suggests a new approach to one of the most controversial concepts in Lurianic thought: the restriction of the infinite light.[43] Generally speaking, post-Lurianic kabbalistic thinkers can be divided into two camps: those who believe that the restriction, contraction, or withdrawal of the infinite light is to be understood literally, and those who believe it should be interpreted figuratively. The difficulty of imagining a divine power that restricts its own presence, decreases its own size, or withdraws from existence, even temporarily, is understandable. From a religious perspective, such a thought might border on blasphemy. In an attempt to keep the omnipresence of the divinity intact, some kabbalistic thinkers argue, therefore, that the restriction of the infinite light is merely a metaphor. Otherwise, the light could not be called infinite. Other voices in kabbalistic thought, however, insist that creation does begin with an ephemeral moment of absolute emptiness, unprecedented and unrepeatable. Echoing the concept of *kenosis*, the divine light, according to this school of thought, empties itself in order to make room for creation.

A dramatic shift in point of view—from the divinity to the vessel, from the creator to the created—allows Ashlagian Kabbalah to propose an elegant solution to the debate. The restriction of the infinite light is a direct result of the increased awareness of the vessel. During the second stage of its development and rectification, the vessel becomes ashamed of its own egotistical needs. Embracing the idea of self-control, the vessel rejects the infinite pleasure of the divine light. From now on, the infinite light can be accepted only if it can be used as an instrument of love. It is during this stage that the restriction, contraction, or withdrawal of the infinite light occurs. From the perspective of the divinity, there is no change in the infinite light. It continues to flow, generously and ceaselessly, whether the vessel accepts or rejects it. It is only from the perspective of the vessel that the light can stop. In other words, it is not the divinity that restricts itself. It is the vessel that chooses to exercise self-restraint. This pivotal choice engenders the screen: an internal force that imposes limitations on the appetite for pleasure. Most importantly, the screen serves as a meeting point between the desire to receive and the desire to give. From now on, the vessel accepts the light only as a compromise between these clashing tendencies: a coupling of colliding powers.[44]

The Screen

While the propelling event in both Lurianic Kabbalah and Ashlagian Kabbalah is identical, the latter is simultaneously more technical and more conceptual, more abstract and more tangible, translating every detail of the supernal worlds into human terms. Both narratives, the Lurianic and the Ashlagian, begin with the divine decision to initiate the creation process. What prompts the divinity to do so is the desire to bestow its goodness on humanity. The next step in the Lurianic narrative is the contraction of the infinite light: the carving of an empty space that will eventually host the physical realm and human life. The next step in the Ashlagian narrative, on the other hand, is the birth of the vessel: the formation of a receptacle that will contain the infinite light and eventually hold the goodness of the divinity. Divided into four stages, the development of the vessel culminates in the burning ambition to receive as much of the infinite light as possible. It is only when the vessel chooses to curb this ambition that the restriction of the infinite light occurs.

At this stage, the Ashlagian vessel foreshadows a series of female elements that play crucial roles in kabbalistic theology: the sphere of royalty, the terminal port of the divinity; the Shekhinah, the heavenly bride; and humanity, the designated recipient of divine bounty. In other words, creation itself is a female entity, represented by the fourth stage in the development of the vessel. After all, if the divine configurations in the world of emanation are conceived as male and female—ZA and the Shekhinah, Father and Mother, and the one-eyed AA, whose female side is included within him—it follows that the infinite light, the earliest element in the kabbalistic narrative, should also be accompanied by a female counterpart: a primeval queen who serves as an archetype of humanity.

More immediately, the fourth stage in the development of the vessel anticipates the clusters of emanations in the primordial structure and the divine configurations in the world of emanation. The numbers and sizes of clusters and configurations are determined by five degrees of craving that mark the fourth stage of the vessel. The bigger the appetite for the divine light, the more powerful the screen that facilitates the coupling of colliding forces. A solid screen can replace a high degree of self-indulgence with an equally high degree of self-control, allowing a generous amount of processed light to enter the vessel. By the same token, a modest yearning for the pleasure of the divine light does not require the most solid screen. Small ambitions can be effectively converted into self-control with a reasonably weaker screen.

In fact, two screens are active inside the vessel, advancing the interplay of thought and action. The first screen is situated in the upper part, the so-called head of the vessel, while a lower screen marks the so-called body of the vessel. The head screen, located in the metaphorical mouth of the vessel, is where the divine intention to offer its unlimited light collides with the decision of the vessel to control its craving for more. The body screen, located in the metaphorical navel of the vessel, is where the surrounding light collides with the inner light. Contained between the head screen and the body screen, the inner light represents only a small part of the potential capacity of the vessel, whose ultimate purpose is to accept the entirety of the infinite light: all the bounty that the divinity has to offer. The surrounding light, having been denied admittance into the vessel, puts pressure on the body screen, urging it to accept more.[45] Aware of its own limitations, the body screen abandons its position and ascends to the upper part of the vessel. Knowing that additional light cannot be converted from hedonistic pleasure into altruistic love, the body screen seeks the company of its superior counterpart, the head screen. Better equipped to identify and reject inconvertible light, the head screen teaches the body screen how to improve its ability to handle the pressure of such light. In kabbalistic terms, the screen, whose ascension signifies a gradual weakening, loses its thickness, its density. When it reaches the upper part of the vessel, it becomes as pure as the head screen. Now it collides directly with the divine light. Having acquired this kind of experience, it is now ready to become the head screen of a new vessel.

The concept of the screen marks a shift to triadic relations. From now on, a third element must be present to negotiate the tension between the ego and the other, the individual and the collective, personal needs and pure love. The head screen, also known as the coupling royalty, rejects the direct light, converts it into reflected light, and admits it into the vessel. The body screen, also known as the demarcating royalty, restricts the inner light that has been accepted into the vessel and resists the pressure to admit the surrounding light. Both screens are female elements. The coupling royalty is the queen of the mouth: the screen from which the head is born.[46] The demarcating royalty is the queen of the navel: the terminal port of the torso, also known as the royalty of royalty.[47] Each of these parts, the head and the torso, is divided into ten spheres. The third part of the vessel, from the navel to the feet, is likewise divided into ten spheres. Its terminal port, marked by the toes, is the royalty of the royalty of royalty: the spot from which humanity is bound to be created. Eventually, at the end of the rectification process, the inner light, which stands for the infinite goodness of the divinity, will spread all the way to the toes of the vessel. Until then, the body screen—the demarcating royalty—functions as a barrier, preventing the inner light from spreading below the navel. At this point, the lower part of the vessel remains dark.

Nevertheless, the pressure on the body screen is essential to the growth of the vessel and the development of creation. It pushes the vessel toward additional progress and motivates it to advance to the next level. The vessel, eager to accept more but afraid of losing what it has already acquired, must be very cautious. The struggle between the surrounding light and the inner light—between the endless pleasure that the divinity offers and the limited capacity to convert hedonism into altruism—encourages the vessel to switch to a lower position, where the pressure is less intense and therefore more manageable.

The thinning of the screen, its ascension to the head, and its subsequent descent to a lower position are developmental stages that signal the transition to the primordial structure. Anticipating the world of emanation, each of the positions of the vessel is now called a configuration.[48] The first configuration, known as the skull, is the largest one. It corresponds to the highest degree of craving, which requires the most powerful screen. When the body screen of this configuration ascends to the head and, after a period of practical training, descends to a lower position, it becomes the head screen of the next configuration. Smaller in size yet still rather lofty, this new configuration corresponds to the numerical value of the highest spelling of the Hebrew letters of the Tetragrammaton: seventy-two. When the body screen of this configuration encounters the pressure of the surrounding light, it ascends, like its predecessor, to the head. When it descends to a lower position, it becomes the head screen of the next configuration, which corresponds to the numerical value of a lower spelling of the Hebrew letters of the Tetragrammaton: sixty-three. The process is repeated twice more, producing the remaining configurations, which correspond to the numerical values of two additional spellings of the Hebrew letters of the Tetragrammaton: forty-five and fifty-two.

The ascension of the screen does not signify a suppression of the desire for the divine light. The craving remains intense, but the screen puts it on hold, so to speak, in order to manufacture better conversion tools: internal checks and balances that, in the future, will help the configuration enjoy the utmost degree of pleasure without the overwhelming sensation that might numb its conscience or render it incapable of seeking anything other than self-gratification. In biblical terms, the surrounding light is a prototype of the serpent. It seduces Adam and Eve, urging them to devour more than they can digest, to consume more than they can contain. The descent of the screen to a lower spot anticipates the expulsion from Eden. Adam and Eve, in order to avoid further temptation, must leave a demanding position and, under less stressful conditions, develop the ability to withstand pressure. The exile from Eden is the essence of rectification. At the end of the process, humanity will perfect its screen, return to a state of expanded consciousness, and delight in its own maturity. According to this narrative, history progresses on a reverse timeline, contrary to the developmental stages of the vessel, the order of the configurations, and the sequence of lights that issue from the metaphorical openings in the primordial structure. The meaning of human development, therefore, is a counterclockwise journey toward complete repair: to the full potential of the vessel.

When the body screen ascends to the head, it carries two major types of information that are necessary for the transition into the next configuration. The first type of information is a record of the light that indwells the body of the configuration.[49] The second type is a record of the power to receive more: the potential to admit additional light.[50] The first is a male element. It is not solid enough to collide with the light and therefore capable of producing only the head of the next configuration: abstract thought that cannot develop into practical terms. The second type of information is a female element. As such, it can spread into the body of the next configuration and fully animate it. If the former stands for the imagination, the latter signifies action. If the former stands for the brain, the latter signifies the heart. If the former stands for cognition, the latter signifies love. By the same token, the heavenly king suggests the idea of creation, while the divine craftswoman is the one who makes it happen.

The Second Contraction

The reflected light processed by the queen of the mouth—the coupling royalty—constitutes the ten spheres of the head of the configuration. In addition, the head stores the surrounding light that awaits its turn to enter the body of the configuration. The inner light that indwells the ten spheres of the body of the configuration, from the mouth to the navel, denotes the purpose of creation: the divine pleasure that humanity is destined to enjoy. The rejection of the light in the lower part of the configuration, from the navel to the feet, signifies the rectification of creation: the pleasure of self-restraint. This self-restraint is considered a light of mercy, while the ability to enjoy it directly, in its purest form, is considered a light of wisdom. Although mostly dark, the lower part of the configuration does receive some light of mercy mixed with wisdom. This is the Ashlagian equivalent of the Lurianic world of *Akudim*: the transitional phase during which the so-called striped emanations, bound in a single receptacle, issue from the mouth of the primordial structure. At this stage, the light of wisdom is bound with the light of mercy. This mixture of lights is received in the first nine spheres of the lower part of the configuration. It denotes the fact that these internal spheres wish to convert additional pleasure into altruistic love but acknowledge the fact that they are not ready to do so. The terminal sphere of the lower part of the configuration, however, is devoid of any light. This is the sphere of royalty: the essence of the craving for the light. The fact that it is utterly dark means that it lacks the potential to develop sparks of altruism. The divine plan to create humanity from this terminal spot—from the royalty of the royalty of royalty—cannot be accomplished if the bottom spot is not illuminated. The problem is that as long as this spot is incapable of using the light for altruistic causes, it cannot be illuminated.

The solution is a second contraction: another withdrawal of the divine light. This contraction occurs in the third configuration of the primordial structure: the one whose numerical value is sixty-three. What facilitates this crucial move is the merging of two female elements: the spheres of royalty and understanding. The royalty of the head of the third configuration ascends from the mouth to the eyes, where the sphere of understanding is located, while the royalty at the bottom of the configuration ascends from the toes to the chest, where the sphere of beauty is located. In this context, the sphere of beauty is considered the understanding of the body. Just as understanding is the third sphere of the head, so is beauty the third sphere of the body. When these parallel mergers occur, understanding, also known as Mother, lends her altruistic sparks to royalty, the younger female sphere. The area below the chest remains empty, and the ascending royalty, with the help of the sparks that she borrows from understanding, engenders the fourth configuration: the one whose numerical value is forty-five. This is the Ashlagian equivalent of the Lurianic world of *Nekudim*: the transitional phase during which the so-called speckled emanations, accompanied by ten independent vessels, issue from the eyes of the primordial structure. This is the configuration that contains the roots of the more stable worlds that follow the transitional phases: the world of emanation, the world of creation, the world of formation, and the world of action.

Now that there is room for the world of action, humanity can be created. The second contraction that empties the body of the third configuration helps the sphere of royalty ascend to understanding, which guarantees that humanity will be endowed with altruistic sparks: the potential to perform the good deeds that will eventually rectify creation. According to this narrative, humanity is born of female bonding: a close collaboration between a mother figure and her daughter. This is how the Kabbalah interprets the vow of loyalty between Ruth and Naomi.

Ruth, who represents the sphere of royalty, clings to Naomi. Naomi, who represents the sphere of understanding, shares her wisdom with Ruth. This act of sharing is the essence of the second contraction. The first contraction renders the daughter—the sphere of royalty, the last of the divine attributes—incapable of receiving the pleasure of the light unless it collides with the screen and undergoes a process of mediation and transformation. As a result of this process, the desire for pleasure is coupled with altruistic love. In other words, the first contraction is the willingness of the daughter to impose limitations on her desire for the light in order to derive a greater pleasure from the ability to share it with others. Mother, on the other hand, represented by the sphere of understanding, is part of the top three spheres: the so-called brains of the divinity, which stand for pure thought. As such, she can receive the light in its purest form, without the danger of losing herself in the pleasure that it brings. Immune to the kind of thoughtlessness that comes with self-indulgence, the sphere of understanding requires no contraction, no limitations, and no screen. In order to help a fellow female sphere, however, she relinquishes her privileged status and temporarily removes herself from her higher position. In the language of the Zohar, Mother lends her garments to her daughter and adorns her with her ornaments.[51] More specifically, in order to allow royalty to enjoy the divine light, understanding suspends her right to receive it directly. She agrees to be fitted with a screen so that the light of wisdom that she normally receives goes instead to royalty.[52] Once royalty receives the light of wisdom, she becomes an independent, more complete, more promising entity. Now she can serve as the progenitor of humanity. Meanwhile, understanding returns to her usual spot and, no longer bound by the second contraction, resumes the uninterrupted reception of the light of wisdom.

If wisdom is the pure, direct, unmitigated spreading of the light, mercy is the desire to receive it. Naomi, who shares her wisdom with her daughter-in-law, specifies the garments that will help Ruth receive what she desires.[53] In terms of divine attributes, the younger female element, royalty, represents uncompromising justice, while the older female element, understanding, represents compassion. Prone to bitter condemnation, the younger female element must be sweetened by the older one in order to sustain humanity. A similar relationship exists between ZA and AA, the younger and older male configurations in

the world of emanation. Eager to exercise his judicial power, ZA must
be counseled and corrected by the patient, forgiving, more mature AA.

The centrality of the female elements, however, is one of the most
interesting innovations of kabbalistic literature. The opening scene of
the Zohar portrays these female figures as two roses. When the sphere
of royalty ascends to the sphere of understanding and achieves a higher
level of maturity, she is called a rose. It is then that her colors are red and
white: a mixture of justice and clemency. When she is in her infancy, she
is called a rose among thistles.[54] In that state, she is mostly red. Only her
top internal sphere, the crown, represents clemency, while the rest of her
nine internal spheres represent justice. The mixture of red and white—
judgment and mercy—means that even in her mature state, when she
ascends to the sphere of understanding, she needs her screen. The judgmental quality of the screen helps her reject the direct light, convert it
into reflected light, and process it successfully.[55] In human terms, one
needs a strong sense of self in order to convert selfishness into selflessness.

In the beginning, the desire for the divine light becomes the body
of the vessel. The body of the vessel, which turns into the most active
part in each of the divine configurations, represents the letters of the
Tetragrammaton, the Hebrew alphabet, the text of the Torah, biblical
and rabbinic literature, and all past, current, and future commentaries
and interpretations. This active part of the configuration becomes the
younger female aspect of the divinity: the tenth sphere, the heavenly
bride who travels up and down to receive the light from the higher
mother—the third sphere—and distribute it below. When the creation
of the physical realm is made possible, she becomes the flesh and blood
of humanity. An important implication of this narrative is that altruistic behavior, which stems from a successful imitation of the divinity,
is not an ecstatic experience that culminates in the denial of the body.
Never does the spiritual bliss that comes with the ability to emulate
the divinity transcend the corporeal dimensions of existence. The pleasures that the corporal dimensions offer are crucial to the fulfillment
of the purpose of creation: the ability to enjoy an infinite degree of
divine opulence. To acquire this ability, humanity must develop a good
screen: a mechanism that will allow the individual to resist avaricious
urges, ascend to a higher level of awareness, espouse the infinitely philanthropic habits of the divinity, descend to the mundane world, and
employ these habits to create a new and improved version of humanity.

The ability of humanity to occupy two positions, represented by the female spheres of royalty and understanding, is a narrative paradigm that typifies the tension between what the Kabbalah calls smallness and greatness.[56] When the Shekhinah is secure in her lofty dwelling place, at the temple in Jerusalem, she is in a state of greatness. When she is banished from her palace by imperial oppressors, she is in a state of smallness. With the devoted protection that the people provide her, she is sustained in exile. At the end of every week, during the Sabbath, she rises again to her elevated position, regains access to the invigorating radiance of the supernal worlds, and returns to the physical realm with the added enlightenment that, in turn, sustains humanity. These alternating settings mirror the duality of the locations that Esther inhabits: one inside the royal court, as a young queen whose mission is to safeguard the Jewish nation, and one outside the palace, among her people. Judith, in her role as the savior of the community, occupies the same positions: one inside the headquarters of the enemy, where she is forced to degrade herself in order to acquire the means with which to protect the nation, and one at home, among her people. In kabbalistic terms, she is willing to contract herself. Like the sphere of understanding, she sacrifices her personal comfort and assumes a temporarily demoted position to secure the future of the congregation. In a similar manner, Tamar contracts herself when she manipulates Judah. In her state of smallness, she is forced to wear a degrading disguise in order to acquire the means with which to produce the next generation of her family. In her state of greatness, she returns home as the future mother of a royal dynasty that is destined to serve as an everlasting sign of hope for the exiled nation.

Conceived and developed in the first decades of the twentieth century, Ashlagian Kabbalah may have maintained some relations, direct or unspoken, with adjacent modernist narratives, especially female-centered ones. Some of these narratives seem to offer playful variations, decidedly secular yet potentially theological, on the Ashlagian concept of the second contraction. In a manner similar to the Ashlagian reading of the Ruth and Naomi story, a 1931 musical comedy—*The Smiling Lieutenant*—features Claudette Colbert in the role of understanding, Miriam Hopkins in the role of royalty.[57] The former is a generous, resilient, independent woman from Vienna, while the latter is a provincial, childish, sexually repressed princess from Flausenthurm, a miniature fictional kingdom across the Austrian border. Both are in love with the same man: a charming army lieutenant, played by Maurice Chevalier, who, despite his commitment to his Viennese lover, is forced by the emperor to marry the princess. At the end of the movie, the elegant, urbane, more experienced woman, attuned to the pain and frustration that the princess endures, abandons the role of a competitor and decides to become a mentor. With her help, the princess transforms from a petulant, supercilious, judgmental character into a radiant, warm, passionate woman. An icon of wisdom, sensitivity, and sisterhood, the more confident woman contracts herself, relinquishes her intimate relationship with the lieutenant, lends her clothes to the small-town princess—literally and figuratively—and teaches her how to secure the attention, admiration, and devotion of the man whom they both desire. What enables her to sacrifice her personal happiness for the sake of a fellow woman whose physical, emotional, and spiritual needs are unfulfilled is her faith in her own ability to find new love.

Such narratives demonstrate the Ashlagian principle of altruistic behavior as the ultimate manifestation of the ongoing effort to minimize dissimilarities between humanity and the divinity.[58] If the vessel is confident of its ability to receive more of the light, it will gladly give the light that it has accumulated to other vessels, refraining from treating it as private, exclusive, nontransferable property. What allows the vessel to do so is the knowledge that other vessels will do the same. In other words, the vessel knows that if it ever found itself in need, other vessels would gladly support it. In theological terms, this kind of social responsibility, based on a permanent mutual guarantee, is the essence of enhanced congruence between the created and the creator: between the shape of the vessel and the divinity that shapes it.

Literary Luminaries

The journey of humanity toward enhanced congruence with the divinity is not a mystical quest. It does not transcend the normal limits of the mind, nor does it expose the so-called mysterious layers of existence. It is based on an ongoing intellectual, psychological, and behavioral effort: a personal and social journey guided by kabbalistic texts. The essence of this journey is intertextual. In many cases, one kabbalistic text offers a radical retelling of another. Ashlagian Kabbalah, for example, changes the definition of sin when it engages with the Zohar. The antagonistic angels, Aza and Azael, are wicked not because they pursue human females but because they operate without a screen, seeking pleasure while disregarding the presence, needs, or potential growth of others. Slaves to the highest degree of desire, which the vessel experiences during the fourth stage of its development, they exploit women to gratify selfish urges. Unlike common interpretations, this reading does not treat the sexual act itself, let alone the idea of woman, as inherently sinful. In that sense, it also offers a new definition of the text. No longer an object whose underpinnings can be adequately charted and classified, the text becomes a subject, an agent, a partner for dialogue: a living entity that readers reconstruct and reimagine every time they engage with it. This new definition allows multiple interpretations to enrich rather than essentialize the text. In addition, it encourages more charitable interpretations: readings that validate the text despite its imperfections. This kind of hospitable interaction embraces the text as a lifelong companion and accentuates its commendable aspects, bracketing interpretations that decry its questionable characteristics.

Disparate frameworks, according to this capacious approach, do not contaminate one another. They enhance one another, allowing neighboring texts to become more complex, more comprehensive, more complete. It is thus possible to offer kabbalistic readings of seemingly dissimilar texts, including the New Testament, modernist literature, and pre-Code cinema. It is also possible to offer new readings of the very kabbalistic texts that serve as interpretive prisms. If the vessel, for example, goes through four developmental stages—passive reception of the light, active rejection of the light, minimal desire for the light, and maximal desire for the light—certain Hasidic readings of this narrative treat the fourth stage, represented by the body of the third configuration in the primordial structure, as the average human being. Generally speaking, the Hasidic movement identifies intellectual pursuits, including Torah study, with elitism. As a counterargument to the elevated social status of the textual scholar, Hasidic thought refrains from dismissing embodied worship, especially when performed by the uneducated. With its roots in eighteenth-century Eastern Europe, the Hasidic movement often clashes with the classic image of overly cerebral Jews who devote themselves to endless Talmudic debates. While the accuracy of this assessment could be contested, especially in view of the fact that the Hasidic movement has never been a unified, consistent, or otherwise easily defined endeavor, it is interesting to note that some Hasidic interpretations of the second contraction in Ashlagian Kabbalah regard the sphere of understanding as the Hasidic movement itself: a light of mercy that spreads into the lowest part of the third configuration, from the navel to the feet, bringing wisdom to the masses and allowing the soul to indwell the body. The body, according to this interpretation, represents the simple people: everyday Jews. Without the Hasidic movement, Judaism would be a head without a body, abstract thought without a congregation.[59] With the help of such readings, familiar narratives acquire fresh meanings, bloom into new possibilities, and shine in new lights.

Resisting compartmentalized textuality, the Kabbalah presents a considerable challenge to those who wish to define it. Attempts to do so, especially in the academic world, often result in heated debates, polarizing viewpoints, and personal attacks. Scholars appeal to a wide variety of concepts and contexts in their efforts to affix telltale labels to the Kabbalah, the most common of which are Jewish mysticism, Jewish theosophy, Jewish magic, and Jewish theurgy. Adjectives such as mythical, symbolic, ecstatic, and experiential are often attached to kabbalistic texts, and rival camps of researchers wrestle for control over the discipline and its methods.[60] Treated as literature, the Kabbalah accommodates all the above labels. It is mystical in the sense that all literature, with its power to induce significant changes in the consciousness of the reader, is mystical. It is mythical in the sense that all literature, with its tendency to generate timeless narratives, is mythical. It is ecstatic in the sense that all literature, with its curious ability to remove readers from their immediate surroundings—to lift them from the mundane circumstances of the physical realm to an imaginary world that seems to exist on a higher sphere—is ecstatic. It is experiential in the sense that all literature, with its propensity to trigger intense emotions, is experiential. Even when approached as theurgy—as a program that, when practiced on earth, introduces changes in the supernal worlds and sustains the entire universe—the Kabbalah embodies a principle that, to a large extent, is true of all literature. If literature has the power to engender hitherto unimagined realities, it is the very acts of reading, interpretation, and rewriting that, by necessity, reshape and maintain these realities. In religious terms, the keeping of the commandments, including daily Torah study, makes the world go round.[61] In kabbalistic terms, an awakening below guarantees and amplifies the flow of divine bounty from above.[62] In literary terms, the text constructs vivid settings, unforgettable characters, striking images, defining moments, and other textual constituents that, as indelible as they may be, rely on active readers for their continuous existence.

On the other hand, it may well be argued that the Kabbalah rejects all the above labels. Rather than submit to multiple definitions, it signals the need for a new definition, which the vessel might provide. Presented as a literary character, the vessel suggests that the Kabbalah itself should be treated in literary terms. Following decades of repeated attempts to define the Kabbalah in terms such as mysticism, myth, and symbol—or magic, ecstasy, and experience—scholarly voices in the late twentieth century called attention to the fact that literary modes of reading had been traditionally excluded from academic Kabbalah studies.[63] Despite a steadily growing academic interest in the Kabbalah, twenty-first-century studies that do emphasize the poetic aspects of kabbalistic literature continue to refer to it as mysticism, myth, or magic.[64] Equally disappointing is the fact that many of these studies focus mainly on Zoharic, pre-Zoharic, and Lurianic texts, neglecting later kabbalistic literature. While the poetic virtuosity of the Zohar, Tikkunei Zohar, and the Lurianic corpus is quite remarkable, later kabbalistic literature— especially the writings of Moses Hayyim Luzzatto, Nachman of Breslov, Abraham Isaac Kook, Yehuda Fetaya, and Yehuda Ashlag—is equally impressive and arguably more versatile, exploring a wider range of literary genres and techniques.

Not surprisingly, academic scholars often mimic the traditional rabbinic desire to control the Kabbalah. In both cases, self-appointed gatekeepers, aware of the endlessly creative nature of the kabbalistic imagination, take it upon themselves to stabilize it, divest it of its literary garments, and harness it into a solid, safe, pseudoscientific field of inquiry. Even among kabbalistic thinkers, certain voices call for a narrower canon and a rejection of imaginative interpretations.[65] The tension between the text and those who study it, which seems to have increased with each additional contribution to kabbalistic literature, may have reached its peak with the appearance of Ashlagian Kabbalah.

Hymn to Love

Uniquely interdisciplinary, Ashlagian Kabbalah stands at the nexus of sociopolitical, ethical, theological, philosophical, and literary platforms. From a political perspective, its emphasis on altruism could be examined in the context of socialist and communist movements. From a literary perspective, and despite its emphasis on the collective rather than the individual, it could be described as unmistakably modernist, often taking the form of interconnected narratives about vessels as broken characters. In keeping with the concept of subjective points of view as alternatives to omniscient perspectives, the death of the Edomite kings, the breaking of the vessels, and the sin of Adam and Eve in the garden of Eden are more than parallel events. Thematically speaking, they are different dimensions of the same crisis. Having experienced the existential aftermath of this crisis, the vessel must leave its comfort zone, so to speak, and undergo a process of self-exploration, growth, and recovery. The purpose of this healing journey is not to find a permanent cure for the damaged individual or the ills of society but to explore structural patterns at the expense of formulaic plot points, acknowledge the hopelessly fragile nature of human existence, and, despite the likelihood of failure, aspire to moments of tenderness, civility, and love, as rare as they may be. These moments, which the vessel must cultivate as more adequate substitutes for its self-obsessed predispositions, are brittle and fragmented rather than unwavering or durable. In fact, the vessel itself is brittle and fragmented, resembling some of the most memorable characters of modernist literature.

In typical modernist fashion, the story of the vessel replaces predictable notions of unity and stability with psychological complexity and the inherently conflicted self. If the goal of the vessel is to convert excessive self-absorption into intimate relations with others, ambiguity and uncertainty are suggested as necessary conditions for such relations. Confusion enhances the capacity for depth, while definitive answers signify the death of discovery. In philosophical terms, the vessel must navigate between positivism and fallibilism: between the conviction that we can know and the possibility that we could be wrong. When it rejects self-serving calculations for the sake of empathy or love, it suspends the quest for validation, verification, or confirmation. Rather than unqualified exactitude, it seeks and embraces the open-endedness of human thoughts, actions, and emotions.

Echoing the sensibilities of modernist fiction and anticipating the rise of speculative cinema, Ashlagian Kabbalah proposes the inescapably perplexing nature of love as an antidote to the impersonal professionalism of order, discipline, and productivity. In many cases, organized efficiency takes the form of mind control, especially in narratives that offer a critique of voracious capitalism. A common trope in such narratives is the depiction of the masses as obedient robots programmed to subscribe to the relentless glorification and commodification of sparkling sedatives: simulated reality, superficial beauty, mechanical fornication, formulaic sentimentality, competitive careers, standardized behaviors, and prepackaged values.[66] As products of pervasive entertainment industries, stupefied populations in dystopian narratives voluntarily espouse the type of comfortable idiocy from which oppressive regimes benefit. The vessel, like the brave protagonist of these narratives, offers active resistance to systems that thrive on self-indulgent subservience. In kabbalistic terms, the commercial nightmare of the modern world and its futuristic exaggerations is a product of the primordial catastrophe: the breaking of the immature vessels. A more developed vessel will eventually begin to suspect that, like the rest of society, it is kept at a shallow, inferior, infantilized level of awareness. At some point, it will rise against the powers that reduce it to an obsessive consumer and fight to repair the cumulative damage of materialistic mindlessness.

The repair of this damage—in kabbalistic terms, *tikkun*—is the primary purpose of humanity. Scholars who acknowledge the centrality of this mending process refer to it as the most powerful idea ever presented in Jewish thought.[67] Religious observance—devotion to the divinity through the daily prayers and the keeping of the commandments—is one of the most important tools of repair. More important, however, are Torah study and acts of loving-kindness.[68] In other words, linguistic practices and intimate relations reaffirm the humanity of indoctrinated and desensitized masses. The language of love is especially crucial when relationships are reduced to virtual profiles, compatibility algorithms, digital images, computerized voices, preprogrammed questions, and rapid response databases. Deeply suspicious of the power of pixels on digital display devices to represent the real, some cultural critics suggest that the strongest resistance to the global virtualization of human life and the ubiquitous destruction of meaning comes from language itself: from the singular, irreducible, vernacular nature of all languages.[69] Insofar as language constructs a self-contained reality, it is powerful and effective precisely because it does not attempt to simulate or reflect an external realm of reference. Furthermore, it exposes the false belief in the ability of signs and symbols to serve as direct or accurate references to designated objects or ideas. In keeping with structural linguistics or immanent semiotics, words, like human beings, are meaningful only when they enter into relations with one another, only when they acknowledge their own failure to signify anything permanent or absolute.

The mission of the vessel, therefore, is to liberate itself through introspection, assert its humanity through language, and emancipate others through love. Love, according to the Kabbalah, has the power to repair the divinity itself. More specifically, regular lovemaking, especially in its conjugal context, both mimics and facilitates the union of the male and female divine configurations in the world of emanation.[70] When men and women neglect to perform this act, ZA and the sphere of royalty—the Blessed Holiness and his beloved Shekhinah—are unable to liberate themselves from the house of bondage to which they are confined in exile. Following the demolition of the First Temple, Father and Mother were separated. Jerusalem was destroyed, and Mother, along with the Jewish nation, was expelled from her celestial palace. Following the demolition of the Second Temple, the Blessed Holiness and his beloved Shekhinah were separated. Jerusalem was destroyed again, and the Shekhinah, along with the Jewish nation, was deported from her holy domain. Consecrated copulation between devoted human lovers guarantees the reunion of the supernal couples, making the divinity whole again.

The divine configurations, like human beings, are linguistic entities. Father and Mother represent the first two letters of the Tetragrammaton, while the Blessed Holiness and the Shekhinah represent the last two letters. The assertion of humanity through the language of love guarantees the transformation of the text into flesh. The union of human flesh in the physical realm facilitates blissful conjugation in the world of emanation. As a result, the divine configurations produce the human souls that inhabit the supernal worlds. When the souls descend to the physical realm and inhabit human flesh, the cycle continues. The union of human flesh, once again, imitates and enables intimate encounters between the divine configurations, allowing them to engender new souls and continue to sustain the supernal worlds and the physical realm. The inescapable fluidity of divine relations, human relations, and human–divine relations validates the complex, inherently volatile, endlessly generative power of imaginative textuality and reciprocal devotion.

The totality of true love—the engulfing sensation of utter devotion—is perhaps what Paul calls Agape.[71] This kind of love renders language itself meaningful. If one speaks both human language and divine language but lacks the capacity for self-abandoning love, one is an empty vessel that clangs and clatters. Such a vessel can be blessed with prophecy, wisdom, or earthshaking faith, but if it lacks the ability to transform hedonism into altruism, it is utterly useless. If a sense of duty rather than devotion prompts the vessel to do charitable deeds, or if a feeling of pride rather than love motivates it to perform self-sacrificing acts, it gains nothing. Mature love is as patient as AA and as gracious as the right side. A rectified vessel that cultivates the capacity for mature love is never envious. It is neither boastful nor conceited. The love that it spreads is never vulgar, never demanding, never crass, never cross, never loud, never smug. A rectified vessel never enters into power games, nor does it stoop to petty scorekeeping. The mature love that the vessel nurtures is all-encompassing and always dependable. Like the humble characters of modernist literature, it endures misfortunes with dignity, losing neither hope nor its temper. Mature love acknowledges its own incompleteness, just as the vessel recognizes its own immaturity. Prophecies may be retracted, human languages may die, and wisdom may be forgotten, but mature love will never regress to infancy. When the vessel was in its infancy, it spoke like a child, grasped like a child, and thought like a child. When it reached adulthood, it abandoned its childish ways. Now it knows that its understanding is partial, as is its foresight, yet it strives for the repair of the disjointed. Its ability to acknowledge other vessels is admittedly limited. It sees them as if through a fog, as if through a mirror. Nevertheless, it hopes to enjoy face-to-face relations and believes in its ability to know its fellow vessels with the utmost intimacy, just as closely as it is known to others. Hope humanizes the vessel, as does the belief in a better future, but it is the language of love that permits it to inspect itself with critical acuity, connect with nearby vessels, bond with the divinity, and share the pleasures and responsibilities of creation.

CHAPTER 3

The Transmigration of Souls

How the Flesh Hosts Multiple Spirits

Tower of Strength

PERSECUTED BY EARLY eighteenth-century rabbinic authorities in Venice and Frankfurt, Moses Hayyim Luzzatto, originally from Padua, sojourned in Amsterdam and died in Acre at the age of thirty-eight. Highly prolific, he composed kabbalistic poems, plays, prayers, parables, letters, allegories, imaginary dialogues, ethical narratives, philosophical treatises, rhetorical handbooks, striking imitations of the Bible, the Zohar, Tikkunei Zohar, and other texts, demonstrating the ability to translate the Kabbalah into a diverse body of literary styles.

At the age of twenty, having written a three-act play, a hundred and fifty biblically inspired psalms, and studies in rhetoric, logic, and poetics, Luzzatto composed *Tower of Strength*, his second play.[1] One of the most inventive accounts of human souls on the road to rectification, it failed to win the attention or recognition of wide audiences, probably because the very idea of theatrical hermeneutics constituted an ostensible departure from the established genres of religious Jewish literature. It is also likely that its premise, plot, and cast of characters were deemed objectionable by community elders, figures of authority, and other suspicious gatekeepers, who later responded with open hostility to the literary virtuosity, avantgarde hermeneutics, and messianic leanings for which Luzzatto became famous. Three hundred years later, critics still struggle to classify, describe, and contextualize his second play.

His first play, an innovative variation on the story of Samson, can be considered a type of midrash: an imaginative expansion of a biblical narrative. As such, and despite the unorthodox form, it remains within the boundaries of rabbinic traditions. The same is true for his third and last play, an intricate allegory that, although stylistically experimental, ultimately evokes the ethical and moral concerns of wisdom literature. All three plays are uncontested masterpieces of Hebrew poetry. *Tower of Strength*, however, remains controversial. Some scholars claim that Luzzatto, anticipating the ruling of religious courts that forced him to renounce some of his own writings, may have written it as a kabbalistic narrative in disguise.[2] Arguing against this assertion, other scholars prefer to see it as a perfectly secular tribute to some of the most famous dramatic works of the Italian Renaissance. Such scholars dismiss the fact that Luzzatto himself, in his preface to the play, cites one of the most memorable parables of the Zohar as the foundation of the drama.[3] In this parable, a princess in a tower stands for the depth and beauty of the Kabbalah: the innermost layers of the Torah. Her secret lover, eager to approach the tower but hesitant to do so, is the dedicated and careful reader who ventures beyond the literal level of the text. The actual play, according to scholars who choose to see the young Luzzatto as a representative of the Enlightenment rather than the Kabbalah, fails to develop the parable to which the author alludes in his preface.

The play opens with a renowned king who owns a fortified tower built on a mountaintop. On the roof of the tower is a beautiful garden. No one, however, has seen the garden, since the tower seems to have no entrance. The king declares that the man who gains access to the rooftop garden will marry his daughter, a princess of exceptional beauty. Unaware of the royal decree, a young prince from a neighboring kingdom visits the area and notices that the tower has no door. He observes the area carefully and discovers a hidden cave in the foothills of the mountain. When he enters the cave, a secret passage leads him to the top of the tower, where he comes upon a camouflaged gate. He opens the gate and walks into the garden. When he notices a sign that promises just deserts to the man who has found his way to this spot, he climbs down and leaves the scene, afraid that he might be punished for trespassing. Another man, who knows about the royal decree and wishes to marry the princess, passes by the tower and spots the open gate. He hurries to the palace and requests an interview with the king, pretending to have visited the garden. The king, unaware of the fact that the man is claiming credit for a task that he did not accomplish, is excited to announce his betrothal to the princess.

The princess despises the great pretender and loves the honest prince. Two other women, Ada and Aya, are in love with the two young men: Ada with the prince, Aya with the pretender. Desperate to marry the prince, Ada claims that the pretender has been lusting after the handmaid who attends to the princess. The handmaid, according to the story that Ada concocts, has been doing everything within her limited power to reject his advances. Ada promises the princess that, if allowed to borrow her handmaid, she will convince her to testify against the pretender in front of the king. The king, Ada says, will find the pretender guilty of betraying the princess and order him executed. With the death of the pretender, Ada explains, the princess will be free to marry the prince. The princess, who does not suspect that Ada is lying, agrees. Having borrowed the obedient handmaid, Ada sends her to deliver a gift of poisoned delicacies to the pretender on behalf of the princess, then dispatches her own servant to warn him not to eat it. If her plot is successful, the princess will be found guilty of attempted murder and sentenced to death, paving the way for Ada herself to marry the prince.

On his way to warn the pretender, the servant dispatched by Ada encounters Aya. When he tells her about the nature of his mission, she asks him to allow her to take his place and deliver the message to the pretender. Aya, who loves the pretender with all her heart, hopes that if she conveys the warning that saves his life, he will realize the extent of her devotion. An earlier display of emotions, genuine but unrequited, does reveal her as a passionate and loyal lover, dedicated to her object of desire despite his unconcealed disdain.

Aya delivers the message to the pretender, who remains unmoved. He tests the validity of the warning by giving some of the gifted delicacies to a dog. When the dog dies, the princess is arrested and condemned to be burned at the stake. The prince, horrified by this turn of events, asks to be put to death instead of the princess, claiming that the idea to poison the pretender was his. The princess insists that he is innocent, but the court decides to have him executed. Prepared to die, he describes his visit to the garden at the top of the tower and confesses to the alleged crime of trespassing. When the king hears his confession, he realizes that it was the prince, not the pretender, who found the entrance to the tower and located the gate to the garden. Questioned by the king, the pretender admits that he has misled the royal family. The king—who represents the infinite patience of AA: the prime divine configuration in the world of emanation—forgives the contrite pretender. He releases the prince, welcomes him as his future son-in-law, and announces the commencement of the wedding celebrations.

At this point, Ada, like the pretender, repents for her duplicity. Filled with shame, she admits that her intention was to incriminate the princess and arrange for her unjust execution. Ready to accept responsibility for her wicked ways, she asks for the punishment that she deserves: death. Moved by the ability to express sincere remorse, the princess forgives her, declares that she loves her, and invites her to join the festivities.

In kabbalistic terms, the three members of the royal family—the king, the prince, and the princess—are the three spheres of the head: crown, wisdom, and understanding. Much more stable than the other spheres, they are immune to temptation. Damaged only partially when the vessels of the other spheres shatter, they are secure in their tower of strength. In terms of human development, they are rectified souls that do not require additional reincarnations. The three other characters— Ada, Aya, and the pretender—are vessels in need of a screen. Each of them is governed by a healthy ambition that must be refined, converted into consideration for others, and redirected into less selfish, more mature channels.

If the princess represents the sphere of understanding, Ada stands for the sphere of royalty. The magnanimous gesture of the princess is the equivalent of the second contraction. Inclusive by nature, she erases her ego and encourages Ada to ascend to a higher level of human decency. Using kabbalistic terminology, this scene can also be interpreted as an example of what the theory of soul inheritance terms *impregnation*: a special type of transmigration that occurs when the repaired soul of a righteous person inhabits the body of a person who struggles to complete the rectification process.[4] Unlike a typical case of reincarnation, in which an incomplete soul inherits a newborn body and continues its personal rectification journey, a perfect soul that impregnates an additional body does so to assist another human being.[5] In this case, two souls inhabit the same body: a host and a visitor. Like a lifelong homeowner, the primary soul operates the body from birth until death, while the visiting soul, like a houseguest, occupies it temporarily. Spiritually speaking, the princess, having identified a fellow soul in need of help, impregnates Ada and serves as her guide and counselor.

The only irredeemably evil character in this play is a depraved sorcerer who covets Ada. Disguised as a hungry beggar, he wins her trust and sympathy, then grabs her throat and reveals his identity. Ada begs for mercy, but the brutal sorcerer responds with verbal abuse. He tightens his grip on her throat and announces his intention to drag her into a cave and rape her. Unable to breathe, she tells him that she is willing to satisfy his lust and asks him, once again, to let go of her throat. If he is afraid that she might run away, she adds, he may grab her hair. When he agrees, she leads him into a secluded cave surrounded by trees, urging him to go ahead and enter it. Eager to satiate his savage lust, he steps forward and falls into a trap: a pit camouflaged with grass. Ada, who clings to the trees, escapes unharmed.

The promise of unlimited transmigration for every soul is a key principle in kabbalistic thought. Only the souls of the utterly wicked are given limited opportunities to inherit new bodies. This concept is based on a biblical expression that, according to rabbinic interpretations, describes the willingness of God to forgive repeat offenders "two or three times."[6] According to kabbalistic interpretations, this biblical expression conveys the idea that God allows the soul of the sinner to start afresh with the body of another person, and another one, and another one. If the soul is corrupt beyond repair, and if the person it inhabits refuses to take even the smallest step toward spiritual growth, it is granted no more than two or three chances. After the third reincarnation, it goes to hell, where hopeless souls are scoured before they ascend to their divine origin. This seems to be the case for the sorcerer. When a sinful person demonstrates a willingness to change, endless reincarnations are available, even if the process of rectification takes a thousand generations.[7]

This, according to the Kabbalah, is the difference between the righteous and the wicked. The righteous are those who, despite their many sins, aspire to self-awareness. Anyone who has started to repair the lifeblood—the most ignoble level of the soul, the basic instincts that animate the body—is given more than three chances. The wicked, on the other hand, are those who do nothing to advance beyond their bestial beginnings. In other words, the principle of three reincarnations, especially according to Lurianic Kabbalah, is applicable only to the lifeblood: the hardest part to repair.[8] Those who manage to extricate themselves from this lowest level of existence are guaranteed an infinite

number of opportunities to rectify the next two levels: the spirit and
the soul itself. Once the soul itself is repaired, the last two levels, the
soul of the soul and the innermost part of the soul, are achieved almost
effortlessly.

The Birth of the Soul

Like the spheres of royalty and understanding, the human soul is a feminine entity, as is each of its five parts: the lifeblood, the spirit, the soul
itself, the so-called soul of the soul, and the highest, purest, innermost
part of the soul. Each of the five worlds—the primordial structure, the
world of emanation, the world of creation, the world of formation, and
the world of action—must be able to host the human souls that inhabit
flesh-and-blood bodies. Common to all souls is their celestial origin.
Manufactured by the divine configurations, the souls are stored in a
special distribution center in the world of creation, from which they
are dispatched to the world of action every time a human being is born.
The future souls of humanity are initially included in Adam and Eve:
male souls in Adam, female souls in Eve. When the vessels shatter, the
holy sparks of the divine light fall from the world of emanation to the
bottom of the physical realm. Similarly, when Adam and Eve eat from
the forbidden tree, the souls of humanity fall from splendid holiness to
bestial drudgery. Now they must begin a long process of rectification: a
journey that will lead them back to holiness.

The internal structure of each world plays an important role in
the journey of the soul. Each world consists of five configurations,
each configuration of ten spheres. Each of the ten spheres is divided
into ten internal spheres. Similarly, each of the five parts of the soul is
divided into five internal parts. The lifeblood, for example, consists of
the lifeblood of the lifeblood, the spirit of the lifeblood, the soul of the
lifeblood, and so on. The spirit consists of the lifeblood of the spirit,
the spirit of the spirit, the soul of the spirit, and so on. This network of
intersecting subdivisions allows the Kabbalah to assign different personalities to different people despite the common root of all human souls.
More accurately, the various parts of the soul represent different stages
in the psychosocial development of every human being.

Several biblical passages serve as points of entry into the kabbalistic
theory of soul inheritance. One such point is the Mosaic Law, which

famously opens with a section that endorses slavery.[9] The kabbalistic worldview revolutionizes the biblical text and translates this legal codex into the story of the human soul: its birth in the supernal worlds, its descent into corporeal existence, its transgenerational journey across time and space, the various stages of its evolution, its correction through reincarnation, its liberation from bondage, and its ultimate ascension to its divine origin.

In some cases, men inherit the souls of women, women the souls of men. For example, Rahab, whose lofty soul wins the approval of both rabbinic and kabbalistic commentators, is born again as Heber the Kenite.[10] Later, after further transmigrations, her soul inhabits Hannah, mother of Samuel.[11] Eli, the priest who facilitates the birth of Samuel, is a reincarnation of Yael, wife of Heber the Kenite. Ultimately, this hermeneutical maneuver suggests that Hannah and Eli were a married couple in a previous life. She was his husband, and he was her wife.

In literary terms, this instance of soul inheritance establishes structural and functional relations between seemingly unrelated characters. Rahab and Hannah are similar in the sense that both, either explicitly or implicitly, are objectified and commodified. As one of two wives who share the same husband, Hannah experiences the kind of emotional and physical distress that could be compared to the daily humiliation that Rahab must suffer as a prostitute. In other words, it is not her inability to conceive that causes Hannah what the biblical text describes as a nervous breakdown. What upsets her to the point of uncontrollable weeping—what triggers such pain that she can neither eat nor sleep—is the fact that, like Rahab, her value is determined by the man who happens to own her. More disturbingly, and as if to corroborate the implied argument that polygamy is synonymous with prostitution, her value is measured and ranked against another woman, as her husband explicitly states.[12] The fact that Elkanah possesses two wives and sleeps with Hannah on a nonexclusive basis accentuates her affinity with Rahab. Referring to herself as a hard-spirited woman, she describes her bitter soul, according to kabbalistic interpretations, as a reincarnation of the habitually violated Rahab.[13] When the opportunity presents itself, both seek to escape from a life marked by loneliness and degradation.

Heber the Kenite is an additional manifestation of a similar situation. Watching from the outskirts of the narrative as his wife invites another man into her bed, he mirrors the voiceless, liminal, passive positions into which Rahab and Hannah are forced prior to their liberation.

In the rabbinic imagination, Yael seduces Sisera into sexual exhaustion before killing him in his sleep.[14] The principle of reincarnation hints at the possibility that, in the kabbalistic imagination, Heber is a helpless husband who experiences the kind of frustration that Rahab and Hannah must endure when dealing with the men in their lives.

The idea that Eli is a reincarnation of Yael is based on the observation that each of them is in charge of a famous tent that signals a turning point in the story. It is in her private tent that Yael eliminates Sisera and secures the survival of the nation. It is in the sanctity of the communal tent—the tent of meeting—that Eli encounters Hannah: another episode that ultimately changes the national narrative. The kabbalistic chronology of souls and their transmigrations portrays Yael as a woman who performs priestly duties. If the killing of Sisera is a symbolic sacrifice, Yael is the clerical authority who presides over this ritual.

Calling further attention to the subtext of the biblical story, the idea of reincarnation translates the taboo layers of the narrative into a new language that allows the unspoken to be explored. The intimate moment that Hannah and Eli share, away from her husband, is followed by a period of pregnancy and the birth of Samuel. When her husband urges her to join him for another pilgrimage, Hannah refuses, as if to say that she must see the priest alone. She waits until Samuel is weaned, then deposits him into the hands of Eli, declaring that the child belongs to God.[15] What this scene seems to imply is that her husband cannot be present when she introduces her son to his father.

To begin its journey toward repair, the soul must reach the lowest point: the engulfing ambition that drives the human vessel to pursue self-serving opportunities. The stronger this ambition, the greater the rectification. Having reached the brink of despair, Rahab and Hannah are motivated to begin new lives. In that sense, they are resilient characters that lend themselves to new interpretations. Similarly, the imperfect souls in *Tower of Strength*—the conniving Ada, the obsessive Aya, and the egotistical pretender—are more vibrant characters than those who are no longer governed by such intense passions: the king, the princess, and the prince. A very strong ambition provides the energy that the soul requires to repair its most impure part: the lifeblood. Once the lifeblood has been repaired, it cannot be damaged again. Now it serves as a stable platform for the next part of the soul: the spirit. While the spirit continues the process of rectification, the lifeblood is immune to regression. In other words, the person who hosts the soul can certainly experience setbacks, succumb to temptation, or commit transgressions, but now it is the spirit that would be injured, not the lifeblood. When the spirit is repaired, the next part of the soul becomes the vulnerable element that undergoes transformation: the soul itself. If the person is especially meritorious, all three parts can be corrected during a single life cycle.

In the cosmological narrative of Ashlagian Kabbalah, the most imperfect part of the soul yields greatness, while the stable parts that transcend temptation yield the quality known as smallness. When the body screen of the third configuration in the primordial structure ascends to the head, it carries, like the screens of the previous configurations, two types of information: a diffusion imprint, which documents the light that indwells the configuration, and a density imprint, which stores data about the thickness of the screen. The latter is a record of the power of the screen to convert hedonism into altruism and admit additional amounts of the divine light. Unique to the screen of the third configuration is the fact that it carries two density imprints. One pertains to the actual body of the third configuration, the other to its extension. This extension, which makes the body of the third configuration grow longer—as long as the body of the first configuration—is followed by the second contraction.

The lower part of the first configuration, from the navel to the feet, represents the full extent of the desire for the light: the burning ambition that remains self-centered. Incapable of using the divine light for altruistic purposes, the lower part of the first configuration remains dark. When the body of the third configuration extends, its lower part becomes identical in size to the lower part of the first configuration. In this position, it is in danger of exposure to the same apportionment of the divine light. The bottom sphere of the third configuration, knowing that it would not be able to reject such light, abandons its post and seeks the protection of the upper spheres: more specifically, the sphere of understanding.

When the sphere of understanding lends a helping hand to the bottom sphere of the third configuration, the second contraction occurs. The screen of the third configuration carries with it an imprint of this contraction: the exposure to an extreme degree of ambition, which becomes the added greatness of the fourth configuration. Its so-called smallness is considered the essence of this new configuration. It stems from the original size of the third configuration, prior to its extension and to the second contraction that ensues. Since this part of the fourth configuration shows little desire for the pleasure of the divine light, its ability to grasp the wisdom of the Torah is limited. More specifically, it is the equivalent of the second level of the soul: the spirit. The greatness of the fourth configuration, which stems from a deep craving for the divine pleasure in its utmost intensity, possesses the ability to grasp much more. Its capacity for wisdom is the equivalent of the fourth level of the soul: the innermost part of the so-called soul of the soul.[16]

Rectification of Imbalances

Despite numerous cases of women whose souls are reborn into new bodies, certain voices in kabbalistic thought insist that reincarnation is a rectification avenue reserved for men alone. Women, according to this view, go straight to hell. Contrary to the common image of hell as a place of eternal damnation, kabbalistic literature, especially in the context of reincarnation, portrays it as a kind of purgatory: a place of redemption that offers an accelerated path to rectification. Once the souls of those who go to hell are purged of their earthly transgressions, they ascend to heaven.

This concept raises the question, openly addressed by Lurianic Kabbalah, whether it is better to skip the arduous process of repeated reincarnations and go straight to hell, where blemished souls are burnished through a relatively brief period of torment.[17] Is it possible that a season in hell is quicker, less daunting, and more efficient than the prospect of a thousand lives? Is it possible that the fire of hell pales in comparison to the hardship, misery, and daily sufferings of the average life, not to mention the agony of death? While the answers to these questions are affirmative, the advantage of reincarnation, according to Lurianic Kabbalah, is that future lives grant human souls additional opportunities to benefit from the daily commandments that they are required to perform. Hopelessly corrupt men who show no intention of keeping the commandments would therefore benefit from a different purification method, especially since additional life cycles would only provide them with additional opportunities to sin. Very quickly, their crimes would outweigh their good deeds, and the damage they would do to their souls would increase rather than diminish. Hell, therefore, is a charitable solution designed to save sinners from further condemnation.

In a value system that treats textual studies as the most important commandment, a man who neglects to labor in the Torah must also pass through hell. Women, for whom Torah study is not a requirement, follow the same rectification shortcut. In this context, the term *ignoramus* is not an insult.[18] It denotes, quite neutrally, a man who has not been able to study the Torah, often due to a lack of aptitude or a pressing need to make a living. A woman who labors in the Torah, according to this view, is still exempt from the toil and trouble of another life. Although her engagement in Torah study is appreciated, she is not officially commanded to do so and therefore not in a position to be rewarded for it.

Obviously, this view is not in keeping with the consistent portrayal of biblical women as equal participants in soul inheritance. For example, Michal, daughter of King Saul, is viewed as a reincarnation of the nameless wife of On, son of Peleth, one of the leaders of the famous revolt against Moses and Aaron.[19] When the revolt fails, some of its leaders are swallowed by the earth, some are consumed by fire. The name of On, however, is not mentioned among the dead. This notable omission leads rabbinic commentators to add a midrashic expansion to the biblical story. Thanks to the insight and ingenuity of his wife, On escapes divine retribution. Aware of the futility of the revolt, she asks him why he is involved in it. "If the current leader stays in power, you will be a subaltern," she says to her husband. "And if another leader replaces him, you will still be a subaltern." When her husband fails to listen to reason, claiming that he has already sworn allegiance to the rebellion, she tells him to sit down and promises to save him. She serves him wine, gets him drunk, puts him in bed, dishevels her hair, and sits outside the tent. When his comrades come to call on him, they notice her messy hair, assume that they are interrupting an intimate moment, and go away. By the time he wakes up, the earth has opened its proverbial mouth, and the rebels are dead.[20] According to this inventive midrash, On did not repent of his own accord. It was his wife who rescued him from death. In her later reincarnation as Michal, she follows the same pattern and saves King David.[21] In this case, kabbalistic literature uses the concept of reincarnation to offer comparative readings of biblical and rabbinic texts, emphasizing the centrality of resourceful female characters. Like the spheres of understanding and royalty, these women—one biblical, the other midrashic—rise to the occasion, alter the course of the plot, and avert calamities at critical junctures in narratives of historical significance.

In many cases, one character rectifies another. Focusing on two other women, kabbalistic literature identifies curious parallels between the biblical story of Hagar and one of the most controversial examples of midrash: the conception of King David. A father of quite a few grown-up children, Jesse has been avoiding his wife for a very long time. After three years, he acquires a young slave woman. Aroused by her beauty, he wishes to possess her as his concubine. He commands her to bathe and beautify herself in preparation for a night of lovemaking. Rather than obey his orders, she approaches his wife. "Save yourself from an impending hell," she says to her mistress. "And save my master and me." Her mistress asks what this is all about, and the slave woman tells her everything. "There is nothing I can do," her mistress says. "My husband has not touched me in three years." The slave woman makes a suggestion. Both will bathe and beautify themselves, and at night, when Jesse says, "Close the door," the slave woman will get out of his bedchamber, and his wife will sneak in. And so they do. Later that night, alone with her master, the slave woman extinguishes the candle, lets her mistress in, and quickly leaves the room. Taking her place, the mistress of the house finally enjoys the physical company of her husband. Jesse makes love to her all night, mistaking her for his slave woman, and as a result of his hot passion, David is born with red hair.[22]

The clever slave woman who devises and executes this bait-and-switch plan is viewed by the Kabbalah as a reincarnation and rectification of Hagar.[23] In the biblical story, Hagar makes two mistakes. She agrees to become a concubine to Abraham and, having conceived, treats Sarah disrespectfully.[24] The nameless slave woman in the midrashic story rectifies these mistakes. She refuses to serve as a concubine to Jesse and treats her mistress with the utmost respect. In kabbalistic terms, Hagar receives her *tikkun* through the nameless slave woman. In literary terms, this new interpretation presents female bonding as the key to the narrative. One woman, like a perfectly mature vessel, is sensitive to the needs of another. Giving birth to the son of the master would have certainly improved the social status of the slave woman, especially since Jesse promises to set her free in exchange for her sexual favors. Nevertheless, in true pre-Code fashion, she arranges for his actual wife to benefit from this situation. As in the case of the Viennese woman and the princess of Flausenthurm in *The Smiling Lieutenant*, the slave woman and her mistress keep the man, literally and figuratively, in the dark.

As a literary technique, the idea of twin souls offers a shift in point of view that reverses the common hierarchies of major and minor characters, most importantly men and women. The empowering of the slave woman allows her to steer the plot, reorient the narrative, and orchestrate its turning point. No longer a marginal element, she manipulates Jesse, assists his wife, rectifies Hagar, and advances her own soul toward rectification. More importantly, she contributes to the rectification of the world, bringing it closer to the operational harmony of the divine attributes and the supernal worlds.

As a semiotic strategy, the concept of soul inheritance serves as a kabbalistic prism through which biblical texts and rabbinic interpretations acquire new meanings. Such is the case of Achsah and Zipporah, another pair of twin souls. Achsah, daughter of Caleb and wife of Othniel, is a reincarnation of Zipporah, daughter of Jethro and wife of Moses.[25] According to the Talmud, Moses was so dedicated to God—or so preoccupied with the Torah—that he neglected his wife.[26] Talmudic literature is highly critical of men who fail to attend to the physical and emotional needs of their spouses.[27] While championing devoted scholars who labor diligently in the Torah, the rabbis of the Talmud chastise those who do not know when to take a break. The inability to balance textual studies with married life is condemned as an act of cruelty, and the Talmud sides with the weeping wife whose husband, immersed in scholastic debates at a faraway educational institution, breaks his promise to come at designated times.[28] As a reincarnation of Zipporah, Achsah is worried that she might find herself in a similar position. What triggers her fear is the Talmudic portrayal of Othniel as the most remarkable scholar of his generation.[29] According to the biblical text, Caleb promises his daughter to the man who captures the town of Kiriat Sefer. Othniel, a successful military commander, accomplishes the task and marries Achsah.[30] According to the Talmud, thousands of laws, logical inferences, linguistic analogies, and other textual nuances were lost when Moses died and restored when Othniel captured Kiriat Sefer. Based on the fact that the literal meaning of Kiriat

Sefer is Book City, the Talmud advocates a metaphorical reading of this biblical episode. To capture Kiriat Sefer, the Talmud argues, is to conquer, grasp, or recover the essence of the text. After the death of Moses, when asked by the people to reconstruct the Torah, several prominent leaders, including Joshua and the priests, attempt to retrieve the missing information but fail to do so. Othniel, with his great analytical acuity, saves the text and wins the beautiful Achsah.

In this interpretive context, the territory that Achsah inherits—the Negev—is arid land: a desert devoid of natural resources. Apprehensive about the prospects of living in material deprivation, she asks her father for springs of water as additional territories. Expanding the hermeneutical metaphor of the Talmud, the Kabbalah suggests that financial insecurity is not what Achsah dreads. After all, the Talmud itself prohibits a working man, unless he secures the permission of his wife, from accepting a new job that carries a higher pay but requires extensive travel. A woman, the Talmud says, would most likely prefer a modest income with regular conjugal intimacy to ten times the money with long periods of celibacy.[31] Achsah, therefore, complains that her husband is an intellectual giant who promises no physical pleasure. Just as Zipporah is frustrated by the fact that Moses is a holy man whose divine affairs tend to come at her expense, so is Achsah troubled by the fact that Othniel is a spiritual soul who might exhaust himself in heavenly pursuits at the expense of earthly delights. According to the Kabbalah, she prays to God that Othniel, her new husband, will not follow in the footsteps of Moses, to whom she was married in an earlier incarnation. In the biblical story, she asks her father for two additional territories: the upper springs and the lower springs. In the kabbalistic imagination, she asks her father in heaven for an all-around man who will divide his time between two domains: the upper world of academic life and the lower world of practical concerns.

In terms of gender relations, female characters with agency, sociopolitical awareness, and the power to change the course of history are rectified souls. What these kabbalistic narratives present is a series of women who refuse to serve the needs of men. Attuned to their own needs, they form intergenerational alliances with other women and liberate themselves from the stereotypical rubrics of ancillary elements that support patriarchal plots. In terms of reincarnation, women whose souls inhabit other women are pivotal characters in the drama of the world, advancing humanity toward complete repair: the correction of ingrained imbalances.

The Reunion of Adam and Eve

As an early model of structural analysis, the Kabbalah rearranges cyclical patterns, thematic paradigms, and other interlaced elements into a new narrative. The juxtaposition of parallel episodes, mirror images, and mutually dependent doubles promotes the principle of relational definitions. According to this principle, the meaning of any textual component, as large as a literary character or as small as a morphological unit, relies on the presence of other components. For example, what supports the assertion that Heber (חבר) is a reincarnation of Rahab (רחב), or that Eli (עלי) is a reincarnation of Yael (יעל), is the fact that, anagrammatically, their Hebrew names are identical.

The new narrative that the Kabbalah constructs begins with the first contraction and a beam of light that enters a globular void. This opening scene serves as a template for a number of subsequent events, including the birth and rebirth of the soul. The infinite light is a representation of the divine will: the decision to initiate the creation process in order to bestow endless bounty on humanity. Inside the globular void, however, the light is no longer infinite. If the globular void is the future recipient of divine opulence, the light must adjust itself to the boundaries of this empty space. In a similar way, when the soul enters the human body, its power is necessarily restricted. Although infinitely spiritual, the soul must operate in accordance with the limitations of its corporeal host.

These principles, as well as the interdependent significance of textual units, including the smallest ones, are emphasized in the following kabbalistic retelling of the creation story. In the beginning, the twenty-two letters of the Hebrew alphabet, one by one, manifested into the reality of creation, giving the world its shape. Halfway through the process, with the eleventh letter, man and woman were created. They were placed with love in the garden of Eden, where the angels above attended to their needs. According to the Talmud, the angels served them roasted meat and chilled wine.[32] The serpent, who observed this scene, was filled with jealousy. According to the Zohar, it was Samael,

the evil angel, who was irritated by the honor with which Adam and
Eve were showered. Riding on the grim serpent, Samael descended from
heaven and revealed himself to the world. As a result, the letters of the
alphabet were mixed. Craftily, working as one, Samael and the serpent
took the rest of the letters and used them to ensnare Adam and Eve.
For example, they exploited the fact that the name of the eighteenth
letter (צד״י) is an anagram of the word *entrapment* (צי״ד). They scram-
bled the letters and used them to ensnare Adam and Eve. They caused
more damage with the next letter, the nineteenth. They exploited the
fact that the name of this letter is identical to the word *monkey* (קוֹף).
They also took advantage of the fact that the shape of this letter is
uneven, as if it has no leg to stand on (ק). They used it to question the
very existence of Adam and Eve, undermining their humanity. Finally,
they exploited the fact that the twentieth letter is the first letter of
the word *evil* (רע). They used it to tempt and deceive Adam and Eve,
causing their fall.

With these last two letters, the nineteenth and the twentieth, Cain
and Abel were born. The serpent, having seduced and defiled Eve, deposited his filth inside her.[33] His seed rattled in her belly but could not
form into a proper living thing. Cain and Abel were born, therefore,
with an inherent instability. Taking after the serpent, whose specialty
was murder, Cain became a killer. Following the death of Abel and the
expulsion of Cain, and after a hundred and thirty years of abstinence,
Adam and Eve renewed their conjugal intimacy. It was then that Seth
was born. Seth, according to the Bible, was made in the image of his
father.[34] This special characterization, which echoes the creation of Adam
and Eve,[35] and which is not used to describe Cain or Abel, corroborates
the kabbalistic view of Seth as fundamentally different from his older
brothers. Apparently, Cain and Abel were not made in the image of their
father. Seth, according to this view, is a rectification of Cain and Abel.
His name, which consists of the two remaining letters of the Hebrew
alphabet, reflects the restoration of order (שת). No longer under the influence of Samael and the serpent, the twenty-first and twenty-second letters are sequentially arranged now, as they should be. The damage caused
by the forces of impurity is repaired through Seth, who personifies these
letters. His body and his soul are correctly formed, as they should be.[36]

The encounter between Eve and the serpent leaves many questions
unanswered. Was it verbal? Physical? Sexual? Was the serpent her lover?
What exactly was the filth that he deposited inside her? The deceptive

words with which he poisoned her mind? The forbidden fruit that he encouraged her to eat? His venom? His sperm? The reality of mortality? The concept of jealousy? Whatever this filth may have been, it had a strong effect on Cain, who was born first. Having diminished with each generation, it dissipated entirely when the people prepared to receive the Torah at Mount Sinai but quickly resurfaced when they committed the sin of the golden calf. This might explain why Adam and Eve avoided each other for a hundred and thirty years. Knowing that time would lessen the effect of the filth, they waited before they conceived Seth. Was the decision to refrain from conjugal intimacy mutual? According to most versions of the story, it was Adam who distanced himself from Eve. And if this is the case, it is likely—as the examples of Moses, Othniel, and Jesse demonstrate—that Adam is guilty of emotional and physical neglect. According to some versions, he repented, then came back to Eve. What was the sin for which he had to repent? Eating the forbidden fruit? Blaming it on Eve? Depriving her of his attention?

What further complicates the relationship between Adam and Eve is the fact that Samael is often considered a male fiend, the serpent his female counterpart. Some versions of the story imagine the serpent as a woman of harlotry who seduces Adam. Adam fails the test and succumbs to her wiles.[37] Later, when he spends a hundred and thirty years away from Eve, female spirits keep him company. He engages in sexual relations with these spirits, who give birth to demons, succubi, and other spirits.[38] These spirits have no bodies. They roam the earth, especially on moonless nights, looking for warmth. When they find a man who sleeps alone, they crawl into his bed. It is because of these spirits that lonely men experience nocturnal emissions. Inseminated by human sperm, these incorporeal spirits produce more of their kind.

From a psychological standpoint, this is the story of the sexual imagination. As soon as the human brain is formed, it develops the ability to produce personal fantasies that can be just as powerful as tangible realities. It would be natural to assume, therefore, that Adam was not the only one visited by such fantasies. According to some versions of the story, while Adam was entertaining female spirits, male spirits sought the company of Eve. Looking for the warmth of a human body, they appeared to her at night. Just as Adam fathered other spirits during those hundred and thirty years, so did Eve give birth to spirits of her own.[39] According to most versions of the story, it was not repentance but jealousy that prompted Adam to return to Eve.

From a kabbalistic perspective, the problematic nature of the relationship between Adam and Eve requires rectification. Once again, reincarnation comes to the rescue. Transmigrating through time and space, the souls of Adam, Eve, and the serpent are eventually hosted by Mordechai, Esther, and Haman.[40] Adam, who deserted Eve for a hundred and thirty years, rectifies his mistake by attending to Esther from childhood to adulthood, staying as close to her as he possibly can, even when she is inside the palace.[41] Eve, who was quick to eat from the forbidden fruit, rectifies her mistake by fasting for three days.[42] Having fallen prey to the manipulative serpent, she now outsmarts the manipulative Haman. Having allowed the serpent to introduce death to the population of the world, she now brings life to the Jewish population of the Persian Kingdom, saving her people from a collective death sentence.

The book of Esther, according to this reading, celebrates the reunion of Adam and Eve. This reunion, however, is not perfect, especially in light of the kabbalistic suggestion that Esther is also a reincarnation of Yael. Forced to degrade herself for the survival of the people, Yael shares her bed with Sisera. Forced to degrade herself for the same cause, Esther shares her bed with the Persian king. In other words, when Esther interacts with Haman, Eve is exonerated from the suspicion of carnal relations with the serpent. On the other hand, when she interacts with the Persian king, the question of sexual compromise emerges again. Similarly, when Mordechai interacts with Esther, Adam is absolved of his resentment for Eve, but when Esther becomes the new queen, his endless patience is replaced by potential detachment, admonition, or jealousy.

Ultimately, reincarnation provides opportunities not only to correct mistakes but also to repeat them. The fact that Esther is a reincarnation of both Eve and Yael contributes to the complexity of what is known in literary terms as round characters: characters who, while growing, changing, or evolving, never enjoy the kind of absolute transformation that often marks predictable, formulaic, so-called flat characters. On a personal level, the idea of reincarnation captures the tension between failure and redemption. While duplicating debilitating patterns is inevitable, progress toward new modes of behavior can be made through a painstaking process of error and improvement. If a state of complete repair is not achievable, enhanced self-awareness might be a more realistic goal.

Disembodied Spirits

If the concept of soul inheritance organizes literary information in terms of conflated personalities, do the biblical characters of kabbalistic hermeneutics know that they must try to avoid duplicating the mistakes of their forerunners? Do they know that they must correct behavioral impediments in order to elevate their souls? Are the rectifications that they perform measurable only inasmuch as they are contrasted with past transgressions recorded in earlier texts? More specifically, does the Esther of the Kabbalah know that she is a reincarnation of Eve? The potentially metafictional nature of such questions is particularly pertinent to the notion of reincarnation as a mode of intertextual reading, especially in the context of character development and the growth of humanity.

In literary terms, Adam and Eve, the principal forerunners who bequeath their souls to the rest of civilization, are conceived as templates for all biblical characters. Nevertheless, in many versions of this narrative, it is Adam alone who damages the future souls of humanity. When he is created, every soul is contained within him. When he sins, the souls sink to the bottom of the physical realm, where they are contaminated by impurities. Human beings, therefore, must labor to cleanse the tainted souls with which they are born and lift them back to their celestial origin. Lurianic Kabbalah further qualifies this narrative by suggesting that some of these original souls managed to escape unharmed. Apparently, the top layer of the souls, known as the upper splendor, ascended to a safer place when Adam sinned.[43] Protected from impurities, this layer serves as a depository of special souls. Cain, the firstborn human being, came from this upper splendor.[44] The soul of the messiah will also come from this undamaged layer.[45]

Personifying the tension between damage and repair, Cain becomes the quintessential human being. Simultaneously vilified and exalted, especially in Lurianic Kabbalah, he is also a prototype of the messianic figure. It is no surprise, therefore, that Hayyim Vital, *de facto* author of the Lurianic corpus, sees himself not only as a reincarnation of Cain but also as a potential messiah.[46] Conflicted, internally tormented, and, in some cases, emotionally addled, Vital oscillates between an eloquent, elegant, confident style and, in contrast, pedantic passages that betray anxieties, obsessions, and self-flagellating tendencies. He

seems to be especially disturbed by the kind of autoeroticism with which
Adam produces additional spirits during the hundred and thirty years
that he spends away from Eve. These disembodied spirits are eventually reincarnated into the Hebrews who are born into slavery in the
Egyptian exile. Through hard labor, the souls of the Hebrew slaves are
rectified and redeemed. Seeking similar redemption, Vital lists different
methods of textual atonement for nuanced types of self-gratification:
while thinking about a woman, while thinking about a man, while using
saliva as a natural lubricant, while pretending to retrieve the missing
foreskin, and other guilty habits.[47]

In each of the above cases, certain combinations of the letters of the
divine names are the means of expiation. Designed to reintroduce order
into the supernal worlds, this remedy is based on the idea that earthly
transgressions damage the divinity by disturbing the conjugal routine
of the male and female configurations in the world of emanation. As a
result, the flow of divine bounty to the physical realm is interrupted.
Known as unifications, advanced textual exercises enhance concord in
the supernal worlds and contribute to the repair of the divinity.

As products of these earthly transgressions, the disembodied spirits
are major characters in the Lurianic corpus.[48] Although referred to as
demonic beings, they are considered lofty souls who suffer from an
enhanced susceptibility to evil. This means that the process of repairing
them is more arduous. Initially incarnated as the people of the flood,
they fail to mend their wicked ways and are consequently destroyed by
God. Translated into Ashlagian terms, the pleasure of self-love, which
originally gives birth to these spirits, is a metaphor for narcissistic tendencies that keep humanity in a hedonistic stage of development, motivated primarily by the satisfaction of self-centered needs.

Lurianic Kabbalah compares the disembodied spirits to gold.
In its natural, unprocessed, unrefined form, gold, like other precious
metals, is intermingled with impurities.[49] Also known as slag, scum,
or dross, these impurities dim the sparkle of the disembodied spirits.
Just like gold, which must be treated again and again before it separates
from its impurities, the disembodied spirits must go through repeated
cycles of purification. With each cycle, additional dross is removed,
and the spirits begin to shine. In the social, psychological, and cosmological terms of Ashlagian Kabbalah, the yearning for pleasure is as
precious as unrefined gold. In its natural form, it is marred by excessive

self-indulgence. Human development is the equivalent of purification. After repeated attempts, maturity is achieved when egocentric impurities are removed, and personal ambitions are converted into the desire to receive for the sake of giving: to enjoy the divine light in order to share it with others.

The second attempt at the purification of the disembodied spirits occurs when they are reincarnated as the conceited builders of the city and tower of Babel. As sinful as those who perished in the flood, they are likewise destroyed. Still unrectified, they are given another chance when they are reincarnated as the people of Sodom and Gomorrah. Once again, they fail to make progress. Apparently, the grip of impurity is very strong, and the disembodied spirits struggle to free themselves from what the Kabbalah labels extraneous admixture.[50] In keeping with the rule that allows the human soul two or three unsuccessful reincarnations, the disembodied spirits are granted one last attempt. Their new hosts are the Hebrew slaves in the Egyptian house of bondage. This time, they manage to break the cycle of sin and begin the rectification process.

The emphasis on underlying parallels that reveal the thematic concerns of the story promotes a literary approach that identifies the formal features of the text as meaning-making mechanisms. According to this approach, form generates content rather than serves as an afterthought that follows it. In structural terms, literary concepts such as plot or character development are functions of internal relations among objects, images, and other textual components. For example, bricks and mortar, mentioned as the instruments of transgression when the city and tower of Babel are built, become the tools of rectification when the disembodied spirits, reincarnated as the Hebrew slaves in Egypt, are forced to build the cities of Pithom and Ramses.[51] Water, the instrument of destruction with which the flood generation is annihilated, resurfaces, so to speak, when Pharaoh commands the people of Egypt to throw the sons of the Hebrew slaves into the river.[52] The only exception in the generation of the Egyptian exile is Moses, whom the Kabbalah considers a reincarnation of Seth. Unlike the disembodied spirits, his soul is a product of physical and emotional intimacy between two flesh-and-blood lovers.

The hardships that are inflicted on this fourth reincarnation are equated with the crucible in which gold is melted and purified.[53]

Contrary to the image of the sinner as a condemned criminal who, rather passively, hopes for mercy, the Kabbalah promotes the idea of wrongdoers whose intentions are essentially good and whose errors must be actively fixed. The essence of repentance, in other words, is not to await forgiveness but to repair the damage. In this case, the damage is repaired both by the disembodied spirits themselves and by the people who are personally responsible for the birth of such spirits. The latter type of repair is divided into two categories.[54] In addition to personal modes of atonement for the inadvertent production of disembodied spirits, one must perform nightly rectifications in order to rescue these spirits from the so-called other side.[55]

According to Lurianic Kabbalah, those who produce disembodied spirits damage the sphere of knowledge in the world of emanation: more specifically, the knowledge of Father and Mother. As a metaphor for lovemaking, the sphere of knowledge is situated between the head and the heart. True carnal knowledge, therefore, is never strictly physical. It is always a synthesis of emotion and action, an interplay of cognitive and corporeal dimensions. In this context, the sphere of knowledge represents the perfect union of mind and body: the lovers who become one flesh, one soul. When this sphere is damaged, Father and Mother are incapable of enjoying the abundant light that guarantees their intimate union. Triggering a chain reaction, this lack of light hinders the intimate union of the younger divine configurations: ZA and his female counterpart, also known as the Blessed Holiness and the Shekhinah.

The solution is to increase the light that emanates from the highest sphere of knowledge: the knowledge of AA, the prime configuration in the world of emanation. This is achieved through the bedtime "Hear O Israel" prayer.[56] While reciting this prayer, one must concentrate on the three consecutive occurrences of the divine name: "the Lord, our God, the Lord."[57] Each of these occurrences corresponds to the highest spelling of the letters of the Tetragrammaton: the one whose numerical value is seventy-two.[58] The highest sphere of knowledge, located behind the metaphorical beard of AA, contains three of these spellings. Three times seventy-two is two hundred and sixteen. Seventy-two plus two hundred and sixteen is two hundred and eighty-eight: the numerical value of the Hebrew word *bloomed*, evoking the biblical image of the morning on which Moses observes that the staff of Aaron, representing

the house of Levi, has bloomed overnight.[59] Aaron and Levi stand for
the two spheres that follow knowledge: Aaron for mercy (חסד), whose
numerical value is seventy-two, and Levi for might (גבורה), whose
numerical value is two hundred and sixteen. The combination of mercy
and might, which equals two hundred and eighty-eight, and which is the
numerical value of *bloomed*, is also the numerical value of the Hebrew
root *hover*. As a reference to the spirit of God, which hovers over the
primordial waters, this root is trapped, so to speak, between a prefix
and a suffix that, put together, signify death (מרחפת).[60] With the help
of such textual acrobatics, the holy spirits are released from the grip of
death. Thanks to the nightly recitation of this prayer, they are revived
and regenerated, like the staff of Aaron.

Lurianic Kabbalah expands this interpretation when it identifies the bedtime prayer with the song of glory that the righteous sing
upon their beds.[61] This joyful song, according to the biblical image,
is in their throats—a reference to the knowledge of AA, located in
his throat—and a sword is in their hands.[62] The sword, according
to this kabbalistic interpretation, is another reference to the three
seventy-two spellings of the divine name, which mark the spot behind
the metaphorical beard of AA, and whose combined numerical value
is two hundred and sixteen. The morphological agglutination *and
a sword*—in Hebrew, one word—carries the same numerical value:
two hundred and sixteen. The righteous derive strength from the
throat of the prime divine configuration, as do Father and Mother,
the Blessed Holiness and the Shekhinah, and the helpless souls that
require healing and support.

This hermeneutical labyrinth, typical of Lurianic rectifications and
unifications, is harnessed to enhance the narrative itself. Imagined as
drops of divine bounty that fail to flow into a female configuration,
the vulnerable souls that are born from acts of self-indulgence wander
into the other side—the unholy domain—where they are tempted to
inhabit impure bodies produced by the serpent: in this case, the female
counterpart of the evil angel Samael. The purpose of the textual rectifications that human beings provide is to eliminate these impure bodies
and restore the souls to their holy roots: to the supernal female configurations in the world of emanation. Once the souls escape to safety, they
will be ready, like all the regular souls, to inhabit human bodies in the
physical realm: the world of action.

Kabbalistic Adoptionism

Where does the soul of the messiah come from? As a self-fashioned messianic figure, Hayyim Vital must wrestle with this question. In true messianic fashion, he must also wrestle with enemies, imaginary or real, who ignore him, reject him, or fail to recognize his historical importance. As a textual commentator who interprets earlier kabbalistic writings, he feels obligated to address apocalyptic narratives that seem to challenge his own messianic identity. According to some of these narratives, the messiah will awake and emerge from heaven, descend to earth, and appear in the land of Galilee. Following the Assyrian capture of Israel, the Galilee marks the beginning of the exile. The messiah, therefore, must begin to reverse this catastrophe from the same location in which it originated. Accompanied by a pillar of fire, the messiah will engage in numerous battles against the enemies of Israel. At some point, the messiah will ascend back to heaven—to receive divine strength and a royal crown—before returning to earth.[63]

Born in the Galilee, Vital cannot claim that he came from heaven. Using the kabbalistic division of the human soul into five developmental stages, he proposes an updated version of this messianic narrative.[64] A righteous human being, born of a woman and a man, the messiah, according to Vital, will acquire all five parts of the soul. His righteousness will increase forever more, until at some point—more specifically, at the end of days—he will achieve complete holiness. On that day, his good deeds will merit the very last part of his soul: the so-called soul of the soul, hitherto stored in heaven. It is only then that he will be designated as a universal redeemer.

Vital cites Moses as an example. A regular human being, Moses acquired righteousness little by little, until all parts of his soul were complete. At that point—more specifically, at the burning bush—the soul of his soul was born in heaven. When the Zohar says that the messiah will awake in the land of Galilee, the meaning, according to Vital, is that his identity as a universal redeemer is dormant. When he earns the soul of his soul, he will rise from his sleep and receive the power of prophecy. This interpretation, according to Vital, is more in keeping with the divine proclamation that bestows sonship on the messiah at the time of his inauguration. On that day, God will beget his anointed king.[65]

This version of the messianic narrative seems to echo the adoptionist view of Jesus: the belief in a flesh-and-blood messiah who is inducted into the divine realm on the day of his baptism. According to this view, Jesus becomes the Christ—in kabbalistic terms, he obtains his messianic soul—neither at the time of his conception, as Luke maintains, nor with the creation of the world, as John suggests.[66] It is at the Jordan River, when the divine spirit descends upon him, that Jesus is adopted into heaven.[67] It is on that day that his messianic identity is confirmed.

Vital, who creates a hermeneutical space for his own messianic biography, continues to develop this narrative. Moses, acknowledged by God as the savior of the Hebrew nation, ascends to heaven, body and soul, where he spends forty days.[68] Similarly, the messiah will be concealed, body and soul, in a pillar of fire. At certain moments in his *Book of Visions*, Vital records the testimonies of women who see a pillar of fire descending on his head.[69] Following this kind of divine endorsement, the future savior of the Hebrew nation, according to Vital, will realize that he is the messiah, although the rest of the people will not recognize him as such. In other words, his identity will be revealed only to himself. Later, after his ascent to heaven and subsequent return to earth, he will be revealed completely and recognized by the rest of the people, who will then follow him.

This interpretive maneuver allows Vital to hint at his own situation. Apparently, he has fulfilled the initial part of this kabbalistic vision. His messianic identity has been revealed in the Galilee, so far only to himself. The fact that members of the Jewish communities in which he lives are unaware of his holy status—especially in Damascus, to which he relocated from the Galilee at a later stage in his life—confirms this messianic narrative. Vital further expands this narrative when he identifies the exact spot in which the soul of the messiah is produced: the sphere of wisdom. Second only to the crown, wisdom occupies a very high place in the divine system. In the poetic imagination of the Zohar, the messiah is a bird that nests in a hidden palace.[70] According to the interpretation that Vital suggests, the nest is the third sphere—understanding—while the bird is the messiah himself: wisdom, the sphere above.

In a sense, Vital associates the nest with the female aspect of the divinity—the sphere of understanding—while the bird itself, the messiah, is perceived as a male entity. A different perspective is offered by

Ashlagian commentary on this section of the Zohar.[71] New signs will be given, and new miracles will happen, according to the Zohar, when the messiah awakes. According to Ashlagian commentary, these miracles will be different from the ones that occurred in Egypt. They will originate from the ascension of the tenth sphere—royalty—to the third sphere: understanding. The miracles in Egypt, on the other hand, originated from understanding alone. In other words, Ashlagian Kabbalah attributes messianic signs and miracles to the collaboration between the two female aspects of the divinity.

This interpretation raises additional questions about the identity of the messiah. If charismatic characters like Esther or Judith, for example, save the nation from its enemies and achieve a certain regal status, can they be seen as messianic figures? Do their queenly roles imply filial relations with God? If male messiahs are adopted into the divinity, can female saviors be considered divine daughters? Lurianic Kabbalah suggests that the soul of the messiah is born of a male–female union between wisdom and understanding. Is it possible that Ashlagian Kabbalah sees the exaltation of the lower female sphere and its merger with the upper one as necessary conditions for the messianic age? As symbols of these female spheres, Ruth and Naomi form a partnership that ultimately facilitates the birth of the anointed king. Does this partnership, according to Ashlagian Kabbalah, shift the focus of the messianic narrative from the man in the spotlight to the women behind the scenes?

In any case, Vital emphasizes the notion that the messiah, while laboring to complete his soul, is unaware of his own identity. After all, if the divinity itself must grow, little by little, until its various aspects—the interdependent configurations in the world of emanation—complete their cognitive development and acquire their so-called brains, so does the messiah. Like the vessel that must learn to hold the divine light, the messiah must achieve maturity to earn salvific power. In the context of the so-called adoptionist heresy, this kabbalistic narrative may be an open counterargument to the common idea that the divine sonship of Jesus is established prior to his incarnation.

In the context of sixteenth-century kabbalistic circles, some scholars identify this portrait of the messiah with Isaac Luria rather than Hayyim Vital.[72] According to this approach, Luria and Vital can be viewed as reincarnations of Moses and Aaron, Jeremiah and Baruch, or Shimon bar Yochai and Rabbi Abba. This duality implies a clear distinction between a senior prophet who assumes a messianic role and a loyal sidekick who serves as a spokesman or scribe. The textual reality of the Lurianic corpus, however, is often more complex. When engaging in eschatological investigations, Hayyim Vital concludes, more than once, that the name of the messiah is, very plainly, Hayyim.[73] While acknowledging Isaac Luria as his venerated mentor, he often envisions himself—or allows others to envision him—as a triumphant king.[74] In that sense, his autobiographical sketch does resemble the story of Jesus. Just as Jesus is destined to overshadow John the Baptist, his immediate forerunner, so is Vital guaranteed to outshine his great predecessor. In some cases, he depicts himself as a wise, sensitive, misunderstood recluse. Foxes have holes, and birds have nests, yet Hayyim Vital has no synagogue that he can call his own. In other cases, he is an angry idealist who imagines the destruction of corrupt societies that fail to repent despite repeated demonstrations of his special powers. Jesus, offended by the wickedness of those who witness the miracles that he performs, predicts that the towns of Chorazin, Bethsaida, and Capernaum will not survive the day of judgment.[75] Vital, equally outraged by desensitized sinners who remain indifferent to his presence, pours out his wrath on larger, international, much more central cities: Jerusalem, Damascus, Cairo, and Venice.[76]

The interplay of humility and rage heightens the humanity of the messiah: an inescapably flawed character who strives for perfection. Those who, like the messiah, aspire to complete their souls—those who are unsatisfied with their current stage of development—are blessed with the ability to imagine themselves fully grown. Viewed from this perspective, the adoptionist position becomes a form of reincarnation. The missing part of the soul—the top level of human consciousness—migrates from the imagination to reality. In metaphorical terms, this missing part is a rare bird. Having left its heavenly nest, it finds a home in deserving individuals who labor to correct their inherent shortcomings. Serving as new nesting places, such individuals are adopted into the divine system. In semiotic terms, they are incorporated into a system that assigns them more mature roles. Contrary to the infancy narratives of Jesus according to Matthew and Luke, the messiah that the Kabbalah imagines, corresponding to the opening episodes of Mark, is a symbol of adulthood.

The Messianic Gap

In theological terms, the kabbalistic approach to the transmigration of souls proposes a more profound reconceptualization of the messianic idea. If time is perceived as a journey toward salvation, each of the reincarnations on the road to personal and collective rectification is a prefiguration of the messiah. While the coming of the messiah will signify the end of the process, the Kabbalah acknowledges the fact that complete repair is unfeasible. Since it is practically impossible to avoid mistakes, every generation, even the most righteous one, will introduce additional setbacks, further delaying the liberation of the characteristically imperfect soul from the tyranny of sin: from the clutches of selfish, harmful, or otherwise impure forces. In typological terms, every prefiguration—and every fulfillment—leaves much to be rectified. Under these circumstances, the Kabbalah proposes a vision of time that acknowledges human limitations and the unlikeliness of conclusion. The great rectification project, which begins with the creation of the world, will reach its end after six thousand years. At that time, anything that humanity fails to accomplish will be completed by God. In other words, it is assumed that we will run out of time. Nevertheless, as long as we make an honest effort, God will take over the project on the due date and finish the work, so to speak.

As blameless as children may be, the Kabbalah treats the absolute inability of a newborn baby to reciprocate the kindness of the caregivers on whom it depends as diametrically opposed to the goodness of the divinity. In biblical terms, humanity is created with the potential to shape itself in the image of God. In the terminology of Ashlagian Kabbalah, the vessel is endowed with the power to emulate the infinitely altruistic light from which it is emanated. The messiah, therefore, is a function of the distance between the vessel and the light. Rather than a constant that secures redemption, the messiah grows more graspable when the incongruity between humanity and the divinity decreases. When one regresses to the limited consciousness of self-serving practices, as one often does, the messiah dissolves into a more elusive image.

It could be argued that this view of the messiah is based on the Lurianic biography of ZA, the youngest male configuration in the world of emanation, whose three stages of development mirror the growth of the human soul: gestation, youth, and maturity.[77] When he enters a period of gestation inside Mother, he is in a stage of limited consciousness.[78] During this period, Mother, the higher female configuration, sustains and constructs him, lending him some of her internal spheres. When he is born, he begins a period of suckling. No longer a total parasite, he still depends on Mother for nourishment. In fact, he is born with six internal spheres instead of ten: an incomplete configuration. The biblical image of Hannah, who makes a small coat for little Samuel, is interpreted by the Kabbalah as a reference to Mother, who clothes the imperfect ZA. His coat is small, according to this interpretation, because it covers the six spheres of his body but not the missing spheres of his head. Upon the transition from childhood to adulthood, he receives his top three spheres. Now he has a fully developed brain, which marks a state of expanded consciousness.[79] His tenth internal sphere is his future female counterpart. Growing inside him, she undergoes a similar process of development.

Lurianic Kabbalah identifies the limited consciousness of youth with cruelty, categorical condemnation, or rigid judicial power, while the expanded consciousness of old age signifies mercy. The adult ZA, like a typical young man, is not a stable configuration. When he leans toward strict censure, he loses his head, so to speak, and reverts to a six-sphere structure. When he leans toward compassion, he regains his full stature. Like humanity itself, he must aspire to emulate AA: the older, more reliable, endlessly forgiving divine configuration. As a liaison whose mission is to bring humanity closer to the divinity, the messiah embodies this aspiration. Not unlike Jesus of Nazareth, the kabbalistic messiah represents the highest degree of congruity between the human and the divine. The difference, however, is that the kabbalistic messiah cannot be used to narrow the gap between the flaws of humanity and the perfection of the divinity. Humanity must labor incessantly to accomplish this task on its own. Even the greatest sins are not detrimental to the point that only the messiah could wash them away. The responsibility of rectification rests solely on humanity, so much so that good progress can hasten the coming of the messiah. The moment all the souls are rectified, even before the end of the designated period of six thousand years, the messiah will come. Although admittedly remote, the very possibility motivates humanity to continue to improve itself, diligently and independently.

The notion that humanity has the power to quicken salvation encourages greater degrees of maturity, accountability, and self-reflection. It also necessitates, especially in the Ashlagian worldview, collective action. To become divinely altruistic is an impractical undertaking if attempted alone. While one may be able to replace cupidity with generosity, extreme altruism could end in bankruptcy. A more effective way would be to operate as a community based on mutually guaranteed support. If individuals exhaust their personal resources, they will be supported by the other members of the community. Knowing that they will never face destitution, they will be able to provide for others wholeheartedly, without the anxiety of poverty. When the entire population of the planet is organized into such communities, every human being will be able to reproduce the kindness that characterizes the highest divine configuration. At that point, the world of action and the world of emanation will become one.

The eschatological implication of this global vision is that humanity may be able to control, at least in theory, the messianic time of arrival. If this scenario fails to materialize, salvation will follow the original schedule and occur after six thousand years. In any event, and contrary to the biblical day of the Lord, the kabbalistic messiah will not come suddenly, like a thief in the night.[80] The image of a displeased authority figure who demands constant vigilance from inattentive followers who tend to disappoint him—a master whose servants are unprepared for his return, a king whose guests are unprepared for his banquet, or a bridegroom whose virgin companions are unprepared for his appearance—is in keeping with neither ZA nor AA.[81] As imprudent as he might be, the young ZA always aspires to be more sagacious, while AA, the epitome of forbearance, would never chastise his servants, admonish his guests, or berate his disciples, even when they make mistakes.

The duality of tempestuous vigor and mature serenity seems to have steered the Kabbalah toward the two-messiah theory. Appropriated and developed by various kabbalistic texts, this midrashic concept tells the story of two messiahs: the son of Joseph and the son of David.[82] Representing the tribe of Ephraim, the son of Joseph is a warrior messiah who signifies the beginning of the last days. Representing the tribe of Judah, the son of David is a stately messiah who signifies the completion of all rectifications. A practical messiah, the son of Joseph harnesses his combative nature to the construction of an efficient administrative

framework. A spiritual messiah, the son of David injects this framework
with meaningful content that promotes loving-kindness. Distinguished
by his zeal, yet somewhat lacking in mercy, the former receives guidance
from the latter.

Like most kabbalistic concepts, the messiah is envisioned as a coop-
erative enterprise rather than a perfect individual. In literary terms, no
kabbalistic narrative is premised on the singularity of a main character.
The ten spheres, the five configurations, and the two messiahs are interdependent agents that must collaborate to advance the collective goal of
humanity: to negotiate the tension between selfishness and selflessness.
In this context, the idea of reincarnation stems from the belief that no
soul is the sole beneficiary of its body. The right to inhabit a domain,
celestial or corporeal, is not granted exclusively. The idea of reincarnation designates the self as a public being whose life is to be shared with
others.

Far from promoting self-denial, the Kabbalah suggests that the tension between selfishness and selflessness should be acknowledged and
addressed rather than dismissed or eradicated. Ashlagian Kabbalah,
for example, with its socialist underpinnings and altruistic tenets, is
careful not to erase the individual or deify the system. No social structure merits reverence, and no individual should be asked to sacrifice
personal happiness for the sake of the nation, the law, or religion itself.
The primary function of such institutions is to serve as temporary means
through which individuals can partake in the divine plan. The achievement of personal happiness is, in fact, the plan: the fulfillment of the
divine desire to bestow endless pleasure on creation. Those who bestow
endless pleasure on their human lovers imitate and rekindle this divine
desire. In order to do so, they must celebrate the unique qualities of the
individuals with whom they are intimate. Similarly, those who love
their neighbors replicate the purpose of creation: to shower humanity
with infinite goodness. In order to do so, they must be attentive to the
special needs of the individuals with whom they interact. The ability
to develop a genuine appreciation for the uniqueness of the other ultimately translates into meaningful relations among people who are rad-
ically different, including people who hold different opinions, promote
different views, or espouse different values. If one of the basic steps
toward rectification is to cultivate empathy for people whose physical
attributes, for example, are unlike our own, a more advanced challenge

would be to befriend someone whose thoughts, beliefs, or convictions are diametrically opposed to ours.

An otherwise controversial proposition, the ephemeral nature of national, legal, and religious systems is essential to a true acknowledgment of the other. When all the souls of humanity are rectified, there will be no need for boundaries, laws, or commandments. With its roots in mainstream rabbinic literature, this vision becomes explicitly pertinent in the context of reincarnation.[83] If the purpose of the human experience is to correct past transgressions and assist the soul in earning credit for commandments that it may have failed to perform in previous life cycles, selective observance could, in fact, hasten the coming of the messiah. Individuals who know which of the six hundred and thirteen commandments are yet to be observed by the souls that they host can concentrate on performing a limited number of tasks. Naturally, when Hayyim Vital offers this idea as a logical implication of reincarnation, conservative commentators are quick to dismiss it as personal doubts or informal speculations.[84] Nevertheless, the fact that it is recorded in the Lurianic corpus itself testifies to the radical scope of the kabbalistic vision: the ability to imagine a world in which immutable regulations will be replaced by the changing needs of the community.

CHAPTER 4

The Characters of the Underworld

How Evil Spirits Return to Good

The Other Side

COMMON INQUIRIES INTO the kabbalistic concept of evil tend to focus on Samael and Lilith: the archangel of destruction and his female counterpart, who function as impure versions of God and the Shekhinah. Just as the celestial realm is inhabited by divine configurations, so is the unholy domain populated by diabolical characters. This domain, known in kabbalistic terms as the other side, is a curious reflection of the supernal worlds. Both sides of the proverbial mirror rely on active collaboration between male and female elements. If the centrality of the Shekhinah in the divine system deprives the familiar Hebrew God of his traditional status as the omnipotent master of the universe, the portrayal of Samael and Lilith as an evil couple presents a similar alternative to the traditional image of the devil as the absolute ruler of the underworld.

The impure territories that mirror the holy worlds are populated by other characters: demons, evil angels, and mischievous spirits who threaten to lead the righteous astray. Famous among these characters is Naamah. Mentioned in the Bible as a descendant of Cain, she is reimagined in the Zohar as the mother of all demons: the quintessential human daughter with whom the divine male beings copulate.[1] More specifically, she proves to Aza and Azael, the demoted angels who find her irresistible, that they are, in spite of their celestial nature, slaves to their desires. Having failed to justify their objection to the creation of humanity, they are chained to the mountains of darkness to prevent them from destroying the world.[2] In a manner similar to Enoch, who begins his life as a human being and, upon his ascent to the supernal worlds, becomes a regular member of the heavenly host, Naamah descends to the other side and acquires the status of an impish matriarch.

Some of the more obscure demonic beings that the Kabbalah introduces are Afrira and Castimon, who rule one of the territories on the so-called other side.[3] The Zohar portrays them as an inseparable couple with a striking resemblance to the holy angels. One is in charge of the darkness, the other of the light. Like the heavenly creatures described by Ezekiel, one takes the form of a bull, the other of an eagle.[4] Each of them has six wings, like the angelic beings described by Isaiah.[5] When the light rules, they work as one. And when they do, they take the form of a single human being. When the darkness rules, they transform into a two-headed snake. In this form, they fly into the abyss and swim in the great sea, all the way to the iron chain that manacles Aza and Azael. Disturbed by Afrira and Castimon, Aza and Azael rise and leap into the mountains of darkness, thinking that God wishes to inflict judgment upon them. Afrira and Castimon continue to explore the great sea, sailing away from the mountains of darkness. When they approach Naamah, mother of the demons, she jumps and travels six thousand leagues: the circumference of the world.[6] She then appears to human beings in various shapes and forms, trying to seduce them. Afrira and Castimon fly away, roaming the world. When they return to their territory, they arouse the descendants of Cain with sinful urges to produce offspring: that is, to generate additional spirits.

What the Kabbalah emphasizes is that demons, spirits, and other nonhuman beings can neither multiply on their own nor sustain themselves without humanity. In other words, these beings are, despite their deceptive appearance, originally and ultimately human. The other side, therefore, hosts the dark aspects of humanity: the embarrassing, the shameful, the horrific, the repulsive, the abject, the taboo. For example, kabbalistic commentators, disturbed by the thought of sexual relations between Esther and the Persian king, invent a doppelganger who takes her place. At night, when she is required to perform her conjugal duties, she summons a female demon who looks exactly like her. While the demon sleeps with the unsuspecting king in the royal bedchamber, Esther stays in her room.[7] This type of ghostly twin can be seen as a defense mechanism against physical acts that compromise her purity. One possibility is that her demonic lookalike is created as a psychological scapegoat on which she can project her own desires. The frightening clash between the deeds of the flesh in which she engages and the angelic image that she has constructed for herself—or that others have constructed for her—forces her to attribute certain aspects of her personality to an alter ego. Another possibility is that this alter ego allows Esther to distance herself from a recurring trauma. Compelled to satisfy the needs of her tormentor, she produces an imaginary understudy that takes her place. From her terrified, subjective, self-protective point of view, it is with this understudy—a mechanical, emotionless, indifferent replica—that the uncouth king sleeps.

This new approach to the other side is further developed by certain branches of kabbalistic literature that present the underworld as the unconscious. Such are the writings of Yehuda Fetaya, an Iraqi rabbi who, in the early decades of the twentieth century, documented and published cases of psychotherapeutic support framed as kabbalistic narratives.[8] Theologically, these narratives, interspersed among vignettes of biblical commentary, offer innovative contributions to the kabbalistic inventory of demonic beings. From an autobiographical perspective, they allow the author to address significant incidents in his professional life. From a literary point of view, they are interconnected episodes in a modernist text that features a first-person narrator: a kabbalistic rabbi who performs mental health interventions. As an alternative version of the author, the rabbi is a typically unreliable narrator. Despite his astute observations when interacting with members of the community who seek his help, he cannot describe the services that he provides in clinical terms. More specifically, he will not translate thoughts, emotions, or actions, neither his own nor those of his patients, into openly psychological terms. It is the role of the reader, therefore, to articulate what the rabbi and his patients are incapable of verbalizing.

One of these patients, a man in his thirties or forties, contacts the rabbi with complaints about outbursts of obsessive thoughts. Apparently, he hears an internal voice urging him to abandon his faith and convert to a different religion. So disturbing are these thoughts that he cannot concentrate on his daily prayers. Twenty years earlier, he contacted another rabbi, the most prominent religious figure in Baghdad at the time, who sent a letter to his own mentor, a famous Iraqi-born rabbinic authority in Hebron, describing the condition of the man and inquiring about possible solutions. Using kabbalistic terminology, the rabbi of Hebron determined that the man was afflicted with a great

impurity—an evil force lodged in his heart—and advised the senior
rabbi of Baghdad not to get involved. Obligated to prescribe some kind
of remedy, the senior rabbi of Baghdad had suggested that the man wear
a special *mezuzah* over his heart: a piece of parchment inscribed with
biblical verses and inserted into a small cylinder. Normally affixed to
domestic doorways, the *mezuzah* is believed to have the power to repel
evil. According to the man, this treatment has been entirely ineffective,
and now he has come to see the new rabbi, asking to be examined again,
wondering if he is possessed by a spirit.[9]

The new rabbi, Yehuda Fetaya, agrees to treat the man and devises
an original course of action. He recites kabbalistic unifications—textual
practices meant to harmonize the divine spheres and hasten the repair of
the world—hoping to arouse the spirit inside the man. In other words,
he understands that the problem is not physical. A spiritual impurity
that cloaks, occludes, or indwells a human heart is a psychological metaphor that cannot be cured by an amulet around the neck. Evil thoughts,
interior voices, or messages from the other side are figures of speech
that express the desire of the patient to communicate something of
extreme personal importance. What the rabbi seems to propose is a new
definition of evil. Rather than an invading force that must be crushed
or expelled, evil is an umbrella term for the shadow mechanisms that
operate within the human mind. Meaningful in themselves, such mechanisms cannot be dismissed as the undesired doings of demonic entities.

In response to the textual unifications that the rabbi chants in his
ear, the man starts laughing. When the rabbi asks what he is laughing
about, the man says that he can hear the voice of another man inside
him, vulgar and vituperative, mocking the old rabbi who advised him,
all those years ago, to carry an amulet. That rabbi, according to the
voice inside the man, should have taken this amulet and shoved it in his
unmentionable orifice. And this new rabbi, the man quotes the voice
inside him, is only half the authority that the other rabbi was.

Ignoring the insult, the rabbi recites additional unifications, while
the man continues to curse and ridicule him. As tempting as it may
be to employ terms like possession or exorcism when commenting on
this narrative, the rabbi does seem to realize that the abusive spirit is a
manifestation of admiration and disdain for male figures of authority,
and that this deep ambivalence is somehow related to certain sexual
experiences, hitherto repressed, that the man is trying to articulate.[10]

It also appears that the man, attuned to the potential insecurities of his therapist, questions the ability of a younger rabbi to succeed where his mentors may have failed. Aware of his own inappropriate behavior, yet unable or reluctant to control it, the man touches upon this sensitive spot in an attempt to make the rabbi uncomfortable: another suggestive performance that might be mimicking an unspeakable sexual act.

When both are exhausted by the unifications, the man asks the rabbi to stop. He needs some time to hear what the spirit inside him has to say. This seems to be the moment for which the rabbi has been waiting. The spirit tells the man to ask the rabbi what he wants.

The Perfect Proxy

In response, the rabbi asks for the full name and birthplace of the spirit inside the man. A psychological interpretation of this request might suggest that the rabbi knows that it would be easier for the man to attribute his terrifying obsessions to an imaginary persona: an alter ego with a different name, a different background, and a different biography. The rabbi warns the spirit not to lie, stating that insolent behavior would result in further unifications, which would be hard to endure. In other words, it is possible that he understands that the only way to discuss the thoughts, memories, or feelings that the man has been trying to suppress is through the so-called spirit that he hosts.

Relentlessly impudent, the spirit says that many men, just like the rabbi himself, have tried to persuade him to tell them his name. "And they all failed," the man says, "for I am stronger than a rock and not afraid of anyone." Once again, it seems that the man, while looking for an outlet to disclose what he perceives as the unnerving details of his identity, is concerned about the consequences of exposure.

Reciprocating the belligerence of the man, the rabbi repeats his threat. "If you are indeed strong," he says to the spirit inside the man, "and if you are accustomed to pain, prepare to suffer the agony of the unifications. These unifications are like fire in a cotton field and more agonizing than hell. I will not leave you alone until you tell me where you come from and who you are. If you don't submit to me, you will suffer in vain. You are the one who is bringing this misery on yourself, not me."

When the spirit refuses to cooperate, the rabbi moves closer to the man. Standing right next to his ear, he resumes the recitation of the unifications and repeatedly blows the trumpet-like ceremonial horn: the shofar. Accompanied by the proper kabbalistic meditations, also known as intentions, the piercing sound of this instrument is meant to rend evil asunder and harmonize the supernal worlds. Like the textual unifications, the kabbalistic meditations associated with the shofar accentuate the integrity of the divine names.[11] More importantly, it is possible to view the auditory ritual that the rabbi orchestrates as a symbolic reenactment of traumatic events. The rabbi explains that the breath of the unifications—the words that come out of his mouth—will enter the man through his ear, reach his internal organs, and awaken the so-called breath of the spirit inside him. In other words, it seems that the treatment is designed to weaken the resistance of the conscious ego, induce a safe, controlled, legitimate resurfacing of blocked memories, and give the alleged spirit the power of speech.

When the man can no longer tolerate this ordeal, he implores the rabbi to stop. The spirit yells inside him, assuring the rabbi that he has had enough, and that he is willing to reveal his identity. The rabbi, however, pays no attention. Based on his experience, so-called spirits are as stiff-necked as Pharaoh. When the pressure is eased, they revert to their stubborn behavior.

When the rabbi finally stops, the man, utterly enervated, begs for a break. Having rested and recovered, the spirit asks the rabbi why he is questioning him about his name and place of origin.

"I would like to rectify your soul," the rabbi replies, "so that you may go to heaven."

Apparently, the rabbi wishes to free the spirit from the hollow of the sling: the twilight zone in which the souls of the sinful dead are trapped.[12] Once released from this harrowing limbo, such souls can start or resume the rectification process, at the end of which they will enter heaven, either straight through hell or after repeated reincarnations.

"You and your rectifications are useless," the spirit says. "I don't want to go to heaven."

The rabbi warns the spirit not to defy him. He brings his mouth closer to the ear of the man who hosts the spirit, ready to chant additional unifications. The spirit screams inside the man. Unable to withstand the unifications, the spirit states his name—David—and says that he comes from the city of Izmir, also known as Smyrna. He presents himself as an apostate who has had sexual relations with foreign women and left no children. He tells the rabbi that it has been seventeen years since he entered the man who now serves as his host. At this point, a conversation between the spirit and the man ensues.

"Why are you screaming bloody murder? Why are you making such a fuss? Have I ever hurt you? If you are so concerned about your own bad thoughts, from now on, I will be careful not to cause you any. Just let me stay. Otherwise, if you force me to leave your body, where will I go? Where would I be able to find rest?"

"Go to hell," the man says to the spirit inside him.

"I am not worthy of entering hell yet," the spirit says, "for I am guilty of sexual relations with menstruating women, gentile women, and prostitutes. And if you make another appointment with this rabbi, I will die. Let me stay, and I promise not to bother you."

In his role as an impromptu psychotherapist, the rabbi observes the internal struggle inside his patient. Minimizing his involvement, he listens as the man negotiates his own identity. The spirit that possesses him, so to speak, cites a biblical verse, comparing the duality of these competing voices to the twin souls of Ruth and Naomi, separable only by death.[13] Translated into psychological terms, the unifications that the rabbi performs are meant to reassemble not only the holy names, the ten spheres, or the divine configurations in the world of emanation but, more pertinently, the split personality of his patient. Confirming the integrity of the man who seeks his help, the rabbi complies with the request of the spirit inside him. He does demand that one condition be observed. If the spirit continues to haunt the man with evil thoughts, he will redress the matter with a firm hand.

Several days later, the man visits the rabbi again and complains that the spirit persists in planting distressing thoughts in his mind. Once again, the reaction of the rabbi indicates that, at least on some intuitive level, he understands the psychological subtext. Prodded by his own unconscious, the patient returns to confess about what he considers further deviations or transgressions. The rabbi recites the unifications and commands the spirit to tell him the truth. In order to ensure the success of this stage of the treatment, he announces that an angel who serves as the minister of unifications has already revealed to him the real name of the spirit. Nevertheless, he intends to continue with the recitation of the unifications until the spirit himself imparts this information. Frightened by the notion that the rabbi might have access to the intimate details of his life, the man says that the name of the spirit is Tzvi, and that he comes, as he stated before, from the city of Izmir. The rabbi calls the attention of the man to the discrepancy between the two names: David, the earlier name provided by the spirit, and Tzvi, the new name. As if to allow the man to ascribe his shadow side to the most scandalous figure in Jewish history, the rabbi asks the spirit if he is, in fact, Sabbatai Tzvi, the infamous seventeenth-century messiah claimant from Izmir. The spirit confirms that this is correct.

A symbol of depravity and blasphemy, Sabbatai Tzvi serves as the perfect proxy: a legendary monster on whom the man can project his own personal history. A messianic pretender whose controversial actions are commonly perceived as bordering on the catastrophic, Sabbatai Tzvi publicly profaned the ineffable name of God, desecrated liturgical practices, married a woman of licentious reputation, fornicated with other women, declared himself king of the Jewish nation, instigated a rebellion against the Ottoman Empire, and converted to Islam when captured by Turkish authorities. Nothing that the man imputes to this notorious character could shock the rabbi. The alleged presence of such a loathsome figure inside his mind might make it easier for the man to discuss his darkest, most shameful, most painful memories or fantasies.

It is interesting to note that at no point does the rabbi employ mystical language. When recounting his invention of the heavenly angel, he openly admits that it was a clever ploy designed to trick the spirit. There is neither a celestial power that allows him to see what the man is trying to conceal nor a supernatural being that animates the man against his will. The rabbi makes it clear that the spirit speaks inside the man—in his heart, in his mind—and that the man reports, in his own voice, what the spirit says.

If this is a case of a dissociative identity disorder, perhaps the rabbi suspects that multiple personalities assist the man in distancing himself from the repressed aspects of his life. When a new personality emerges, the rabbi addresses it very logically. "If you are Sabbatai Tzvi," he says to the spirit, "you have been gone since 1666. That was two hundred and thirty-seven years ago. What have you been doing since? Where have you been reincarnated? What forms of expiation have you undergone since your departure?"

"Go buy yourself a ream of paper and a bunch of pens, sit down, and write all the things that I have been through," the spirit replies, rather sarcastically. "Do you have nothing better to do? Look at the time. You're late for your class at the house of study. Your students are waiting for you. How much longer are you going to waste your time with me?"

The rabbi realizes that the spirit is right. He leaves for the house of study, postponing the rest of the treatment until the following day. Upon his arrival at the house of study, he greets a fellow rabbi, to whom he proceeds to relate the story of his current patient and the spirit of Sabbatai Tzvi. The other rabbi, an authority on the transmigration of souls, repeats the story to the same senior rabbi with whom the patient consulted twenty years earlier.[14] As concerned colleagues, they advise the younger rabbi to abandon the case. Dealing with Sabbatai Tzvi, they warn him, could be dangerous.

It is also interesting to observe the ways in which the rabbi weaves his own psychological struggle into the story of the man and his spirit. Eager to establish himself as a new kabbalistic authority, the rabbi must wrestle with what has been famously called the anxiety of influence: the sense that he is overshadowed by his celebrated precursors.[15] In a symbolic act that destroys these precursors, he defies the authority of the older rabbis and continues to treat his patient, determined to communicate with the spirit of Sabbatai Tzvi. It is possible, therefore, that he secretly admires, respects, or identifies with the rebellious nature of his patient. The sympathy that he develops for the recalcitrant side of the man could explain his insightful decision to experiment with a different therapeutic approach: a shift in the narrative that yields a dramatic breakthrough.

Spirits in the Material World

The next day, when the man comes to see him again, the rabbi starts the session with special unifications meant for Sabbatai Tzvi. Predictably contentious, the so-called spirit curses the rabbi, while the man repeats the foul language of the voice inside him. This time, however, the rabbi responds very softly, addressing the spirit with gentle words that he hopes will touch his heart. Having failed to institute a meaningful communication channel with the spirit, the rabbi seems to realize that the man who seeks his help expects to be dominated, disciplined, or humiliated. Used to such mistreatment, the man duplicates these patterns with his contemptuous, confrontational, abusive conduct, which he attributes to the spirit inside him. Rather than interrogate the man directly, the rabbi initiates a conversation about the therapeutic process itself. He stops reciting the unifications and asks the reincarnated Sabbatai Tzvi a series of rhetorical questions. "Why do you think I am doing this? Is there an old feud between us? Am I motivated by revenge? Am I retaliating for something that you did to me when you were alive? Is it because you were an enemy of my father?"

"Of course not," the spirit of Sabbatai Tzvi replies. "Were you even alive back then? Besides, you people are not from Izmir."

"Then why do you think I am causing you such pain with all these unifications? Is it because I expect to be generously paid by the man who hosts you?"

"Of course not," the spirit replies. "You know that this man is poor. He will not give you a penny."

Apparently, it is important for the man to make it clear—indirectly, yet quite explicitly, using the third-person voice of the spirit inside him—that he does not intend to pay the rabbi for his services. It is also important for the rabbi himself, as the first-person narrator of this episode, to make it known that his work is entirely voluntary: a purely philanthropic undertaking, for which he expects no reward.

"Think about it," the rabbi says to the spirit. "The reason I am putting my studies on hold, neglecting all the other things I normally do, is that I care about your soul. Your soul is part of the divinity above.[16] It shines like a pearl. The problem is that sins tarnish it. God, the reason of all reasons, the cause of all causes, has arranged it so that you would enter the body of this man. This turn of events gives me a chance to perform the necessary rectification procedures and bring the repair of your soul to completion. And if this is the case, what is my crime that you curse me so vilely?"

"I cannot stand the pain of these unifications," the spirit says.

"This is the way of the world," the rabbi says. "If a patient suffers from a lesion somewhere in the abdomen, for example, and the doctor must make an incision and perform surgery, the patient does not curse the doctor, even if the procedure is painful, and especially if the doctor is doing it for free. You must know that I usually try to avoid elaborate conversations with spirits. Most spirits are completely ignorant and cannot distinguish between friend and foe. You, on the other hand, are intelligent and observant. You are smart enough to tell the difference between someone who wishes to help you and someone who wishes to harm you, which is why I am taking the time and trouble to explain my methodology. To be honest, I don't mind your insults, because I know that deep down in your soul, you don't want to curse me. It is the outer layer of your soul that compels you to do so, and I forgive you."

The rabbi soon discovers that his calm, respectful, conciliatory tone has produced the desired results. In a kind and appreciative voice that echoes the words of the rabbi, the so-called spirit of Sabbatai Tzvi says that although the treatment hurts, he feels much better at the end of each unification session. Having framed this metatherapeutic discussion in paramedical terms, the rabbi allows the patient to use similar language. The man compares himself to someone who suffers from multiple cuts. When the doctor disinfects the cuts, the pain is almost unbearable, but when the skin heals, the patient feels a great sense of relief. He says that he perfectly understands what the rabbi must do and begs him to continue with the treatment. "Even if I scream and protest," the man says to the rabbi, "do not pay attention to me."

The rabbi tells the man that this is not enough. The most immediate goal is to give the patient the agency that he feels he lacks. Having complimented his wisdom and commended his willingness to make some sacrifices for the sake of recovery, the rabbi, using a poignant parable, assigns the man an active role in his own treatment. A drunk man who stumbles, falls in the mud, and cries for help will undoubtedly make an effort to lift himself up when passersby come to his assistance rather than remain passive, placing his full weight on them. "By the same token," the rabbi says to the man, "I am asking you not to rely on me to do the bulk of the work. While I am purifying your soul from without, try your best to do the same from within."

Enthusiastic about this collaborative project, the man urges the rabbi to continue with the unifications. The rabbi, who declares that he wants to demonstrate to the unruly spirit the power of the holy names, convinces the man of his own power—the power of the patient—to repair the schism in his soul.

Another series of unifications follows, which the rabbi describes as physically and emotionally draining, not only for his patient but also for himself. When the man regains his strength, he says that he feels that the burden of the outer layer, although still very heavy, has been somewhat lifted from his soul. The rabbi asks him how thick his outer layer normally is.

"Without exaggeration," the man replies, "a whole cubit."

It seems that the purpose of this question is to allow the patient to contribute to his own diagnosis. Common kabbalistic terms such as outer layers—also known as husks, shells, or peels—are no longer euphemisms for impure forces or evil beings. What the rabbi suggests is that such expressions can be used to denote measurable degrees of mental discomfort.

The next question that the rabbi asks the man seems rather whimsical. "Does the disc of the sun roll like a ball across the firmament, slice and emerge through the firmament, or hang in the air under the firmament?"

"If I stick my head among the giants of wisdom," the man replies, "I might get my skull crushed. Whatever the books say. You can always go and look it up. Such debates are none of my business."

It is possible that the question is meant to gauge the extent to which the man is inclined to squander his inner resources on frivolous, digressive, or otherwise futile arguments. His refusal to respond to what could be described as a capricious challenge is a good sign. He seems less volatile, more focused, and ready to consider more meaningful questions. Speaking as Sabbatai Tzvi, he revisits his own past and examines some defining moments that appear to have shaped his personality. He says that he was conceived in an unholy manner, attributing his so-called wickedness to the sexual behavior of his parents. His soul, he says, has transmigrated many times, gradually acquiring its first two levels: the lifeblood and the spirit. When the third level—the soul itself—began to gleam inside him, a breakdown occurred. Although somewhat vague, these statements suggest that the first few years of his life, although outwardly tranquil, may have masked some unspoken trauma. The only way he can speak about the turmoil in his soul, at least at this stage of the treatment, is through references to Sabbatai Tzvi. Describing what could be construed as a sense of suffocation and isolation, he says that he died by strangulation and, having never repented, was buried in a foreign grave. The fact that he describes his final resting place as a gentile cemetery may indicate that he feels contaminated, shunned by his immediate social environment, and ultimately hopeless. While he was alive, the forces of impurity—the outer layers—habitually appeared to him. He says that now, in retrospect, he can see that Moses and the Torah are, in fact, the truth. He claims, however, that this admission comes too late. Quoting the Talmud, he says that since the dead are exempt from performing the commandments, his confession is useless.[17] Even the commandments that he did observe, he says, cannot be counted to his credit. Another, more righteous man has already been rewarded for the good deeds that he had performed. He says that he tries to keep the spirit inside him under control through Torah study. Torah study, according to the man, forces the spirit to speak silently, internally, and not through his mouth. The problem is that the spirit, fighting back, interrupts his Torah study with disturbing thoughts.

In a parenthetical note, the rabbi adds that his patient is incorrect. It is true, the rabbi admits, that Torah study is a good way to control evil spirits. That is not the reason, however, that such spirits speak in the hearts rather than from the throats of the people they inhabit. As evidence, he cites the case of a woman who hosted the spirit of a recently deceased, ill-reputed local rabbinic scholar. Single, thirty-five years old, and blind, the woman was urged by the spirit inside her to engage in sexual relations with another rabbinic scholar. Even though her blindness prevented her from studying the Torah, the spirit, who tried to tempt her by suggesting that from such sexual congress the messiah would be born, spoke only inside her, never through her mouth.

Referring to the Lurianic *Gate of Reincarnations*, the rabbi explains that the souls of the sinful dead often inhabit their living hosts secretly.[18] They do so, according to the interpretation that the rabbi suggests, because they do not wish to be recognized or ridiculed. In other words, the rabbi seems to acknowledge that so-called impure thoughts, wicked ways, or sinful behaviors are, in many cases, closely linked to feelings of shame, guilt, or failure. If his current patient is a man who, like many other victims, blames himself for the actions of others, the sadness and despair with which he tells his story accentuate the possibility of sexual abuse.

It is in this context that the self-deprecating statements made by the man can be understood. Corroborating the hypothesis that he

is a reincarnation of a false messiah, he says that while the spirit of
Sabbatai Tzvi does reside within him, the lower aspect of his soul—the
lifeblood—lives in a wild animal. He says that he yearns to leave his own
body and dwell in the forest, never to be reincarnated as a human being
again. He refuses to answer more questions, stating, once again, that the
evil element that cloaks him is a cubit thick. The rabbi, who terminates
the session, may be aware that the rapid shift from manic behavior to a
depressive episode—from talkative, aggressive, overconfident patterns
to feelings of worthlessness, disinterest in communication, and potentially suicidal thoughts—is typical of the initial stages of the therapeutic
program. The patient, who becomes aware of his condition, is evidently
mortified, petrified, or otherwise incapacitated by his own discoveries.

Restoration of Humanity

Five days later, the rabbi and the man meet for another session. The rabbi,
who continues to speak softly, notices an improvement. Remorseful
for what he refers to as his own wrongdoings, the man greets the rabbi
warmly and asks him to proceed with the rectification of his soul. He
declares that in appreciation for the work that the rabbi is doing, he will
now speak nothing but the truth. Assuming the persona of Sabbatai
Tzvi, he says that his first sin was an illicit love affair with a married
woman. He then lists two other transgressions, attributing them to
Sabbatai Tzvi. First, he had sexual relations with a man while wearing
phylacteries and a prayer shawl. Second, he sent a young man to perform sexual acts with his promiscuous wife, explicitly instructing him
to obey all her orders. Finally, speaking in terms of cause and effect,
he says that it has been thirty years since Sabbatai Tzvi entered his
body, and that it happened on the day that, as a boy, he kissed a girl.
Based on a similar case, it is implied that he kissed her private parts.[19]
According to the man, Sabbatai Tzvi had always been hovering over his
head, so to speak, but entered his body because of that forbidden kiss.
Quoting the Lurianic corpus again, the rabbi remarks that it is usually
close relatives—an uncle or a cousin—who enter other bodies in such
a way.[20] A seemingly casual reference to the principles of reincarnation
and rectification, this comment suggests that the story of the man could
be interpreted as an etiology of incestuous abuse.

Another story that the rabbi records—and that may support this reading—is the case of a pregnant woman who, in addition to violent seizures, suffers from nightmares in which she is violated by a strange man.[21] The rabbi examines her and, using the kind of language that makes it possible for her to talk about the abusive man in her recurring dreams, determines that she is possessed by a spirit. When interviewed by the rabbi, the spirit reveals that he is her dead brother. Like the spirit of Sabbatai Tzvi, he is in the hollow of the sling, waiting to be admitted into hell. While alive, he was known as an exceptionally handsome man with uncontrollable carnal urges who provided sexual services to Turkish army officers and their wives during World War I. He would also have his way with prostitutes, subjecting them to every imaginable sexual act. He died at the age of twenty-four, yet his presence continues to torture his sister every night. Speaking on his behalf, she exposes his bestial character, to which her mother, who is present in the room during the interview with the rabbi, responds with a categorical denial. She accuses the spirit of spreading lies about her son and demands a sign: a personal detail from his childhood that would serve as proof. Her daughter, on behalf of the spirit inside her, describes the room in which the family used to sleep. Speaking as her brother, she mentions a certain lullaby that her mother used to sing to him whenever he woke up crying in the middle of the night. She also mentions a certain bedtime story that she herself told him once, when again he was crying. Her mother admits that all this information is correct.

When the rabbi asks the spirit of the abusive brother if he is wearing anything, he says that he is completely naked. From a technical point of view, nakedness represents the initial stages of the sentence that a sinful spirit has to serve. Gradually, as the abusive brother advances toward repentance, he will acquire various articles of clothing. More significantly, the fact that his sister describes him in such a way is a telltale attempt to communicate the unspeakable. The rabbi treats the spirit inside her with the same unifications to which he subjects the spirit of Sabbatai Tzvi. After numerous setbacks, the abusive spirit seems to develop the ability to curb his sexual appetite, only to regress to his old patterns and defile his sister in her dreams again. At some point, he decides to complain to his dead father about the pain that the rabbi inflicts on him. He visits his father in his grave and returns after a short while. He reports to the rabbi that his father was grieved to learn that

he had died but glad to see that he was making progress with the rectification of his soul. Unlike his son, the father has yet to begin the process
of rectification. It has been fifteen years since the day of his death, yet he
is still in the hollow of the sling. When the rabbi asks the spirit what his
father was wearing, he says that spirits can make themselves invisible to
one another. He could speak with his father but not see him. The rabbi
concludes that the father, ashamed of his appearance, was also naked.

The rabbi asks the woman if she would permit the spirit of her
father to indwell her temporarily, so that he, too, can be rectified. She
agrees, and the rabbi asks him about his sins. The father claims that,
while alive, he committed only one sin, which he was too embarrassed
to repent. Seduced by a married woman, he succumbed to his desire
and slept with her. This happened, according to the father, in her house,
while her husband was away. Is he telling the truth? Is that his only
crime? Is he talking, indirectly, about his own daughter?

The fact that the patient, speaking on behalf of the spirit that tor-
tures her, mentions her father, then gives her consent to interview him,
could suggest that her incestuous ordeal did not begin or end with her
brother. Again and again, the text deconstructs itself, revealing what
the author hesitates to address explicitly. Refraining from translating
the confessions of the brother and the father into diagnostic terms, the
rabbi records one of his own dreams, in which he sees two dogs—one
big, the other smaller—barking at each other. When he looks closely,
he realizes that a man is reincarnated in each of them. The dream takes
place at the grain market of Baghdad, and both men, when alive, were
bakers. Their beards have been singed by the fire of the oven, and they
seem to know that they are human souls who inhabit dogs. When they
look at the rabbi, they can tell that he knows who they are. Ashamed,
they bury their faces in the ground and go their separate ways.[22]

In a sense, the dream is a visual ratification of the observations and
discoveries that the rabbi has made during his conversations with the
woman. Visibly embarrassed, the men in the dream serve as a literal
enactment of a rabbinic saying, according to which a face as blackened
as the bottom of a pot is a sign of disgrace.[23] Twice displaced—first as
bakers, then as dogs—the abusive relatives evoke the biblical and rabbinic image of Ahab, son of Kolaiah, and Zedekiah, son of Maaseiah:
two false prophets who, having slept with married women and seduced
young daughters, are burned in a fiery furnace.[24] According to the rabbi,

the dogs in his dream try to talk. In their current reincarnation, however, they are only able to bark. In the context of the spirits of the father and the brother that torment the woman, the dogs represent sexual offenders who, ashamed of their crimes, find it impossible to confess. At the same time, it is possible that they represent another pair of interlocutors who struggle to communicate: the victim and her therapist. According to this type of condensation, the woman and the rabbi, who find it difficult to discuss the traumatic events that they have probed and uncovered, must resort to circumspect speech.

Although it is the rabbi who dreams about the dogs, the fact that they attempt to talk is a classic case of wish fulfillment. The woman, who witnesses the incredulous reaction of her mother, seeks a long overdue validation of her own traumatic memories. As a victim of intrafamilial abuse, she must have been told, either by others or by her own second-guessing self, that such memories are not to be trusted. The men inside the dogs, despite the obvious struggle, are willing to admit that these memories are neither fanciful fabrications nor false accusations. The rabbi, who knows that they are actual experiences, understands that the woman wishes to terminate this cycle of denial: the allegedly safe script that her mother expects her to follow.

As if alarmed by his own discoveries, the rabbi subjects his dream to what is known in Freudian terms as secondary revision. In an attempt to impose a less alarming narrative on the images and events of the dream, the rabbi explains that men who sleep with gentile women are reincarnated, according to the Lurianic corpus, into dogs.[25] As a form of censorship, this kind of revision deprives the dream of its latent content and presents it as a more palatable story of crime and punishment. The evil deeds of the father and the brother are converted into victimless transgressions whose consequences only the offenders suffer.

While the psychoanalytic vocabulary of this reading might seem anachronistic, the idea of later interpretations that reveal the so-called secrets of earlier texts is quite common. Just as the cosmological and theological dimensions of the Zohar are made apparent centuries after its composition, when approached from a Lurianic perspective, so are the psychological dimensions of the kabbalistic underworld explored and exposed when approached from modern perspectives. By the same token, it is when Freud reads Shakespeare that Hamlet becomes a more complex character. Based on the semiotic principle of infinite sign action, the text acquires additional meanings—sometimes its most profound meaning—when new perspectives find their way into it. This type of deconstruction highlights the radical dependence of the text on its implicit layers. It is precisely when the text is destabilized—when it is disassembled and rephrased as a series of questions about its own premise—that its growth potential peaks.

It is in 1903 that the rabbi treats the tortured man of Baghdad who hosts the spirit of Sabbatai Tzvi. In 1918, against the backdrop of Freudian and Jungian theories, he begins to treat the pregnant woman. It could be argued, therefore, that a psychoanalytic reading of these cases is not at all anachronistic. Many contemporaneous narratives explore similar mechanisms, inviting audiences to draw the conclusions that storytellers or characters stop short of articulating. A notable example is a 1927 movie—*The Unknown*—in which Joan Crawford portrays a young circus performer who suffers from a morbid fear of hands.[26] So debilitating is her phobia that she recoils even from the touch of the man she loves. Certain scenes in which her father, the circus owner, is depicted as a brutal and possessive character imply that her condition is the result of childhood abuse. In typical Hollywood fashion, the attractive circus performer, following the death of her father, is cured of her phobia. No longer afraid of men and their hands, she spends most of her time in the arms of her fiancé, enjoying his caresses.

The rabbi of Baghdad, on the other hand, fails to cure his patient of her nightmares. A certain remission is achieved when, after years of treatment, she is able to wake up from the dreams in which her brother appears just in time to prevent his apparition from forcing her to relive the same trauma. Does the rabbi acknowledge his own failure to diagnose and document such cases more overtly, more courageously? Is it possible that his official role as a religious authority prevents him from publishing a manifestly psychological study that documents cases of sexual abuse in the community that he serves? Does he cleverly disguise his investigations and findings as an unassuming book of biblical commentary? In any event, he admits that the treatment was not a complete success, and that he was ultimately unable, despite considerable effort, to save the woman from the terror of her dead brother.

He does describe more positive results with the man who hosts the so-called spirit of Sabbatai Tzvi. Following a mutually introspective trial-and-error process, a more ethical clinician–client code of conduct is implemented. The patient, who now regards his therapist with appreciation rather than contempt, is much more comfortable with a collaborative plan of action based on caring and trust rather than reproach or compliance. The rabbi agrees with the man that laboring in the Torah is an effective intellectual pursuit that should help him bracket, dispatch, or otherwise cope with obsessive thoughts. More importantly, he tells him to study the Zohar several times a day as a means of rectification for the soul of Sabbatai Tzvi. From now on, such textual practices will save rather than subdue the spirit inside him. In other words, the rabbi communicates to the man the idea that the spirit inside him, as evil as it may be, could benefit rather than suffer from the treatment that he prescribes.

The immediate result, as recorded by the rabbi, is that the spirit of Sabbatai Tzvi now beseeches the man to study more of the Zohar. The man tells the rabbi that the spirit wakes him up early in the morning, urging him to go to the house of prayer. He wishes to see the rabbi for regular unification sessions every day and asks for additional study assignments, expressing his hope that such projects will help the spirit inside him enter hell and complete the rectification process. The rabbi inquires when the spirit expects to leave the man. The spirit replies, "Please don't ask me about that. When I consider myself worthy and deserving of entering hell, I will leave this man without a word."

A few days go by, and it appears that the spirit, as promised, has left the man. When no one wakes him up in the morning, he goes to see the rabbi. The rabbi examines him and finds no spirit inside him other than his own. What the rabbi may have demonstrated is that when victims name the evil spirits that torment them, the pain is converted from a petrifying obstacle into a manageable condition. It is the ability to identify, examine, and process the trauma that diminishes its power. Contrary to the happy endings that popular narratives tend to boast, the pain does not subside when the monster that causes it is punished or eliminated. Evil returns to good when its victims restore their own humanity.

The Souls of the World of Chaos

The notion of the other side as a divinely endorsed dark realm that reveals the unconscious is suggested by another major kabbalistic figure: Abraham Isaac Kook. In keeping with modernist sensibilities, and

echoing Freudian and Jungian psychology, Kook composed his most
poetic, most experimental, most influential texts in the early decades
of the twentieth century—while serving as chief rabbi of Jaffa, then of
Jerusalem—before his appointment as chief rabbi of Israel. A notable
example is "The Souls of the World of Chaos," a short essay published
in 1913, in which Kook writes—with a great deal of admiration, and
much to the surprise of his observant disciples—about secular Jews who
forsake religious practices for socialist ideas. This unlikely hymn to dedicated delinquents is an insightful portrait of the violently passionate,
painfully sincere, socially shipwrecked protagonists that modernist
fiction often explores:

> Regular observance of codes of decency, good morals, and the
> law is characteristic of the world of rectification. Any devia-
> tion from these norms, whether triggered by foolishness and
> recklessness or heightened awareness and spiritual awakening,
> is typical of the world of chaos. There is, however, a significant
> difference between opposing elements in the world of chaos.
> The great idealists, who dream of a new order, magnificent
> and monumental yet entirely unprecedented, destroy all exist-
> ing structures. Some of these visionaries know how to rebuild
> the world that they destroy, while others, motivated only su-
> perficially by idealistic inclinations, cause nothing but dam-
> age and destruction. Those are the ones who are rooted in the
> lower level of the world of chaos.
>
> The souls of chaos are higher than the souls of rectifica-
> tion. Majestic by nature, they put great demands on reality
> and crave more than their vessels can sustain. They pursue a
> supreme light and cannot tolerate anything that is regiment-
> ed, regulated, or restricted. They descended from their lofty
> standing at the genesis of existence, soared like a flame, and
> dwindled. Their infinite ambition refuses to die. Cloaked in
> various vessels, they always overreach, always aspire to more.
> They rise above and fall. When they realize that they are impris-
> oned by laws, confined by conditions that prevent them from
> expanding indefinitely, all the way to the boundless heavens,
> they collapse in sadness, in despair, in rage. Their anger yields
> malice, spite, squalor, hostility, disgust, devastation, and utter

negativity. Their restlessness is vigorous and incessant. They
are to be found in the most audacious rebels of the generation.
Outlaws guided by strong convictions—those who break
the rules out of principle rather than self-serving pleasure—
possess superior souls, straight from the lights of chaos. They
have chosen destruction, and they do destroy. While dissolv-
ing the world, they bring about their own dissolution. Yet
the essence of courage represented by their willpower is the
spot of holiness. When ordinary souls are transfused with this
holiness, they acquire the force of life. The souls of chaos are
especially dominant at the end of an epoch, prior to the birth
of a new world, right before the creation of a wonderful and
unique reality, on the verge of expanding frontiers, heralding
the inception of a system to surpass all others.

When salvation approaches, defiance peaks.[27] A storm
rises and rages on, one outburst after another, growing increasingly more defiant, marked by dissatisfaction with the
measured amount of good light: the limited light that fails to
fulfill all wishes, lift all masks, unlock all secrets, quench all
desires. The souls of chaos renounce everything, including the
good: the kernel of happiness that leads to tranquil pastures
and permanent repose, to eternal joy and everlasting exhilara-
tion. Forever restless, they kick and fume, break and annihi-
late, seeking sustenance in foreign fields and nourishment in
strange places, disparaging all established authority.

These fiery souls demonstrate their strength, making it
clear that no fence or boundary can stop them. At their sight,
the meek of the conventional world, those who are reserved
and refined, are frightened: "Who can withstand such con-
suming fire? Who can withstand such eternal flame?"[28] The
truth, however, is that there should be no fear. Only the sinful and the spineless, whose souls are frail, are seized by fear.
The mighty ones, on the other hand, know that this display
of strength is one of the revelations that are designed to bring
creation closer to perfection and fortify the nation, humanity,
and the world. At first, this strength is revealed in the form of
chaos. Eventually, it will be taken away from the wicked and
placed in the hands of the righteous: the lionlike heroes who

will unveil the true nature of rectification and construction. They will do so with a clear and resolute mind, emotional courage, and decisive, consistent, valiant action.

These storms will produce bountiful showers. These dark clouds will facilitate great lights. "Out of shadow and darkness, the eyes of the blind shall see."[29]

Antagonistic yet apprehensive, affectionate yet acrimonious, cordial yet cruel, confident yet confused, cautious yet capricious, bursting with vitality yet hopelessly morbid, the souls of chaos undermine the predictable dichotomies of moralistic literature. Heroes and villains are replaced with self-tortured, self-destructive, often self-sacrificing characters who fail to generate transparent sympathy. The all-consuming passions with which such characters burn correspond to the most crucial phase in the Ashlagian version of kabbalistic cosmology: the fourth stage in the development of the vessel. This is the point at which the female aspect of the divinity—the royalty of the infinite light—experiences absolute desire and, startled by its consequences, decides to curb it. Such an intense degree of desire is essential for self-awareness, despite the fact that it stands in sharp contrast with the giving qualities of the light itself and, by necessity, with the purpose of creation: the perfection of humanity, the abandonment of selfishness, and the development of altruistic vessels. Eager to become completely independent, the souls of chaos reject the light. When the light disappears, they experience a great sense of loss, which triggers a lifelong, exasperating, manic search for meaning.[30]

The memorable malcontents of modernist literature are characters whose nightmares, cravings, or convictions compel them into such journeys: Melanctha Herbert, Malte Laurids Brigge, Harry Haller, Matthew O'Connor, and—perhaps most quintessentially—Hazel Motes.[31] Each of them is a broken vessel: a lonely individual incapable of accepting their allotted amount of light, incapable of receiving, sustaining, or reciprocating love. While struggling to reform the world, they desperately try to repair themselves. Chronically frustrated, they dream of restoring creation to its intended perfection, to its prelapsarian state of maximum illumination. Anxiously searching for that ever-elusive utopia, they are ready to demolish anything that threatens to delay the fulfillment of their far-reaching fantasies. In kabbalistic terms, their declared goal is to reconstruct the world of chaos—what would have been the original world of emanation—and prevent it, with hard work and uncompromising devotion, from collapsing.

At that stage of the cosmogenic narrative, also known as the world of *Nekudim*, the vessels of the divine spheres are arranged in a speckled pattern: small, individuated, unstable dots that fail to collaborate with one another. In a sense, the souls of chaos believe in their ability to reverse time. If they could only goad those isolated vessels into growing somewhat faster, they would prevent them from shattering so quickly upon contact with the blissful light. If they could only convince humanity that words of wisdom etched in stone are more precious than a large chunk of gold, they would stop Moses from smashing the first tablets. At some point, they realize that significant progress, despite their herculean efforts, might not be feasible during their lifetime. In the context of reincarnation, they acknowledge the impossibility of immediate repair. In many cases, partial rectification of past traumas can only occur several generations later.

In the meantime, the souls of chaos refrain from excommunicating the unconscious, as terrifying as it may be. Rather than suppress the appetite for destruction, they harness it for the construction of a larger whole. The spot of holiness that they embody is revealed when this larger whole becomes a uniquely creative project. The souls of chaos despise unimaginative competency. In literary terms, they subvert familiar reading patterns and reinvent modes of writing. In the context of biblical interpretation, they liberate, expand, and repurpose the text. Highly aware of the probability of failure, they are never deterred by the prospect of rejection or ridicule. Natural aspects of the human mind that are often dismissed as indecent or abhorrent serve as their building blocks. The refusal to deny, devalue, or expunge these aspects is a daring challenge to the binary structure of the supernal worlds and the other side. The souls of chaos rage against the machinery of complacency, the flattening of human emotions, and the sanctimonious certitude with which people discuss God. Contemptuous of the common tendency to beat an inherent complexity into a flattened coherence, they overturn hermeneutical tables. As a counterargument to businesslike theology, they insist on the inevitable ambiguity of demanding narratives. Unhappy with a simplistic systematization of multifaceted concepts, they destabilize the boundaries between the past and the future, the self and the collective, the center and the periphery, the signifier and the signified, the sacred and the impure, the virtuous and the corrupt, the regular and the abnormal, the essence and the shell, the light and the vessel.

The Optimistic Illusion

Despite the recurring image of transformative concord between opposing aspects of the divinity and the self, many kabbalistic narratives are powered by the impossibility of such an optimistic vision. Espousing a more realistic view, Ashlag, for example, admits that people will not lift a finger to help others unless they are certain of some personal reward.[32] Even those who devote themselves to acts of charity are inescapably motivated by their own righteousness: public applause, social recognition, some self-congratulatory sense of satisfaction, or other egotistical concerns. The mere knowledge that good deeds are likely to be met with gratitude or appreciation renders such deeds selfish rather than altruistic.

The irresolvable nature of this paradox cannot be ignored, just as Fetaya, the rabbi of Baghdad, cannot deny his inability to introduce a satisfactory reintegration of the conflicting forces that operate inside some of his patients. While the story of the tortured man who hosts the spirit of Sabbatai Tzvi features a happy, cathartic, somewhat sentimental ending, the narrative of the woman who hosts the soul of her abusive brother rejects the rosy picture of rupture and repair. In paradigmatic terms, the desire to translate the stations of her ordeal into the familiar language of Lurianic cosmology remains unfulfilled. There is no constriction of her infinite pain, no safe space for the creation of a new reality, no primordial structure from which pure light can emanate, no rectification for the broken vessels of her being, no rebuilding of more stable configurations, and no middle ground—in kabbalistic terms, no middle pillar—between judgment and mercy: between categorical condemnation and unconditional forgiveness. Ultimately, her narrative resists the common oversimplification of kabbalistic principles, refusing to make the transition from the inherently fragile world of chaos to the beautiful fantasy of strength, stability, reconciliation, restoration, renewal, rebirth, and redemption.

In similar fashion, Kook emphasizes the irreparable schisms that mark the commendable souls of chaos. What makes these souls exceptional is the wild mixture of discordant temperaments that drives them into action. The narrative that Kook suggests does not culminate in the unification of internal polarities. The souls of chaos remain deeply conflicted, as do Cain, Korah, and other biblical characters who tend to be condemned as thoroughly evil. Traditional narratives denounce these characters as ungodly sinners. Bound to suffer eternal punishment, they are labeled brute beasts, filthy dreamers, clouds without rain, trees without fruit, wandering stars that drift in utter darkness, ocean waves that foam with shame, or disgruntled faultfinders who defy authority.[33] The kabbalistic view of these characters, on the other hand, replaces didactic castigation with observation and analysis. The derogatory labels listed above become accurate metaphors for those who register honest, fervent, heart-wrenching complaints against an imperfect world. The inevitability of such complaints is often the result of acute self-awareness. Uprooted, lonely, and highly critical, these characters crash against the shore of reality again and again, unwilling to exchange their broken dreams for meaningless conveniences. Alienated from society, from themselves, and from God, they spend their lives wrestling with the existential, psychological, and theological distress that ordinary souls—the souls of the world of rectification—are content to ignore or repress. In many cases, ordinary souls delude themselves with visions of healthy growth or a harmonious life: a sugarcoated, self-soothing, self-deceptive narrative. The souls of chaos are valued precisely for their refusal to submit to this comfortable illusion.

In hermeneutical terms, this popular illusion fosters the belief in the Bible as a symbol of perfection, authority, and verity. In contrast, the very act of interpretation is a creative endeavor that undermines notions of stability, certitude, and completion. Every interpretation manufactures its own grammar, its own vocabulary, its own style. Every interpretation promotes its own vision, its own agenda, its own engagement with the text. Commentators are commanded to rewrite the Bible endlessly in order to arrive at a deeper understanding, as elusive as it may be. Encompassing a steadily increasing number of interpretive possibilities, the Kabbalah accommodates the slippery nature of meaning. As a literary framework, the Kabbalah magnifies certain textual elements, disassembles them, and reconstructs them to create new narratives. According to this framework, it would be a sin to imprison the Bible in authorized, ossified, pre-approved readings. Readers are required to develop innovative interpretations that would illuminate the Bible in surprising ways and unearth its previously obscured layers. Despite their alarming effect, unconventional interpretations become part of the Bible itself: a living text that anticipates and absorbs all its future interpretations, an ever-growing system that welcomes new combinations, new perspectives, new ideas. In that sense, the biblical text is forever incomplete, as are God, creation, and the human self. It is the role of daring readers to complete the text, the role of idealistic thinkers to complete creation, and the role of new interpretations to complete the divinity.

Kabbalistic narratives that offer alternatives to pedestrian optimism acknowledge the fact that a lifelong commitment to this kind of repair is a Sisyphean undertaking. After many failed attempts, the souls of chaos might realize that partial emendation is possible only through literary creativity. It is when Luria reinvents the Zohar that readers can ascend to a higher level of consciousness. It is when Ashlag reinvents Lurianic Kabbalah that readers can gain more profound insights into the psyche of the individual, social interaction, and the complexity of the divinity. It is when Luzzatto dresses kabbalistic ideas in poetic clothes that the drama of creation, human strife, and ultimate forgiveness unfolds in more vivid colors. It is when Fetaya translates the concept of reincarnation into an original cycle of short stories that readers can experience the redemptive power of the imagination. It is when Kook develops the souls of chaos that the problem of evil approaches an eye-opening solution.

The intertextual dimensions of creative interpretation are emphasized by kabbalistic commentators who record their own hermeneutical practices. Fetaya, for example, interrupts the story of the woman who hosts the spirit of her abusive brother with a curiously self-referential digression. After two years of treatment, the woman experiences a period of remission, during which the intensity of the sexual urges that govern the naked spirit of her brother subsides. The progression of his rectification is marked by the gradual acquisition of clothes. First, he appears in trousers. Another week goes by, and now he is wearing a shirt; next, a hat and coat; and finally, after three years of unifications, socks and shoes.[34] As if sensing that the miraculous transition from disgrace to dignity is only temporary, the rabbi takes advantage of this opportunity and sends the reformed spirit to the heavenly court. Apparently, the rabbi is anxious to ask the court some practical, theoretical, and textual questions to which he has been unable to find good answers on his own.[35]

The spirit of the abusive brother says that he is scared. More specifically, he is afraid that the court might punish him. The rabbi assures him that he will not be punished. After all, he will be going merely as a messenger. Reluctant to accept this assignment, the spirit says that the court guard would not admit him. The rabbi instructs him to tell the guard that he was sent by Yehuda Fetaya. He gives him a list of questions and sends him on his way.

Apparently, Fetaya is a name that opens every door. When the spirit mentions it, he is admitted into the heavenly courtroom without delay. Upon his entrance, he bows four times on behalf of Fetaya: before God, before the messiah, before the court scribe, and before the court itself. Impressed by these gestures, the court invites him to ask his questions.

The first question that has been troubling Fetaya is whether the court would disapprove of a successful rectification process, especially if it shortened the number of years that a convicted spirit spends in the hollow of the sling: the purgatory of souls in transit. In other words, if a sinful spirit has been sentenced to a certain period of liminal punishment, does Fetaya have the right, through sessions of unifications, to nullify the decision of the court?

The court replies that its intentions are not vindictive. The purpose of the punishment is to cleanse the lifeblood, the spirit, and the soul of the evildoer. At the end of the process, the evildoer will enter heaven. If the rabbi can perform this cleansing more quickly, the court has no objection.

Fetaya says that later, after this ruling had been conveyed to him by the spirit of the abusive brother, he found support for it in the Zohar. Somewhat controversially, the Zohar states that the righteous can revoke divine decrees.[36] What the ruling of the court suggests is that every effort should be made to convert evil into a constructive force. Phrased in Jungian terms, the process of individuation—the blending of opposites that leads to psychological integration—can be accomplished only when evil impulses are acknowledged rather than eliminated.

Equally important is the emphasis that Fetaya places on the text as a meaning-making mechanism. The seal of approval that a heavenly authority provides is not enough. It must be validated by an earthly engagement of the human mind with relevant literature. This principle is corroborated by another question that the abusive spirit, on behalf of Fetaya, raises before the court. Immersed in the study of the *Tree of Life*, the primary Lurianic text, Fetaya has been struggling to understand a particularly puzzling passage about the development of ZA, the younger male divine configuration. Unable to resolve a certain logical inconsistency, he sends the spirit to the heavenly court with a detailed inquiry about the text, including quotations and references. The court replies that answers to such questions cannot be delivered by a messenger. The court promises, however, to grant Fetaya the wisdom to understand the text on his own.

What the heavenly court asserts here is that the Kabbalah is not a mystical discipline. Contrary to the notion of a revelation from above, kabbalistic knowledge cannot be acquired instantaneously. Far from a supernatural experience, a thorough comprehension of divine matters demands an intellectual effort.

It is on a Sunday in the spring of 1921 that Fetaya sends the spirit of the abusive brother to the heavenly court. The following night, while the spirit appears before the court, Fetaya spends a few hours reviewing that Lurianic conundrum. Reading the text again and again, a good interpretation finally occurs to him. Interviewing the spirit upon his return, Fetaya learns that his long-awaited insight coincided with the exact moment at which the court had declared that he would be granted the wisdom to solve the problem without divine assistance.

Shortly after this episode, the spirit of the abusive brother regresses to his old behavior. As he resumes torturing his sister, he loses all his clothes. Nevertheless, his proverbial moment of fame in the heavenly courtroom, however brief, testifies to the ability of repeat offenders, even the most corrupt ones, to regain some of their humanity.

Forgiveness for God

The psychological complexity that Fetaya explores is enhanced by an extensive use of everyday dialogue. Typical of modernist fiction, this literary technique allows the author to investigate the lives of lowly characters in the world of action, often at the expense of the divine configurations and other celestial beings that populate the supernal worlds of emanation, creation, and formation. Equally significant is the narrative device known as nesting, embedding, or encapsulation: stories within stories that echo the journey toward the center of the self, revealing layers of meaning that grow deeper and deeper. Such is the story of the otherworldly officer who oversees the spirit of the abusive brother. In a manner similar to the angels of destruction that sinners acquire every time they commit a transgression, officers are appointed by the heavenly court to supervise the correction of criminal souls.[37] With each successful step toward rectification, the supervising officer in charge of the abusive brother is replaced with a better one. At some point, the rabbi asks the spirit of the brother about his current officer. The spirit says that the name of his officer is Joseph. The rabbi announces that he wishes to speak to Joseph and asks the spirit to step aside. In response, the woman who hosts the spirit experiences a fifteen-second fainting spell, during which the supervising officer takes the place of her brother. When she regains consciousness, she speaks on behalf of the officer. Needless to say, the frame narrative features two characters: Fetaya himself—or the rabbi who serves as his literary version—and the woman. Fetaya, who reminds his readers of this fact, seems to be making repeated efforts to prevent other characters from dominating the woman or controlling her narrative. The other characters—her dead brother, her dead father, and now the officer—are internal voices that communicate her story. Unlike earlier kabbalistic texts that concern the correction of sinful spirits, the focus in the cases that Fetaya recounts shifts from the misadventures of diabolical creatures to the concrete details of human suffering: debilitating emotional states, the etiologies of mental conditions, and the psychological struggle for remission and recovery.[38]

Speaking through the woman, Joseph identifies himself and, reluctant to cooperate, questions the decision of the rabbi to summon him. "Why did you call me? I don't know you at all," he says. "I was appointed three days ago, and I have never seen you. I don't think I would like to talk to you. It is very unusual for a rabbi to speak to a supervising officer. A rabbi can only communicate with a spirit. I want nothing to do with you."

"What if the court gives you permission?"

"If you can make it happen," the officer says to the rabbi, "fine."

It is the woman who, indirectly, communicates her reluctance, or at least her hesitation, to expose additional aspects of her mental anguish. Although the rabbi never states this explicitly, he seems to understand that she is looking for validation, encouragement, or reassurance. He lifts his eyes to heaven and improvises a short prayer, asking God to grant Officer Joseph permission to talk with him. As he utters these words, he notices the so-called officer pricking up his ears, then whispering, "Yes."

Turning to the rabbi, the officer says, "Please forgive me. I didn't know who you were. From now on, I will do my best to answer your questions."

What the reader might be asked to surmise is that the woman, before allowing herself to reveal new information to the rabbi, must consult with the voices in her head. The rabbi, who seems to understand the situation, asks the so-called officer if he was given permission to speak.

"Yes," the officer says. "They told me not to hide anything from you."

As if to celebrate the unprecedented deviation from the elevated language of earlier kabbalistic texts, Fetaya tells his readers that the ensuing conversation with Officer Joseph was conducted in the Jewish dialect of Iraqi Arabic. In fact, he says, all the officers who are commissioned to supervise sinful spirits speak eloquent and lucid Arabic, which, for the benefit of his readers, he renders in Hebrew. Once again, the subtext is clear. It is the woman who speaks, not a figure of authority: a regular human being whose colloquial language is authentic, articulate, and perfectly suitable for kabbalistic literature.

Joseph begins by describing the physical appearance and daily routine of the officers. They never sleep. They stand all day and all night, although they never feel tired. Their legs are straight, with no knees, and their feet look like donkey hooves. They eat two meals a day: one in the morning and one in the evening. Every meal consists of a full cup of sweet red lentils, which materializes on its own, suspended in the air, served in a bowl right in front of them. This portion is exactly enough to keep them full, and they eat the whole serving, leaving not a single lentil. At the end of the meal, the bowls disappear into thin air, yet they do not know who removes them.

The spirits, on the other hand, do not eat. Instead, they breathe the air, which serves as their sustenance. When the officers flog the spirits, their hands, in which canes or belts materialize, move on their own. Sometimes they punish the spirits forcefully, sometimes softly, sometimes copiously, sometimes sparingly. When they are done, the canes or belts disappear from their hands.

When the rabbi asks Joseph to show himself, he refuses to do so. The rabbi says that he wishes to see his face, as well as the shape of his body, but Joseph is afraid that the rabbi might be horrified by the sight.

"Don't worry," the rabbi says. "Your face would not scare me. I'm used to things like that."

"I'm too ashamed to reveal myself," the officer says. "Our faces are very different from those of regular people, from those who are made in the proper image and likeness."

"In that case," the rabbi says, "please describe your face to me."

The officer sighs and says that his face sprouts from his shoulder, and that his nose is very long and very crooked, reaching all the way down to his chest. Keeping in mind that it is the woman herself who plays the role of Officer Joseph, it is likely that she is trying to communicate important information about her emotions, sensations, and self-image. Not surprisingly, she sees herself as some kind of monster. She cannot sleep, objects around her seem unreal, and some of her movements feel involuntary.

In psychotherapeutic terms, the role-playing techniques that the rabbi suggests mimic the shifting relations among the divine configuration and employ the kabbalistic clothing metaphor in imaginative ways. The woman is invited to wear, so to speak, the costume of the officer. When she does, she discovers new ways to voice the unexpressed. Without the figure of the officer, it would have been very hard for her to tell the rabbi that she sees herself as disfigured, that she wishes to harm herself, or that she fantasizes about punishing her brother.

In literary terms, the storytelling strategies with which the rabbi equips the woman produce a wider range of narrative possibilities. It seems that when the rabbi realizes that the woman is quick to adopt the persona of the officer, he creates yet another opportunity for vicarious performance, asking Joseph to tell him about some of his previous assignments.

Joseph says that he is still astonished by an incident that occurred during his tenure as an officer in charge of another spirit. That spirit had entered a certain woman and, in order to cause her great discomfort, lodged itself in her throat. It was very painful for that woman to breathe, talk, eat, or drink. She assumed that it was a physical illness, as did her husband and other relatives. They took her to the hospital, where the doctors labored in vain to alleviate her suffering.

She had three children, young and beautiful, whom she adored. They wanted to see her very much. Her husband brought them to the hospital, but at the sight of their mother, whose condition had not improved, they burst into tears. Seeing them in such a miserable state, she cried and cried.

Later that day, after her husband and children had left the hospital, she swallowed an overdose of arsenic. When the spirit inside her saw what she had done, it jumped and left her body. She immediately felt better, as if she had been cured, and regretted having taken that toxic drug. Unfortunately, it was too late. Her intestines had been irreparably damaged, and she died.

When she reported to the heavenly court, she was questioned and reproached: "How dare you commit suicide?"

She prostrated herself on the ground and wept. "I confess before God and before this court of justice," she said, "and admit that I have sinned. I took my own life and spilled my own blood, and I deserve any punishment that you impose on me. In fact, I probably deserve worse than the punishment to which you will sentence me, and I await your verdict with acceptance and love. God knows, however, that I did it out of deep sorrow for myself and for my children. God only knows the extent of my anguish, which was unbearable. Nevertheless, I am ready and willing to accept your verdict."

The members of the court were driven to tears by her speech, but what could they do? Although they felt her pain, they were not allowed to reduce her sentence. At that moment, a voice from the supernal world was heard: "Forgive her for this crime."

"And that is what amazes me," Officer Joseph concludes his story. "Never before had it happened that the heavenly court itself felt sorry for a sinner, let alone shed tears."

"That would be all," the rabbi says to the officer. "You may leave now."

This growing labyrinth of stories within stories has culminated in a new doppelganger: a woman whose mental distress is so acute that she chooses to end her life. Embodying the interplay of chaos and rectification—in Hebrew, *tohu* and *tikkun*—she is torn between action and reflection, impulse and remorse, defiance and submission. Acknowledging the perpetual nature of this conflict, the Kabbalah advocates divine forgiveness for the imperfect souls of those who suffer, even when they are transgressive, destructive, or self-destructive. The implied narrative of this kabbalistic vision is that the divinity itself is imperfect. This admission of deficiency expands the definition of theurgy—in kabbalistic terms, the raising of feminine water—to include the souls of chaos. There is no question about the role that the souls of rectification play in the improvement of the divinity. Those who obey the law, exercise compassion, and study the Kabbalah increase harmony in the world of emanation. Equally instrumental in the rectification of the supernal worlds are the souls of chaos. The things that they do on earth, however controversial, ameliorate the doings of heaven. Phrased more bluntly, theurgy is based on the idea that the role of humanity is to entice God into acting more lovingly. After all, if AA—the older, more patient, more composed divine configuration—can forgive the hypercritical reactions of ZA, the younger male deity, and steer him toward a greater degree of grace, so can humanity.

CHAPTER 5

The God of the Future

How Humanity Returns to Genesis

The Quiddity of the Word

NOWHERE IN KABBALISTIC literature itself is the Kabbalah referred to as mysticism, yet academic circles are, by and large, eager to define it as such. One wonders what prompts these circles to impose on the Kabbalah a label that kabbalistic thinkers and observant readers are likely to reject? A possible explanation could be gleaned from the structure of the psyche that Jung proposed in 1918, especially the controversial distinction between Aryan psychology and Jewish psychology. Jung identifies the Christian ideal of goodness with the upper half of the Aryan psyche, while the lower half represents the dark, pagan, primitive side of the collective unconscious. In other words, the savage element in the Germanic mind—the part that connects the nation to its folkish, chthonic, barbarous roots—is very strong. In contrast, the Jewish mind, according to Jung, consists not of culture and nature but of two cultures: that of the host country, which constitutes the upper half of the psyche, and an ancient, biblical, religious culture that corresponds to the unconscious: three thousand years of Jewish traditions, beliefs, and practices.[1]

While the modern, secular, assimilated Jew of the diaspora might fit this description, it would be inaccurate to apply the duality that Jung describes to millions of Jews, especially observant ones, who never saw themselves—or were never allowed to identify—as ordinary citizens of their host countries. It would also be inaccurate to apply it to millions of Jews, especially secular ones, who became citizens of twentieth-century Israel: a new geopolitical apparatus that has brought the myth and language of the religious past to the national foreground.

As a new academic discipline, the ostensibly scientific study of the Kabbalah seems to have adopted the Jungian model. Created and steered by Gershom Scholem, a German Jew who moved to Jerusalem in 1923, the discipline attempted to adjust the Jungian model to the historically informed, territorially oriented, Hebrew-speaking Jew of modern Israel. The biblical past, therefore, was reassigned to the upper half of the psyche: the conscious ego. This paradigm shift meant that some other framework had to take the place of the lower half. In order to complete this move, the Kabbalah was conscripted to play the part of the ancient, the arcane, the allegedly untamed: the beast underneath the surface, the primeval force behind the educated, cultivated, rational Jew. And in order to secure this reshuffle, the Kabbalah—an unmistakably textual, intellectual, linguistically sophisticated tradition—was rebranded as Jewish mysticism.

In its role as the shadow side, the Kabbalah occupies the slot that has been traditionally reserved for the occult: the spiritual, the esoteric, the transcendentally symbolic. This role might explain why scholars of so-called Jewish mysticism find it difficult to read the Kabbalah as literature. For example, it is hard for such scholars to treat the *maggid* of kabbalistic literature—a celestial teacher who reveals the secrets of the narrative to a seemingly passive author—as a basic framing device. Writers who wish to distance themselves from their own work often employ this literary convention, presenting highly inventive narratives as if they were told to them by mysterious figures that are external to the text or revealed to them in dreams and visions. Naturally, such devices are not to be taken literally. Readers are expected to understand that these common conceits are meant to endow the text with an aura of authority and importance. Nevertheless, when the Kabbalah is relegated—or romantically elevated—to a mystical domain that defies reason, elementary storytelling strategies are interpreted as towering attempts to bond with the miraculous.

The idea that the Kabbalah occupies the place of the collective unconscious could also explain why the divine configurations in the world of emanation are rarely treated as literary characters, despite the fact that the Lurianic narrative portrays AA as a distant but sympathetic mentor, Father and Mother as a dynamic but ultimately stable couple, ZA as a tempestuous young man, and the Shekhinah as a passionate, loyal, independent woman. Like other kabbalistic characters, the divine configurations are often understood, especially in the academic world, as archetypes. Like other textual constituents, they become victims of excessive symbolism. Armed with allegorical approaches, scholars comb the text in an attempt to detect one-to-one parallels between kabbalistic literature and other frames of reference: Greek mythology, Platonic philosophy, Christian theology, Gnosticism, Hinduism, alchemy, astrology, Euclidean geometry, fractal theory, quantum physics, and so on. The world of emanation, according to such approaches, cannot be understood as the special place in which the divine configurations interact. In other words, it cannot be regarded as a literary setting. It must represent something other than itself.

In a sense, all literature suffers from the aggressive desire of solution-driven consumers to subject it to symbolic interpretations. Misinformed by the notion that literature should provide a unified set of facts, ideas, and values, many readers feel the need to impose some simple sense of order on inherently polyphonic narratives. A comforting recipe to alleviate ambiguity is the belief that characters, events, and images stand for things that exist outside the scope of the text. Faced with the terrifying white whale, readers of *Moby-Dick*, for example, are likely to convince themselves that it represents life, death, evil, innocence, heaven, hell, truth, nature, the unknown, the unknowable, homosexuality, Jesus, the persecuted Christian, the persecuted Jew, and so on. More terrifying than the whale, however, is the bold rejection of narrative unity and the relentless exploration of literary genres that the novel presents: lists, lectures, anecdotes, manuals, biographies, geographies, legal documents, biblical sermons, and pages upon pages of detailed information on whaling, paleontology, anthropology, philosophy, marine biology, art history, oil manufacturing, and other topics that have very little to do with the so-called plot. At some point, it becomes clear that these purported digressions overshadow the adventures of the Pequod. As a structural statement, this captivating labyrinth, like the never-ending labyrinth of the Kabbalah, questions the common dichotomy between focus and departure, celebrates form and style rather than straightforward storytelling, and insists, more than anything else, on the construction of a gigantic textual organism: a literary leviathan, a massive collage of narrative techniques, a one-of-a-kind creation that readers, much like Captain Ahab and his crew, struggle to grasp, harness, contain, and comprehend.

The instant gratification of solving a riddle is powerful enough to reduce even the most complex novel to a giant crossword puzzle. To develop an appreciation for the incomparable qualities of literary components is a painstaking task that usually demands years of reading and rereading. To tackle the text as a code that can be correctly cracked is an immediately rewarding undertaking. In psychological terms, it promises the kind of pleasure that a child might derive from the ability to recite the right answers to a geography quiz that requires matching countries to capital cities. Maturity is the realization that the joy of successful decryption limits the power of the interpretive mind. To impose restrictions on the ability of the text to generate additional meanings is an infantile instinct that the Zohar denounces as unforgivable stupidity.[2] Spiritual growth—or, in kabbalistic terms, the ascension to the primordial structure after six thousand years of creation—is to capture the infinite scope of narrative possibilities that preceded the restriction of the divine light: a state of being that encompasses all imaginable interpretations. This expanded consciousness acknowledges the irreducibility of the written word to an easily identifiable signifier that perfectly corresponds to a clear and stable signified.

Without the contraction and restriction of the divine light, the letters of the alphabet would not exist: the preliminary building blocks of writing, reading, and comprehension. While necessary for basic understanding, the curtailment of infinite wisdom must ultimately yield enhanced thought patterns rather than conditioned decoding. As an expression of this principle, the primordial structure contains an element that is designated as incomparable. The kabbalistic term for the primordial structure—*Adam Kadmon*—denotes the earliest human form. Again and again, kabbalistic thinkers emphasize the idea that the uppermost part of this metaphorical human form, its hair, remains protected from symbolic interpretations.

The eschatological journey to the genesis of the cosmos will be marked by the gradual ascension of a rectified humanity to the mouth of the primordial structure and beyond. The penultimate station of the journey will be the hair of the primordial structure. And the final stop: the infinite light itself. As interdependent pieces that maintain their autonomy, the infinite light and the hair of the primordial structure do not represent any objects other than themselves. They cannot be explained by an appeal to familiar concepts. They can be understood only insofar as they interact with other elements in Lurianic literature and its ongoing expansions. In the future, all literary components will be acknowledged as autonomous and relational. In the future, the meaning of such components will be derived not from external frames of reference but from the internal relations that they hold with one another.

Scholars who, following Gershom Scholem, refer to the Kabbalah as a set of symbols might find it hard to admit that the primordial structure itself is incomparable, irreducible to analogy, or incomprehensible when disengaged from its own literary context. This is not to dismiss or devalue the attempts to equate the primordial structure with other things. For example, the primordial structure is similar to the way in which Hesiod describes Pandora: an amalgamation of opposites endowed with every gift and weakness, a beautiful but degradable matrix that dictates the shape of humanity. Pandora, according to Hesiod, is a stratified specimen that precipitates the deterioration from gold to silver to bronze to iron. Similarly, the primordial structure of Lurianic Kabbalah is a divinely assembled organism that embodies the descent from pure emanation to a corporeal existence marked by tension, toil, and mortality.[3]

In Platonic terms, the primordial structure is the equivalent of the Demiurge: an auxiliary creator that, unlike the perfect oneness of the infinite light, shapes a physical, fragmentary, ever-changing world. In Johannine and Pauline terms, the primordial structure is the Logos, the Son, the Christ: the divine firstborn who reconciles heaven and earth, life and death, the ephemeral and the eternal, the beginning and the end, the spirit and the flesh, the body and the soul, the visible and the invisible, incarnation and resurrection.[4] In Gnostic terms, the primordial structure resembles the Anthropos: the prototypical Adam, the earliest personification of humanity. For the alchemists, the primordial structure represents the blending of polarities: the merging of metal and liquid, fire and water, male and female, human and divine, being and nothingness. In Freudian terms, the primordial structure is a metaphor for the intersecting components of the mind: the creation of human personality. In Jungian terms, it signifies the process of individuation: the formation of an integrated self. In folkloristic terms, it is the Golem: a fabricated humanoid powered by divine knowledge.

Common to all the above parallels is the view of the primordial structure as a conglomerate of all things: the soul of all souls, the world of all possible worlds, a union of contradictions that signals the initial point of existence, the essence of human development, and the desired transformation of individuals and communities. The attractive power of these parallels is understandable. They can convert the act of reading from a slow, cerebral, essentially solitary effort into a communal experience that triggers a sense of quick satisfaction and connects the lonely reader, sometimes on an emotional level, with millions of other lonely readers. The effect is a stupefying sense of comfort and safety, which transcends the cumulative, contemplative, and often confusing nature of textual investigation. In most cases, however, these parallels, as valid as they may be, fail to develop a deep involvement with the unique actuality of the primordial structure.

This failure compromises the agency, particularity, and self-sufficiency of the Kabbalah. Writers who cherish the intimate connection that the reader must build with the idiosyncrasy of a beloved text present the act of comparing it to other texts as a form of adultery: the temptation to translate a neglected lover into other terms, into other people.[5] True lovers, on the other hand, are invested in the rareness of a singular partner: in the irreplaceable otherness of a treasured companion. This is the relationship between the text and the reader that the Zohar describes when it portrays the Kabbalah itself as a medieval Lady Wisdom. Ignored by superficial observers, she invites the attentive devotee, a true lover who has been admiring her from afar, to approach her, learn her special language, and appreciate her quiddity.[6]

How exactly does the Kabbalah become a textual partner? How does the attentive reader form an intimate bond with the distinctive qualities of the Lurianic narrative? How does one discuss the primordial structure, for example, on its own terms?

Theater of Possibilities

The most significant event that occurs in the primordial structure is the formation of vessels. Made of thicker light, the vessels are formed when one aspect of the light, known in kabbalistic terms as the surrounding light, encounters another: the inner light. The elaborate sequence of Lurianic settings, characters, and events is a textual edifice that invites readers to reciprocate its imaginative energy with their own creative comprehension. Readers who enter this edifice are expected to explore its internal structure rather than look for familiar symbols that could serve as road signs, secret passages, or convenient shortcuts. A careful investigation of the primordial structure will begin with the repetitions and variations that function as the formal features of the text.

Since the hair of the primordial structure remains ineffable, the first channels that transmit visible light are the ears. Ten pulses of light—ten clusters of emanations, ten spheres—issue from each ear. The next pair of channels is the nose: ten pulses of light from each nostril. Naturally, the distance between the lights that issue from the right nostril and the lights that issue from the left nostril is smaller than the distance between the lights that issue from the right ear and the lights that issue from the left ear. The distance between the lights that issue from the next opening in the primordial structure, the mouth, is even smaller. The fact that the lights of the mouth issue from a single opening means that contact between them is inevitable. At this stage, a vessel begins to form. Growing proximity between the surrounding light and the inner light is necessary for the development of a vessel.

Another feature that distinguishes the lights of the mouth is their lower location. The lights that emerge from the ears of the primordial structure descend to its chin. The lights of the nose emerge from a lower point in the face of the primordial structure and descend to its chest. The lights of the mouth emerge from the lowest opening in the face of the primordial structure and descend to its navel. A lower site is also necessary for the development of a vessel.

Yet another feature that distinguishes the lights of the mouth is the order of their appearance. The first to emerge from the mouth is the light of royalty: the last of the ten spheres. Next is the light of foundation: the ninth sphere. Then the light of the eighth sphere, the seventh sphere, and so on, until the light of the top sphere comes out: the crown. The inevitable contact between its inner and surrounding aspects means that the light of the mouth is accompanied by would-be vessels: particles of thicker light that hold the potential to exist independently and serve as receptacles for the pure form of the light. The ten pulses of light that emerge from the mouth of the primordial structure and illuminate their potential vessels are inherently incomplete. Feeling the need to be forti-fied with additional light, they backtrack toward the emanating source and return to the mouth. When they do, their potential vessels grow thicker and more independent. Each of these original pulses leaves an impression of its light to illuminate the vessel of the sphere below it.[7] For example, the crown leaves an impression of its light for the second sphere, wisdom. Wisdom leaves an impression of its light for the third sphere, understanding. The only light that does not leave an impression is the bottom one: royalty, which has no sphere below it.

Having retraced their steps, the lights are ready to emerge again. This time, they do so in descending order: from top to bottom. The crown, however, stays in the mouth, and the first to emerge is the light of wisdom. It occupies the spot of the crown and indwells its vessel. Had the lights returned to indwell their own vessels, their pure intensity would have absorbed the thicker light and dissolved the vessel. In order to solidify the fragile, unstable, newly formed vessels, a lesser light goes into each of them: the light of wisdom into the vessel of the crown, the light of understanding into the vessel of wisdom, and so on, until the light of royalty indwells the vessel of foundation, the penultimate sphere. And since only nine lights emerge during this iteration, the vessel of royalty remains empty, illuminated only by the impression that the light of foundation has left on its way up.[8]

The sphere of royalty, therefore, is referred to as a mirror that has no light of its own: a potentiality in search of fulfillment. In theological terms, the sphere of royalty is the Shekhinah: the female aspect of the divinity. In national terms, it is the congregation of Israel: a civilization in exile. In universal terms, it is the human race: the part of creation that requires rectification. All are embodiments of the ultimate vessel. All must be fortified with additional illumination. And while certain divine elements can provide some support, most of the work is the responsibility of humanity itself. It is the role of the people to strengthen the Shekhinah, the role of the individual to repair society, and the role of the human mind to seek its own psychological development.

In literary terms, the sphere of royalty is the text itself: the letters of the alphabet, the books of the Bible, and the very pages in which this kabbalistic narrative unfolds.[9] This self-referential reading evokes the traditional designation of Torah study—in this case, Kabbalah study—as the center of human activity: an indispensable prism that shapes our perception of the world and continues to grow as humanity labors to increase its own cognitive and emotional powers. A book, according to this reading, is the ultimate vessel: a textual body that begs for additional illumination from careful readers. In the context of kabbalistic texts, the sphere of royalty—the domain of sovereignty—is the creative mind: the branch of human imagination that engages in literary experimentation. An essentially subversive mode of expression, the Kabbalah revolutionizes hermeneutical practices, giving commentators a legitimate outlet to record unorthodox interpretations.

An initial account of the events that take place in the mouth of the primordial structure, also known as the world of *Akudim*, is provided in the sixth chapter of the *Tree of Life*, the primary Lurianic text. Compiled and composed by Hayyim Vital in the late sixteenth century, the *Tree of Life*—in Hebrew, *Etz Hayyim*—consists of fifty chapters that begin with the contraction of the infinite light and end in the underworld: the realm of the impure forces. The lights that emanate from various openings in the primordial structure are presented as choreographed characters that enter the stage from different directions. In a curious way, the lights of the mouth anticipate the lights of the eyes. At some point, they leave their vessels and return to the mouth. Similarly, the lights of the eyes retreat and climb back to the expanded vessels of the top three spheres. The lights of the mouth, however, do so with the intention of reinforcing their vessels, while the lights of the eyes abandon their broken vessels. In other words, both groups deploy and retreat, but their motives are different. From a performative perspective, the primordial structure is a theater of possibilities. Sets of doors, dramatic actors, driving forces, and other cardinal units form the grammar of the text: the presupposed system behind the visible process, the paradigmatic plane that produces syntagmatic sequences, the deep structure that generates surface patterns. Readers are invited to register the options embedded in this proverbial motherboard, observe the operations and combinations that yield successions of scenes, and follow the progression of the cosmological narrative.

As if to remind audiences that symbolic correspondences cannot substitute a careful reading and rereading of the text, the seventh chapter of the *Tree of Life* revisits the events that take place in the mouth of the primordial structure and offers a much more detailed version of this scene. When the pure light emanates from the hair, ears, and nose of the primordial structure, no vessel can tolerate its intensity. When it emanates from the mouth, it is slightly thicker—or somewhat coarser—and a vessel is formed. This vessel consists of ten compartments, which will later develop into the independent vessels of the ten spheres. Still frail, these potential vessels cannot withstand the disappearance of the light. Lined up outside the body of the primordial structure in a row that stretches from the mouth to the navel, they turn their faces and look away when the light leaves them and climbs back to the mouth. The first to be emptied is the bottom one: the vessel of royalty. When it is no longer illuminated, it turns its head and faces downward. At this point, it is in a back-to-back position with the light. Now it must wait for the light to leave the vessel of the sphere directly above it—foundation—before it can look upward again and face the back of the light.

This process is repeated nine more times. When the vessel of foundation is emptied, it turns its head and faces downward. At this point, the feminine vessel of royalty and the masculine vessel of foundation are standing face to face: a position that foreshadows the most intimate type of union between the male and female divine configurations. In other words, when there is a gap of one sphere between the vessel and the light, the vessel can face the light again. When there is a gap of two spheres between the vessel and the light, the vessel, farther in the dark and thicker still, becomes a complete vessel. In this case, when the light leaves the vessel of the sphere directly above foundation—glory— the vessel of royalty becomes a complete vessel. Once again, this scene emphasizes the centrality of the bottom sphere: the heavenly queen. She is the first to emerge from the mouth, the first to become independent when the light disappears, and the first to develop a real vessel.

The vessel of foundation waits until the light leaves the sphere above it, then turns around to look upward, facing the back of the light. In this position, royalty faces the back of foundation, while foundation is standing face to face with the vessel of glory. When the light leaves the vessel of the sphere directly above glory—endurance—the vessel of foundation becomes a complete vessel. And so on, until the light leaves the top vessel: the crown. At the end of this chain of events, the vessels of the bottom seven spheres are complete, while those of the top three spheres are not.[10] More accurately, the top two spheres, crown and wisdom, do not have complete vessels at this point, while the vessel of the third sphere, understanding, is slightly closer to completion. Still under the influence of the strong light of the crown, it is not, unlike the lower vessels, entirely in the dark.

When the light comes out of the mouth for the second time, it spreads into each vessel and immediately recedes. This repeated act of spreading and withdrawal is essential to the fortification of the vessels. The light enters the vessel of the crown and retreats, enters the vessel of wisdom and retreats, enters the vessel of understanding and retreats, and so on. In fact, it never ceases to enter and retreat, like the flame of a candle that keeps flickering. In more modern terms, the light that comes out of the mouth for the second time flows like an alternating electrical current, constantly reversing direction. Although complete, the vessels of the lower spheres are still weak. Light that flows in one direction and stays in the vessel—the equivalent of a direct current— would break them right away. Aware of this inherent weakness, the light outsmarts the vessels. It reaches and reaches not, using this special invention—this unique method of emanation—to keep the vessels from shattering until they are strong enough to sustain a steady flow of light.[11] This is achieved neither at this stage, in the world of *Akudim*, nor in the world of *Nekudim*, also known as the world of chaos, where the vessels collapse when attempting to hold the light of the eyes. It is only in the world of *Brudim*, also known as the world of rectification—which then becomes the world of emanation—that the repaired vessels are strong enough to retain their lights.

Lights Made Letters

The worlds of *Akudim*, *Nekudim*, and *Brudim*—the lights of the mouth, the eyes, and the forehead—are the last three acts in the drama of the primordial structure. Contrary to common readings of the Lurianic narrative, it is the formation of the vessels, not the breaking of the vessels, that constitutes its most earthshaking episode. From a literary perspective, it is clear that the vessels are bound to break. The plot is peppered with clues that communicate the volatile condition of the vessels and prepare the reader for an inevitable catastrophe. The truly momentous event, which borders on the outrageous, is the gradual conversion of the divine light into an autonomous vessel that becomes synonymous not only with humanity but with the Kabbalah itself. The act of contraction—*tzimtzum*—is a statement of purpose. The divinity expresses an unprecedented desire to share its assets and reveal its name.

The vessel signifies the transition from intention to action, from thought to thing: a concept that captures the process of writing.

The first assets that the divinity shares are the letters of the alphabet. The four movements that the light of the mouth performs—two expansions and two withdrawals—represent the four letters of the Tetragrammaton. The first advent of the light and its would-be vessels represents the first letter of the divine name. The return to the mouth in order to be fitted with additional illumination represents the second letter. The second descent from the mouth, during which the light spreads into the compartments of its vessel, represents the third letter. The innovative withdrawal that marks the alternating direction of the second advent of the light represents the fourth letter.[12] The appearance of the alphabet at this early stage of creation could be construed as divine endorsement of textual practices. An understanding of the sacred, according to this view, comes from a relationship with literature. The ability to follow the thought patterns of narrators or identify with the consciousness of literary characters is the essence of empathy for others. As the lights indwell the vessels, so do the words of writers indwell readers. The willingness to make room for different perspectives is what the divinity demonstrates when it contracts its infinite light to create a space for beings other than itself. The vessel expresses the same disposition when it contains the light, as does the reader whose perception is readily replaced by the consciousness of an imaginative author. Just as God becomes a capacious concept that welcomes multiple divine configurations, so does the Kabbalah develop into a hermeneutical receptacle that accommodates an expansive selection of interpretations. In that sense, the vessel is both the text and the reader.

During the first descent from the mouth of the primordial structure, the would-be vessels begin to thicken and prepare to separate from their respective lights. During the return of the lights to the mouth, the vessels, away from their primary source of illumination, grow darker, thicker, and more independent. When all ten lights have returned to the mouth, the vessels of the bottom seven spheres are complete. During the second descent, the vessels of the top three spheres become independent. This is a more complex process that requires greater degrees of cooperation and coordination among different types of lights and vessels.

Since the light of the first sphere, the crown, stays in the mouth and does not participate in the second descent, the light of the second sphere, wisdom, comes out first and enters the would-be vessel of the first sphere, the crown. Waiting inside this potential vessel is the impression that illuminates the sphere below it: the residual light that the crown has left for the vessel of wisdom on its way up during the return to the mouth. Normally, a light is stronger than an impression. In this case, however, the impression of the crown is of a higher origin and therefore more powerful than the light of wisdom. The sphere of wisdom, which later develops into the divine configuration known as Father, is a masculine entity, as is its light. Nevertheless, when the light of wisdom meets the impression of the crown, it is the former that plays a feminine role. When they mate, so to speak, the impression of the crown is dimmed by the light of wisdom. In its role as a male partner, the impression of the crown enters the light of wisdom. The light of wisdom envelops the impression of the crown and blocks its strong light. In other words, the light of wisdom functions as a barrier between the impression and the would-be vessel: the thicker part of the original light. This state of reduced illumination further thickens this part, solidifying it into a complete vessel that holds two kinds of light: one feminine, one masculine.

A similar chain of events occurs when the light of the third sphere, understanding, descends from the mouth and enters the would-be vessel of the second sphere: wisdom. In this case, the light and the impression retain their original gender identities. The impression of wisdom, a higher light lodged in its would-be vessel, welcomes the descending light of understanding. The sphere of understanding, which later develops into the divine configuration known as Mother, is a feminine entity, as is its light. It envelops the impression of wisdom, softening its harsh light. This is how Lurianic Kabbalah interprets the biblical description of a female element that encircles a male one.[13] When the masculine impression is diminished by the feminine light, the vessel of wisdom is strengthened. At the end of the process, it contains, like the first vessel, a male light and a female light.

Next to descend from the mouth is the light of mercy, the fourth sphere. When it meets the impression of the third sphere, understanding, the narrative pattern changes. The impression of understanding—or, in other terms, the residual light of Mother—is a feminine element. Since the distance between understanding and its original light is longer, its impression is not as bright as the ones above it. More specifically, the gap between wisdom and its original light is only one sphere, while the crown is right next to the mouth, where its light rests. During the return to the mouth, the gap between understanding and its original light was two spheres, which made its vessel stronger but its impression weaker. In this condition, the impression of understating lacks the power to enter the light of mercy. In other words, it cannot perform the role of the male. And neither can the light of mercy, which is, in fact, the child of understanding: the first of the six spheres that will collectively become ZA, the younger male divine configuration, who spends a period of gestation inside Mother.

This situation means that a new light must be produced: a light that will serve as a male partner for the impression of understanding. It is the male and female elements in wisdom, the sphere directly above understanding, that produce this new light. When it is born, it descends to the sphere of understanding and mates with the impression that has been left there. This intimate union solidifies the vessel of understanding, which, like the two vessels above it, holds two kinds of light: a female light, which comes from its own impression, and the new male light that it receives from the sphere of wisdom. It also holds a third light: the light of mercy. It may appear that its inability to function as a conjugal consort leaves the light of mercy redundant. In fact, it retains its original role: the role of a child. It stays with its parents in the vessel of understanding and raises feminine water to guarantee their permanent union. In theological terms, it represents the spiritual awakening of humanity that encourages the younger divine configurations to enter into intimate relations and bestow their bounty on the physical world.

Theoretically, the light of mercy, now that it has been replaced by a new male light, could have descended farther on its own to illuminate the sphere directly below understanding: mercy, its own sphere. This would have solved the problem of nine lights that need to fit into ten vessels. Since the vessels of the lower seven spheres are farther from their original lights and much stronger, they do not require lesser lights. Each could have received its own light. According to this scenario, the vessel of mercy would have received the light of mercy, the vessel of might the light of might, and so on, until the last light, the light of royalty, would enter the vessel of royalty. But this is not what happens. Unlike the younger divine configurations, Father and Mother are always in a state of intimate union, which guarantees a tenured position for mercy. It

must remain in the vessel of understanding, like manna in a jar: a fixture
that ensures a steady flow of divine opulence.[14] ZA and the Shekhinah,
the heavenly king and queen, do not enjoy this type of stability. Often
exiled from each other, they rely on humanity to bring them together.

Now that the sphere of understanding is complete, the next light
can descend to the fourth sphere: mercy. The light of might, a masculine
entity, enters the impression of mercy, a masculine entity that plays a
feminine role. This means that mercy is the first sphere that holds two
lights of the same kind: both male. The next four spheres follow the
same pattern. The light of beauty enters the impression of might, the
light of endurance enters the impression of beauty, the light of glory
enters the impression of endurance, and the light of foundation enters
the impression of glory. All these domains belong to the six-sphere configuration that later develops into ZA. All become male–male spheres.

The last domain that belongs to this six-part configuration is the
ninth sphere: foundation. When the light of the very last sphere goes
into the vessel of the penultimate one—that is, when the descending
light of royalty meets the impression of foundation—the pattern
changes again. The light of royalty is a feminine entity. It cannot play
a male role. And neither can the impression of foundation. Although
it is a masculine entity, the great distance from its original light makes
it very weak. This impasse necessitates, once again, a new light. It is
the male and female elements in the third sphere, understanding, that
produce this new light.

Earlier, the male and female elements in the second sphere, wisdom,
produced a new light for understanding. Now it is the sphere of understanding that helps the sphere of foundation. The new light engendered
by the male and female aspects of understanding consists of two parts:
one male, one female. The male part descends to the vessel of foundation, where it mates with the female light of royalty. This means that
foundation becomes the fourth sphere to hold both male and female
lights.

At this point, the vessel of the terminal sphere, royalty, is devoid of
light. Since there is no sphere below it for which to provide illumination,
it has left no impression during the return of the lights to the mouth.
In addition, no light goes into it during the second descent. Yet it does
not remain empty. The female part of the new light that the sphere of
understanding has produced descends to the vessel of royalty, and now

all ten spheres of the mouth are complete. Four of them, the top three and the ninth, are female–male spheres: crown, wisdom, understanding, and foundation. Five of them—the fourth, fifth, sixth, seventh, and eighth—are male–male spheres: mercy, might, beauty, endurance, and glory. The tenth sphere, royalty, consists of a female light inside a female vessel.

This interplay of constants and variables brings the world of *Akudim* to completion. During the second descent from the mouth, the lights, like the impressions with which they mate, are very dynamic. Ready to make quick decisions in response to changing circumstances, they do not perceive the necessity to switch roles as a threat to their masculine or feminine identities. This remarkable elasticity is also evident when certain lights and impressions—more specifically, the light of mercy and the impression of foundation—admit that they can neither perform their masculine roles nor easily play feminine parts. No sense of shame or failure accompanies the need to be replaced by a new element that is better equipped to handle the task. The vessel, on the other hand, is envisioned as a stable space that hosts the light. Earlier, however, during the return of the lights to the mouth, it is much more pliable, exhibiting a wide range of emotional responses. It yearns for the light, feels devastated when the light leaves, turns its back to the light when separation becomes unbearable, then develops a sense of confidence and faces the light again, watching it grow more distant, awaiting its second descent with an increasing sense of independence. When the light comes back and enters it again, it feels revitalized. Like the flexible light that animates the vessel, the sensitive reader animates the text.

Back to the Future

The meticulous delineation of each light, each impression, and each vessel seems to suggest that insight into the primordial structure is to be found in the details of the text. While analogies and archetypes might be able to provide partial answers, a studious commitment to the particulars of the narrative could capture its essence or totality. As a counterargument, academic communities often challenge the traditional loyalty to the written word, dismissing it as outmoded. Fueled by the thrill of new partners, contemporary research agendas tend to advocate the replacement of primary sources, both sacred and secular, with fashionable theories that are perceived as fresh, more attractive, and more likely to satisfy the current needs of readers and scholars. In some cases, primary sources, especially canonical ones, are condemned as anthropocentric, androcentric, ethnocentric, or otherwise biased: instruments of oppression that should be dissected with corrective tools and superseded by more relevant narratives, including nonlinguistic ones. To extend the metaphor, those who consider it their duty to reject the text see it as a privileged patriarch whose shortcomings must be exposed, while the Kabbalah views it as a struggling vessel that seeks illumination from lovers of literature who remain devoted to it despite its weaknesses.

Ultimately, theories of literature are easier to control than literature itself. The inherent ambiguity of literary texts stands in stark contrast with ongoing attempts to harness such texts into social, political, or self-improvement programs. Despite its focus on the rectification of creation and the individual, the Kabbalah is not a toolkit that teaches readers how to reform the world or how to find their inner selves. Despite its bold subversion of rigid gender roles, the narrative of the primordial structure is not a univocal set of values that can be enlisted to serve as a manifesto of progress. The story of the lights, the impressions, and the vessels does promote gender fluidity and the willingness to accept change, yet it performs these principles with a built-in vagueness that declares its presence from the very start.

One of the manifestations of this vagueness is the sheer flexibility of the Hebrew letters. The four movements of the lights of the mouth—two advents and two withdrawals—are not the only elements that signify the divine letters. The new lights that the spheres of wisdom and understanding produce are also linked to the divine letters. The new light that wisdom produces is synonymous with the first letter of the Tetragrammaton, while the new light that understanding produces is synonymous with the second letter. Some of these letters are further divided into separate orthographic components, which, in turn, signify other letters of the alphabet. For example, the second letter of the Tetragrammaton, which happens to be identical to the fourth, is *hey* (ה). Visually, it resembles a small *vav* (ו) inside a larger *dalet* (ד). The small *vav* is the masculine part of the new light that the sphere of understanding produces: the part that mates with the light of royalty in the vessel of foundation. The *dalet* that surrounds the *vav* is the feminine part of this new light: the part that enters the vessel of royalty.

Vocalized differently, the *dalet* would turn into *dalat*, the genitive form of the feminine adjective *dalah*: in Hebrew, *poor*. Poorly illuminated, the only light that the sphere of royalty possesses is the one that she receives from understanding, her fellow female sphere. In her role as the Shekhinah, the sphere of royalty is a queen in exile, downtrodden and destitute, who relies on humanity to lift her from the gutter, adorn her with new clothes, and restore her to her heavenly spouse. In self-referential terms, the sphere of royalty is the Kabbalah: a derelict text that relies on conscientious readers to save it from hermeneutical poverty and celebrate its inherent richness.

Another vocalization would turn the letter *dalet* into the noun *delet*, with the stress falling on the first syllable: in Hebrew, *door*. The sphere of royalty at the end of every world is a door that opens to the crown of the next world: from the primordial structure to the world of emanation, from the world of emanation to the world of creation, from the world of creation to the world of formation, and from the world of formation to the world of action. Each of these doors connects a bottom sphere to a top one. More accurately, each of these doors is a path to a future in which the belittled female will rise to a position higher than the male crown. This is how the Kabbalah understands the biblical proverb that describes the superior woman as the crown on top of her man: the force above him.[15]

Yet another vocalization would turn the *dalet* into *delet*, with the stress falling on the second syllable: in Aramaic, *that which has not*. More specifically, *delet* is the first word of the Aramaic expression that describes the sphere of royalty as a mirror that, like the moon, has no light to call its own.[16] In the future, the moon will shine as brightly as the sun.[17] According to this kabbalistic narrative, the meaning of the rectification of the world—in Hebrew, *tikkun olam*—is the correction of gender imbalance.

The fact that the letters of the alphabet are revealed orthographically, not phonetically, emphasizes the centrality of the written word. Unlike the God of Genesis, the kabbalistic emanator—the infinite light—does not speak. Devoid of vowels, the written word can be pronounced in various ways. The shapeshifting qualities of the letters prevent any single reading from dominating the text or becoming a fetish object that commands uncritical reverence. A multivalent narrative, the story of the primordial structure explores the elastic identities of cosmological components, the possibilities of collaboration among the constituents of creation, reciprocal modes of assistance and support, and the constantly evolving nature of family dynamics, social interaction, and intimate relations.

It is to this pleroma of possibilities that humanity will return after six thousand years. The return of the lights to the mouth of the primordial structure prefigures the eschatological elevation of humanity to the exact same spot: from the corporeal to the ethereal, from the actual to the imaginative, from the obvious limitations of the physical world to the boundless creativity that characterizes the divine. If the first act of withdrawal, the contraction of the infinite light, is akin to *kenosis*—a self-emptying gesture that signals the beginning of all possibilities—the return of humanity to the primordial structure is similar to the idea of *apocatastasis*: the ultimate gathering of all things, the restoration of all beings to the initial state in which they were created. In the context of Christian theology, universal restitution is rarely considered a valid option. Not consistent with mainstream doctrine, *apocatastasis* is tolerated only as an impossible utopia for which believers are merely permitted to hope. The history of ideas, human–divine relations, and the future of creation, according to this worldview, are restricted areas into which products of an aberrant imagination are denied entrance. Hell, in other words, is real, but *apocatastasis* is a fantasy. The implication of this dichotomy is that certain notions are accepted as objectively true, while others are banished as imaginary. Given the fact that both hell and *apocatastasis* are products of textual traditions, a different theology would suggest that both are imaginary. The fact that eternal torment and universal restitution are captivating fabrications is precisely what makes them such important ideas in the lives of those who cherish sacred narratives. Phrased in more general terms, it is the fictitious nature of sacred narratives that makes them sacred. To argue that God, the garden of Eden, Noah and his ark, or the lengthy conversations between Job and his friends exist as characters, places, objects, and documented dialogues in factual realities that operate independently of the texts in which they appear is to replace the authority of Scripture with a nonlinguistic domain that is somehow considered more real, more axiomatic, and more authoritative.

As alternatives to the distinction between the real and the unreal—
or, in theological terms, between realism and antirealism—*referential*
and *self-referential* might be better, more useful, more accurate terms.
Those who denounce antirealism are often eager to prove, demonstrate,
or affirm the existence of God. A self-referential approach, on the other
hand, would suggest that there is no need to prove that God exists.
More specifically, there is no need to match the God of Scripture to a
living God who resides outside the text. Sacred texts are not scientific
reports, news stories, or novels with keys. They do not refer to things
that are more concrete, more enduring, or more important. They are
texts that announce their own importance: autonomous cycles of poetic
compositions that require no external validation. God could not hope
for a more resounding affirmation than the daily reading, rereading,
and rewriting of these ever-growing yet self-contained texts. According
to this theology, God is not unimaginable. According to this theology,
hoping for the impossible is not an act of faith. God is best demonstrated through linguistic practices that celebrate the imagination and
explore new literary possibilities.

This theology affirms the identification of the text with the
Shekhinah: the sphere of royalty, monarchy, or—perhaps most
accurately—sovereignty. It is the sovereignty, autonomy, and authority
of the text that gives birth to concepts like God and humanity. Without
textual traditions or other products of the imagination, human beings
would live, like all the other animals on the planet, entirely in the
present, never concerned with the past or the future. The very concept
of humanity is a construct of the imagination, as are individual identities. Appellations like *Jew* or *Christian* do not occur naturally. They
do not exist in any text-independent reality. Similarly, God does not
live on Mount Moriah, Mount Sinai, or Mount Gerizim. The biblical
Olympus is the text itself. The questionable belief in a physical temple
as the dwelling place of God, repeatedly attacked by the prophets, was
abandoned after the destruction of Jerusalem for the sake of a literary
theology that refrains from finding signs of the divinity outside the texts
that continue to actualize it.

The relocation of the divinity from the temple to the text is a recurring image in kabbalistic literature.[18] When the Kabbalah describes the
ascension of humanity to the primordial structure, it imagines a return
to the core of the text: to the birthplace of the written word. Further

into the future, humanity will rise to the very top: to the infinite light. What the Kabbalah proposes is that the infinite light itself, like other elements in the supernal worlds, and despite its characterization as the epitome of unity, could be divided into ten internal spheres, the most important of which is the last one: the sphere of royalty, which signifies the very beginning of the creation process. This is the spot in which the first act of contraction occurs and to which humanity will be restored. The nexus of the divinity, this spot signifies utter sovereignty: the ability to imagine all conceivable things. Perhaps this is what Paul means when he describes a future in which the distinction between Jew and gentile, master and servant, or male and female will no longer exist.[19] Absolute permission to imagine and reimagine the self, the world, and the divinity will be celebrated as the source of all potentialities and the ultimate achievement of humanity.

The Emperor's Daughter

Other voices in kabbalistic literature continue to explore gender identities, the centrality of female elements, and the ability of the text to accommodate or generate innovative interpretations. One such voice is Nachman of Breslov, widely revered post-Lurianic rabbi, whose innovative literary approach could be seen as a missing link between the early eighteenth-century work of Luzzatto and the early twentieth-century writings of Fetaya, Kook, and Ashlag. After extensive travel through Eastern Europe, often marked by strained relations with other rabbinic figures, Nachman of Breslov composed—in the early nineteenth century, during the last years of his life—a series of kabbalistic fairy tales, short stories, and novellas. He died, like Luzzatto and Isaac Luria, at the age of thirty-eight, as if in defiance of the semi-official rabbinic decree that restricts the dissemination of the Kabbalah and discourages people under the age of forty from studying it. To use the terminology coined by Kook, those who censor kabbalistic texts, those who feel the need to protect the public from exposure to potentially controversial ideas, are souls that belong to the world of rectification. In many cases, these souls feel safer, or at least more comfortable, when kabbalistic concepts are accompanied by diagrams, flowcharts, rubrics, illustrations, or other schematic aids. Literary pioneers, on the other hand, refuse to satisfy the popular demand for friendly visualizations of sophisticated narratives. The refusal to do so—in other words, the unshakable belief in the textuality of the text—is typical of what Kook calls the souls of chaos: a bold, impudent, subversive stance, which compliant readers and writers tend to interpret as an act of violence against common decency.

Foreshadowing surrealist modes of expression, the unique brand of fiction for which Nachman of Breslov is famous advances kabbalistic literature in new, often surprising directions. A prominent example is "The King and the Emperor." Despite the title, the tale focuses on a young female character who outsmarts and overshadows the seemingly more powerful male characters that surround her. The tale does open with an emperor and a king, who quickly disappear from the narrative. Both are childless, and although they do not know each other, they experience similar difficulties. The fact that they leave their wives at home and travel the world in search of a remedy implies that both men might be suffering from infertility. Upon a chance meeting at a roadside inn, they share their feelings of sadness and make a pact, promising to each other that if one of them fathers a boy, and the other a girl, they will arrange for their children to marry each other. When they return home, the emperor's wife conceives and gives birth to a daughter. The king's wife conceives as well, giving birth to a son. The marriage pact, however, is forgotten.

When the children grow up, they are sent, quite coincidentally, to be educated at the same place, by the same tutor. They fall in love, secretly exchanging wedding rings. Recalled to their respective palaces, they pine for each other desperately. It is then that their fathers remember the marriage pact. The emperor, however, expresses some reservations, asking for the king's son to be sent to his palace to be tested in matters of government. At the emperor's palace, lovesick to the point of physical weakness, the king's son faints. The emperor's daughter revives him and decides that they can no longer be apart. They hire a ship and escape together.

After sailing for a while, they anchor at a forested shore, where they disembark and, after a series of unfortunate mistakes, ultimately lose each other. The king's son eventually finds his way to a populated area, where, having no professional skills, he finds employment as a servant. The emperor's daughter remains on the shore, hoping to be rescued by a passing ship, relying on the trees of the forest for food and shelter. A young merchant, whose rich father has given him a ship with which to learn how to conduct business, sails by, spots her hiding in the trees, approaches in a small boat, and tells her to come down. The emperor's daughter says that she will do so only on condition that he refrain from touching her until they are properly married in his home country. She tells him that she is an important woman who prefers not to reveal her identity until after the wedding. The young merchant agrees. He is especially excited when he discovers that she can play multiple musical instruments and speak several languages.

When they approach his home country, she tells him to go ashore on his own, summon all his relatives, and bring them back to the ship to welcome her. At that point, she says, she will reveal her identity. She also asks him to celebrate the occasion by offering wine to his sailors. The young merchant agrees. While he is away, the sailors get drunk on shore. Alone, the emperor's daughter unties the ship and sails away. The young merchant returns with his father and the rest of his family, only to find the ship gone, the sailors inebriated. Furious about the loss of a ship full of expensive merchandise, the father banishes his son and refuses to see him again.

From her stolen ship, the emperor's daughter observes a shoreline palace. The ruler of the palace, a bachelor king, sees her ship approaching. He notices that it has neither sailors nor passengers. Curious about the palace, the emperor's daughter draws near, then changes her mind. "Why would I want to go into this palace?" she asks herself, but the bachelor king notices her and orders his men to sail out and bring her to him. Having spent years searching for the right woman, he shows immediate interest in her. Having no choice but to pretend that she is willing to relinquish her freedom, she employs the same ruse and asks him to promise not to touch her until they are legally married. She also requests that her ship remain at sea, untouched until the wedding day. At that time, she will reveal the wealth that is stored in her ship. She also asks for eleven young ladies to keep her company. The king agrees to all these stipulations. He announces his forthcoming wedding and gathers eleven ladies, daughters of the aristocracy, to accompany his future wife. He builds a private palace for each of them. The emperor's daughter spends her time with her lady friends, making music and playing games.

One day, she invites her eleven companions to play at sea. They climb aboard her ship, where she offers them some of the same wine with

which she tricked the young merchant and his sailors. When her lady
friends drink and fall asleep, she unties the ship and flees. Meanwhile,
the king discovers that she is missing. When it is discovered that her
eleven companions are also missing, their fathers, influential noblemen
who control the affairs of the kingdom, impeach the king and send him
into exile.

The eleven ladies wake up and, thinking that they are close to shore,
ask to return to their palaces. The emperor's daughter urges them to stay
on the ship and play some more. When they realize that they are at sea,
they demand to know why the emperor's daughter untied the ship. She
lies to them, saying that, due to a coming storm, she was forced to spread
the sails to save the ship from breaking into pieces. What she probably
means to communicate, using an appropriate metaphor, is her need to
spread her wings, so to speak, and run away from an impending personal
disaster: the pressure to marry a man against her will.

They sail on. When they sight another palace, her lady friends ask
if they could take a closer look, but the emperor's daughter refuses,
saying that she still regrets the temptation to inspect the palace of that
bachelor king. At this point, it is obvious that she associates the idea of
a palace with danger: a beautiful prison controlled by a male figure of
authority who, in all probability, will try to tame her, domesticate her,
and deprive her of the independence for which she strives.

Next, they sight an island. On approach, they are captured by
twelve pirates. The pirates make it clear that they intend to kill the
women. The emperor's daughter tells their leader that she and her lady
friends are also pirates.

"The difference," she says, "is that you rob by force, whereas we use
our wisdom, for we are trained in languages and musical instruments.
What would you gain, therefore, from killing us? You might as well
marry us. If you did, you would gain not only wives but quite a bit of
wealth."

She shows the pirates the contents of her ship, and they accept her
proposal. They give her a tour of their treasure troves and boast about
their own wealth. The pirates decide that each of them, based on size
and preferences, will select his bride. To celebrate the occasion, she
invites the pirates to taste the exquisite wine that she keeps aboard her
ship. She pours twelve cups and asks for each pirate to drink for each of
the twelve women. When they get drunk and fall asleep, she tells each

of her eleven companions to kill her would-be-husband. They slaughter the pirates and take away their gold and precious stones, leaving the copper and silver behind. After loading the ship with the loot, they decide not to dress like women anymore. They sew themselves modern men's clothes and set sail again.

Next, they encounter a ship that carries a vainglorious young king, accompanied by his wife and an entourage of ministers. Frolicking on the deck, the young king and his ministers remove their clothes and engage in a contest to see who can climb to the top of the mast. When the king himself, who happens to be bald, reaches the top of the mast, the emperor's daughter aims a solar concentrator at his head and burns his skull. His brain destroyed, he falls into the sea. Unsuspecting, the ministers approach the ship that carries the emperor's daughter and her companions, asking if there is a doctor on board. The emperor's daughter, dressed as a man, tells them to retrieve the body of the king from the water and bring it to her. When they do, she pretends to gauge his pulse and informs them that his brain was incinerated. When they examine his brain and confirm her diagnosis, they express their admiration for her medical knowledge and ask her to accompany them to their kingdom, inviting her to serve as royal physician to the retired father of the dead king. She turns them down, explaining that she is not a real doctor. Afraid to return home with their dead king, the ministers sail alongside her ship. Not realizing that the emperor's daughter is a woman disguised as a man, they decide that it would be a good idea for their widowed queen to marry this great physician. They are worried, however, that it would be inappropriate for their queen to betroth a common doctor. At the same time, the queen herself wants to marry the alleged physician but is afraid that her people would not accept him as a king. To put the plan into action, the ministers propose a series of banquets, hoping that the matter could be more easily discussed at a time of merriment.

The emperor's daughter agrees. When it is her turn to host a banquet, she serves her guests some of her special wine. While inebriated, they all decide that it would be lovely if the queen married the doctor, despite the breach of protocol. Playing the role of the alluring male doctor, the emperor's daughter asks them, including the queen herself, to repeat their wish while sober. When they do, her engagement to the queen is officially declared.

Greeted by the people as their new king, the emperor's daughter orders every visitor, sojourner, fugitive, and refugee to attend the royal wedding. She also orders drinking fountains to be installed all around the city, with her portrait next to each. She appoints guards to keep vigils, instructing them to apprehend those who, when looking at her image, show visible signs that they recognize her face.

Three people are arrested: the impeached king, who was dethroned by his ministers following the disappearance of their eleven daughters; the young merchant, whose father disinherited him after the loss of his valuable ship; and her true love, the prince, who has been working as a servant. Even though they recognize her image at the drinking fountains, they cannot see through her disguise when brought before her on her wedding day. Addressing each of them, she makes it known that she is familiar with the details of their personal misfortunes.

"You," she says to the impeached king, "were overthrown because of the missing noble ladies. Here are these ladies. Now you can return to your country and to your throne."

"You," she says to the young merchant, "were banished by your father because of the missing ship. Here is your ship, now worth much more than its original value." She gives him his ship, filled with the additional treasures that she has taken from the pirates.

"And you," she says to her true love. "Let's go home."

Literature as Kabbalah

Many attempts have been made to match elements in this tale to familiar concepts in other kabbalistic texts. The emperor, for example, can be seen as a literary representation of divine wisdom, the laws of nature, the angels of the supernal worlds, the angels of the underworld, and so on. His daughter, the undisputed main character, can be considered the embodiment of the primordial structure, the sphere of royalty, the vessel, the messiah, and other key entities.[20] Common to all these readings is the implied argument against the alleged immutability of the divinity. The overwhelming number of interpretive possibilities challenges the idea of God as an immovable mover: a transcendent, unreachable, unchanging force. It also defies the notion of a stable human identity. The rapid transformations that the main character undergoes question the efficacy of unbending personal convictions as coping mechanisms for the anxiety of change. And if God and humanity are perceived as inescapably flexible, so is the text itself. The impossibility of harnessing this tale to a stable hermeneutical framework exposes the illusion of an unequivocal truth.

For example, the duality of an emperor and a king has been interpreted as the concomitance of two types of divine governance: one based on moral codes, the other on the laws of nature. In a manner akin to a light that occupies a vessel, moral governance, considered higher or internal, uses natural governance as a vehicle. At the same time, it is not the emperor but his daughter who plays the role of the vessel. While it is hard for the vessel to survive without illumination, it is the absence of light that makes it stronger, more secure, and more independent. In the context of this tale, separation from an intimate companion is necessary for the emperor's daughter to embark on her own voyage, discover her strength, and navigate the tension between the desire to be fulfilled by someone else and the value of self-reliance. The spreading of the light into the vessel is based on the idea of push–pull interaction—or a cloak-and-indwell relationship—between external forces and internal resources. While yearning for invigorating connections with its surroundings, the vessel must be careful not to allow the light to flood it. The king's son might be able to make the world of the emperor's daughter richer, but he cannot control her, and neither can any of the other characters. Lights, impressions, vessels, spheres, and divine configurations that communicate and collaborate with one another are cosmological versions of characters, scenes, stories, and larger literary texts that are made more autonomous and more complete when they enter into conversations with one another. The attentive reader facilitates such conversations, exposing hitherto unrealized relations among texts that grow and develop as they encounter additional texts.

The emperor's daughter and the king's son also stand for the two messiahs: the son of Joseph and the son of David. Joseph is Rachel's son, while David is a descendant of the controversial union between Tamar and Judah. In view of the fact that Judah is Leah's son, the tale can be interpreted as the all-important encounter between the two female spheres: understanding and royalty. And if the land, according to common kabbalistic interpretations, represents the sphere of royalty, the sea, where most of the tale takes place, is the royalty of royalty:

the sphere of royalty after it has been sweetened, so to speak, by the sphere of understanding, after it has successfully replaced some of its inherent judgmental tendencies with compassion from above. In this state, the emperor's daughter has the power to conquer the forest. The loss of her true love, however, is the equivalent of the historical exile. With the destruction of the temple in Jerusalem, God, like the king's son, becomes a servant: a deity in disguise. The trees that sustain the emperor's daughter and give her shelter are the righteous who support the Shekhinah in exile with their good deeds.

According to this interpretive thread, the young merchant, a representation of King Saul, is an element that mediates between the two messiahs. Saul takes the monarchy away from the judges—the legendary warriors who represent the son of Joseph, the warrior messiah—and transfers it to the house of David. His father, an older, more experienced merchant, is Samuel, the man who orchestrates the transition from the judges to the monarchy.

Other interpretations view the emperor's daughter and the king's son as representations of the Shekhinah and ZA: the younger male and female divine configurations in the world of emanation. According to these interpretations, their tutor, who facilitates their first meeting, is AA, the older divine configuration: the element that brings the younger ones together. But if the desired outcome is the merger of moral governance and natural governance, or the union of the divine configurations, why does the emperor object to the marriage? The fact that natural governance is considered lower or external means that the emperor, even though his status is higher than that of the king, can also be seen, surprisingly, as a representation of the evil angel Samael. In charge of external wisdom—physics, biology, and other natural sciences—Samael rebels and objects to the idea of internal wisdom using him as a vehicle. In this context, the concept of internal wisdom is associated with the Torah: more specifically, with the Kabbalah.

Along these lines, other interpretations identify the emperor and the king as two of the top three spheres: wisdom and understanding. The objection of the emperor to the marriage reflects the ability of wisdom to see into the future and tell that humanity will sin and not be worthy of the Torah. In any case, the desire to father children can be seen as the divine wish to create humanity, while the fact that both men forget the pact might be an allusion to the angels who object to the idea.

Another representation of Samael—the ruler of the impure forces, who wishes to drain the power of royalty for the construction of the other side—is the bachelor king. The emperor's daughter, who enters his palace, channels Esther, who enters the royal court of Persia. Her mission is to extract the holy sparks from the impure forces and eliminate evil in its own domain. Aided by her eleven companions, she ultimately causes the impeachment of the king.

A different reading of this scene would emphasize the liberation of female characters. The emperor's daughter extracts her lady friends from typically patriarchal territory and saves them from limited conciseness, highlighting their autonomy through a broad education and imaginative play, transforming them from passive women who spend their lives in waiting into active protagonists in control of their own journey.

Other representations of the impure forces are the twelve pirates. The gold and precious stones that they hide are the holy sparks that have fallen to the other side and that must be extracted and restored to the supernal worlds. Certain interpretations see the copper and silver that the emperor's daughter and her eleven companions leave behind as excessive religiosity: the unnecessary strictness of daily rituals. Gold and precious stones, on the other hand, represent the superior value of linguistic practices: prayer and Torah study.

The bald king, whose brain is destroyed, is yet another representation of Samael. His widow, whom the emperor's daughter intends to marry, plays the role of Lilith. In terms of biblical parallels, the bald king and his wife are Ahab and Jezebel, while the emperor's daughter is Elijah, who rebukes King Ahab and burns his prophets with fire from the sky.[21] And while the emperor's daughter kills the pirates and the bald king, she welcomes the young merchant and the impeached king as sinners who return to good: men who ultimately accept the fact that they cannot possess her. Similarly, the widowed queen, assuming that she stands for Jezebel or Lilith, is not punished. The fact that she is embraced by the emperor's daughter makes it possible to see her as a twelfth female companion: a woman who escapes the authority of her husband and completes the transition from darkness to light, from subservience to self-worth.

Saving herself from danger and advancing her quest, the emperor's daughter uses wine four times: to render the sailors incapacitated and steal the ship from the young merchant, to take the ladies away from the bachelor king, to kill the pirates and steal their loot, and to obtain—or secure her marriage to—the widowed queen. It is possible to see these four episodes as representations of the impure layers of the underworld—the four *klippot* of the other side—as well as the four empires that have controlled the nation of Israel. The young merchant represents the first impure layer: the *klippah* known as windstorm, which corresponds to Babylon. The bachelor king represents the second *klippah*: great cloud, which corresponds to Persia. The twelve pirates represent the third *klippah*: blazing fire, which corresponds to Rome. The bald king represents the fourth *klippah*: glow, which corresponds to Greece.[22] When he climbs to the top of the mast, he epitomizes pride: the desire of the impure forces to siphon energy from the world of emanation.

In metafictional terms, the emperor's daughter is the text itself: a work of literature looking for the ideal reader. The fact that she does not want to marry the men who wish to own her signifies the refusal of the text to subject itself to readers who are likely to confine it to manacled interpretations. Like the emperor's daughter, the text resists the small-mindedness of readers who wish to dominate it rather than appreciate its autonomous complexity. The tale concludes with the reunion of soulmates: the joining of text and reader that marks the completion of the rectification process. Having gone to school together, the emperor's daughter and the king's son are mentally compatible. Their homecoming foreshadows the ascension of humanity to the primordial structure and the return to the genesis of creation.

The other men who recognize the image of the emperor's daughter, the impeached king and the young merchant, could also be counted as observant readers. Although initially perceived as representatives of impure forces, they are eventually forgiven and rewarded. In eschatological terms, evil will be rectified rather than eliminated. In any case, all three, like the prodigal son, must endure humiliation and destitution before they can be appreciated again. All three, like the holy sparks, must hit rock bottom before they are readmitted into the divine system.

Throughout the tale, the emperor's daughter emerges as a warrior messiah who embodies the strength and cunning—or the might and wisdom—of several women: Tamar, Rahab, Deborah, Yael, Ruth, Naomi, Esther, Judith. Quite appropriately, this endless labyrinth of intertextual possibilities leaves its readers with a myriad of questions. Does the fact that the emperor's daughter herself arranges her marriage to the widowed queen mean that, at least on some level, she is interested in a same-sex relationship? Is this foreshadowed by her request that eleven ladies provide her with permanent companionship? Does the widowed queen know that behind the façade of a medical doctor hides a determined woman? Is the queen eager to remarry precisely because her future spouse is not a man? Is that the reason she is ashamed to articulate her wish to the ministers? Is that why she needs a drink or two before she can admit her secret desire? Do the ministers know that marriage to an ordinary man is not the truly unconventional aspect of this proposal? Does the wedding take place? Is the emperor's daughter officially married to the queen? And if so, does she get to keep her newly wedded wife when she goes home with the king's son? Is she officially married to the king's son? Is this deliberate vagueness yet another expression of her independence?

Rather than answers, what Nachman of Breslov seems to offer is a brilliant exercise in literature as Kabbalah. Each of the characters in this tale plays multiple divine roles. Equally important are the multiple human roles that the main character plays. In the course of her adventures, the emperor's daughter discovers that she can perfectly function in a variety of capacities—woman, man, sailor, captain, pirate, doctor, princess, king—without sacrificing her true self. Like the primordial structure, she demonstrates her potential to be all things: a complete human being, unrestricted by norms or expectations.

Back to Genesis

At its most inventive, the Kabbalah is metafictional in the sense that its self-professed goal is to teach readers how to approach the text, how to read it intertextually, and how to translate interpretive potentialities into literary actualities. When readers and writers use one text to expand another, the narrative is never in danger of stagnation. When they invite multiple texts to interact with one another, the narrative advances toward a full realization of its literary promise. This is what Ashlag emphasizes when he calls his extensive and innovative Zohar commentary *The Ladder*. The purpose, he explains, is to construct a textual stairway that will allow readers to climb the vast edifice of kabbalistic literature, explore its upper levels, and reach the heights of understanding on their own. His goal, in other words, is not to explicate kabbalistic writings but to equip readers with creative comprehension skills and encourage independent expansions of the text.

Contemporary kabbalistic commentator David Steinberg demonstrates these principles when he offers an Ashlagian reading of Genesis 1:1, unearthing a treasury of new meanings.[23] Orthographically, the Bible opens with an oversized version of the second letter of the Hebrew alphabet: a preposition writ large. This big B alludes to the second contraction: the ascension of royalty to understanding in the primordial structure, which Ashlag calls Contraction B.[24] The nominal phrase that follows this preposition, *the beginning*, alludes to the wisdom of the infinite light. This interpretation is based on the kabbalistic reading of Psalm 111:10, which replaces the genitive construction *the beginning of wisdom* with a nominal clause: the beginning *is* wisdom. The appellation *God*—in Hebrew, *Elohim*—alludes to the sphere of understanding. The verb *created* alludes to the process by which the sphere of understanding descends from the head to the throat in order to transmit wisdom to the elements below. In this context, understanding is called the ears, nose, and mouth—that is, the lower half of the face—while the crown and wisdom, the upper half of the face, are called the skull and the eyes.

The nominal phrases *the heavens* and *the earth* allude to ZA and the Shekhinah: the elements that are directly below, on whom wisdom is bestowed through the sphere of understanding, also known as Mother. ZA and the Shekhinah, the younger divine configurations, are initially emanated without their top three spheres. In other words, they are born headless. Representing the older configurations, Mother gives her children, ZA and the Shekhinah, the brains that they are missing. When they are fully developed, they become the royal couple of the supernal worlds. Omitted from English translations of Genesis 1:1 are the accusative markers that precede *the heavens* and *the earth*, which allude to the cognitive growth of ZA and the Shekhinah. Each of these markers consists of the first and last letter of the Hebrew alphabet, referring to the text itself, the Torah, as the means by which the consciousness of ZA and the Shekhinah is enhanced.[25] Crucial to creation, according to this interpretation, is the collaboration between the two female elements in the primordial structure: royalty and understanding. It is through this collaboration that wisdom can be transmitted to the heavenly king and queen in the world of emanation. Mother is in charge of bestowing wisdom on her divine children, while her daughter transmits it further down, all the way to the physical realm, in which humanity resides.

Essential to the transition from the primordial structure to the world of emanation is the return of understanding to its upper position: from the throat to the head. This happens in two stages. First, the top sphere, the crown, uses its light to lift the fallen sphere of understanding and restore it to its regular place. The second stage, however, is more significant. The sphere of understanding uses its own light to repair itself. This internal light, like the light that revitalizes the vessel, foreshadows the ability of human readers to study and understand the Kabbalah on their own, without the assistance of a revelation from above.[26] The purpose of creation, therefore, is to encourage humanity to acquire maturity and independence through sincere mental effort.

When the Zohar offers its experimental rendition of Genesis 1:1, medieval audiences, although enamored with its poetic beauty, admit that it is largely incomprehensible.[27] In the sixteenth century, when Luria offers his own interpretation of the Zohar, certain elements in this retelling of creation become much clearer. Informed by Lurianic cosmology, a new translation of the Aramaic of the Zohar might look like this:

> *By the very power of the king,*
> *A spark of darkness carved*
> *A space in the supernal light.*
> *From the innermost spot*
> *In the actual infinite,*
> *A primordial shape emerged,*
> *Pinned to the center of a circle:*
> *Neither white nor black,*
> *Neither red nor green,*
> *Nor any color at all.*
> *When it measured a boundary,*
> *It produced colors to illuminate*
> *The space inside. Inside the spark*
> *A fountainhead formed, from which*
> *Colors flowed further down.*

The contraction of divine power, which occurs in the terminal sphere of the infinite light, seems to be the propelling event in this poetic narrative, followed by the beam that enters the globular void and produces the primordial structure and the supernal worlds. Certain elements in this narrative, however, remain entirely obscure. In the twentieth century, when Ashlag offers a new reading of the Zohar, these elements become meaningful. The spark of darkness is the coupling royalty: the queen of the mouth, located in the head of each vessel or configuration. Using a powerful filter—the screen, which the Zohar calls a fountainhead—the queen of the mouth rejects the direct light that emanates from above, converts it into reflected light, and transmits it to the vessels, which the Zohar calls colors. Initially, the primordial structure contains no vessels. The lack of shades or colors—neither white nor black, neither red nor green—conveys this situation. At this stage, according to the Lurianic narrative, there are no independent vessels. According to the Ashlagian version of this narrative, unselfish vessels, ones that would not be engulfed by the bounty of the light, do not exist yet. It is only after the development of the screen that the vessels can accept and share the light, using it for altruistic rather than narcissistic purposes. In this context, the movement further down that the Zohar describes is the spreading of the light to the body of the vessel.

Theologically, such interpretations replace the portrayal of God as a single deity—omnipresent, omnipotent, and indivisible—with a creation process that decentralizes the divinity. What the Kabbalah argues is that these provocative readings of Genesis have always been part of the biblical text. In semiotic terms, the text is a sign that contains all its future meanings, including those that are currently dormant. The idea that changing circumstances will produce new hermeneutical insights is especially instrumental to eschatological and post-eschatological literature. According to the Jewish calendar, six thousand years of creation will reach its conclusion sometime in the twenty-third century: in the year 2240, to be exact. At that point, if the messiah fails to come, and if the physical world in which we live does not ascend to the mouth of the primordial structure—in other words, if life as we know it does not reach a certain end—existing kabbalistic texts are bound to be amended. Far from being discarded as irrelevant, these texts would be enhanced with new interpretations, updated to communicate new meanings, and invited to participate in the creation of new narratives.

From a psychological point of view, the personification of the text is an expression of the lifelong search for the smarter self: the more aware, more mature, more capable version of the personality which we currently possess, let alone the one with which we are born. Readers who aspire to this maturity revisit the text again and again, hoping to notice things that they could not see before. Failure to do so—the inability to gain a new appreciation for the unique subtleties of the text—is merely a temporary setback: an invitation to try again. In a sense, this is what Luria writes about when he traces the formation, collapse, and repair of the vessels. This is what Vital writes about when he records his visions of grandeur, the reality of his rejection and humiliation in Damascus, and his dreams of restitution and recognition. This is what Luzzatto writes about when he describes the elevated status of the princess in *Tower of Strength*, her unjust discreditation and death sentence, and her ultimate rehabilitation. This is what Fetaya writes about when he documents the euphoric aggression of tormented souls, their subsequent regression to depression and despair, and the rekindled hope for future amelioration. This is what Kook writes about when he portrays the rise, the fall, and the potential recuperation of the souls of chaos. This is what Nachman of Breslov writes about when he chronicles the twists and turns that characterize the journey of the emperor's daughter.

Like the text itself, and like the kabbalistic divinity, the emperor's daughter invents and reinvents herself, reminding readers that she is always more than one thing. At the end of the tale, she does not shed her disguise. In fact, her so-called disguise becomes part of her new, ever-changing self. Comfortable with ambiguities and confident in her enhanced complexity, she makes no attempt to present a more coherent front. This self-possession is reciprocated by the fact that no one seems to question her noncompliance with gender categories. No one suggests that she commit to a more consistent agenda, display a more easily classi- fied style, or relinquish any of the various identities that she has acquired along the way. As a spokesperson for the Kabbalah, she conveys the sheer value of new perspectives and demonstrates the ability to embrace chaos: to recognize the ups and downs of the divinity, the volatile nature of creation, the elasticity of the self, the instability of the text.

What the Kabbalah reminds its readers is that the schisms, chasms, and quandaries of human existence cannot be navigated with the spu- rious safety of a single narrative. When a community demands that all its members share the same values, think alike, or speak unanimously, it is likely to ban books, boycott ideas, punish creative endeavors for the crimes of their creators, or otherwise try to protect itself from voices that come from the proverbial other side. The kabbalistic vision, on the other hand, celebrates the kind of carnivalesque textuality that keeps sacred literature alive, the divinity dynamic, and the anxiety of disintegration at bay. Approaching the unknown as an exciting quest rather than a petrifying threat, the Kabbalah speaks in different voices, each resonating with its idiosyncratic timbre. This diversity of narratives allows the Kabbalah to operate as an interlaced enterprise whose beauty stems not from the concept of coerced harmony but from genuine curiosity about future questions, possible counterarguments, and evermore challenging modes of reading and writing.

NOTES

CHAPTER 1

1. Zohar III (בהעלותך) 152a.
2. Proverbs 8:22–31.
3. Jeremiah 23:29; *b.Sanhedrin* 34a.
4. Esther 4:11; 5:1–8.
5. Esther 5:1. The Hebrew preposition נִכַח is an acronym of נִשְׁמַת כָּל חַי.
6. *Gate of Intentions* (שער הכוונות), On the Sabbath Morning Prayer (ענין שחרית של שבת); Mordechai Sheinberger, *At the King's Gate: Four-Layered Commentary and Essays on Esther* (בשער המלך: לקט פירושים וביאורים על מגילת אסתר בדרך הפרד"ס) (Or Ganuz, Israel: Or Daat, 2017), 91 [Hebrew].
7. Hebrew: ספירות. Common transliterations: *sefirot, sephiroth*.
8. Genesis 1:16; *b.Chullin* 60b.
9. Isaiah 30:26.
10. Psalm 118:22; Esther 4:17.
11. Proverbs 12:4; Yehuda Leib Ashlag (1884–1954), the Ladder commentary (פירוש הסולם) on Zohar I (בראשית) 25b, par. 234; Sheinberger, *At the King's Gate*, 86, 156.
12. Michael Raposa, "Some Applications of the Law of Mind," paper presented at the 5th Biennial Philosophy of Communication Conference, June 7, 2022, sponsored by the Department of Communication and Rhetorical Studies and the Communication Ethics Institute at Duquesne University.
13. A recurring theme in the theological thought of Walter Brueggemann. For example, *Texts under Negotiation: The Bible and Postmodern Imagination* (Minneapolis: Fortress Press, 1993); "Fidelity and the Seduction of Certitude," lecture given at the University of Findlay, Ohio, October 17, 2014, https://youtu.be/Cs2aHsbUBZw.
14. Aramaic: אריך אנפין. Common transliteration: *Arikh Anpin*.
15. Aramaic: זעיר אנפין. Common transliteration: *Zeir Anpin*.

16. Ashlag on Zohar III (אמור) 102b, par. 255.

17. Exodus 17:16 (כִּי יָד עַל כֵּס יָהּ).

18. Esther 4:1; 8:15.

19. Moses David Valle (1696–1776) on Esther 5:1–3 (ספר הישועה);
    Sheinberger, *At the King's Gate*, 161–62.

20. Tikkunei Zohar 21:57b.

21. Exodus 28:36–41.

22. Tikkunei Zohar 3b.

23. Esther 5:1.

24. Esther 5:1.

25. Esther 5:2.

26. Genesis 9:16.

27. Daniel 9:19.

28. Hebrew: Purim.

29. Hebrew: *yom kipurim*. Vocalized differently: *yom kepurim* (a day like
    Purim).

30. Song of Songs 7:2.

31. Tikkunei Zohar 3b.

32. Ashlag on Zohar I (בראשית) 20a, pars. 111–15; Yehuda Tzvi Brandwein
    (1903–69), Steps of the Ladder commentary (פירוש מעלות הסולם) on
    Tikkunei Zohar 3b, par. 63; 10a, par. 211; 21:58b, par. 436; Mordechai
    Sheinberger, Labor of the Ladder commentary (פירוש מלאכת הסולם) on
    Tikkunei Zohar 40:80a, par. 2; 69:106b, par. 188; Sheinberger, Labor
    of the Ladder commentary on New Tikkunei Zohar 109d, par. 431.

33. Genesis 1:16; *b.Chullin* 60b.

34. Psalm 45:13 (45:14 MT).

35. Psalm 45:14 (45:15 MT).

36. *b.Megillah* 14b.

37. Judges 6:34.

38. 1 Chronicles 12:18 (12:19 MT).

39. 2 Chronicles 24:20.

40. *b.Sukkah* 27b.

41. *Midrash Tadshe* 8.

42. Genesis 34:25–30; 49:5–7.

43. Numbers 25:14.

44. Deuteronomy 33.

45. Judith 9:2–4.

46. Jubilees 30.

47. *The Story of Judith* (מעשה יהודית), in *Bet ha-Midrasch* (בית המדרש), a
    landmark anthology of lesser-known midrashic texts collected by Adolf
    Jellinek (1821–93) (Jerusalem: Wahrmann Books, 1967), 1:130–31
    [Hebrew].

48. Judith 11:6–9.
49. Judith 5:5–6:20.
50. Judith 14:5–7.
51. Christopher S. Morrissey, "The Greek and Latin Dress of Judith: '*Ex Virtute Pendebat*'? (Idt 10:4 Vg)," paper presented at the virtual Pacific Northwest regional conference of the American Academy of Religion and the Society of Biblical Literature, May 14, 2022.
52. Judith 12:12.
53. Judith 11:5–19.
54. Genesis 38:14–15.
55. Ruth 3:2.
56. Judith 10:3–4; 15:7–9.
57. Esther 5:1–3; Additions to Esther 15.
58. Isaiah Tishby, *Paths of Faith and Heresy: Essays on Kabbalah and Sabbateanism* (נתיבי אמונה ומינות: מסות ומחקרים בספרות הקבלה והשבתאות) (Jerusalem: The Magnes Press at the Hebrew University, 1964), 23–29 [Hebrew].
59. Bracha Sack, *The Kabbalah of Rabbi Moshe Cordovero* (בשערי הקבלה של רבי משה קורדובירו) (Beersheba: Ben-Gurion University of the Negev Press, 1995), 30 [Hebrew].
60. Joseph Ben-Shlomo, *The Mystical Theology of Moses Cordovero* (תורת האלוהות של ר' משה קורדובירו) (Jerusalem: The Bialik Institute, 1965), 13 [Hebrew]. For more on the tension between Cordovero and Luria, see Isaiah Tishby, "The Debate between the Kabbalah of Isaac Luria and the Kabbalah of Moses Cordovero in the Life and Work of Rabbi Aaron Berechiah of Modena," originally published in 1974, in *Studies in Kabbalah and Its Branches* (חקרי קבלה ושלוחותיה: מחקרים ומקורות) (Jerusalem: The Magnes Press at the Hebrew University, 1982), 1:177–254 [Hebrew].
61. Hayyim Vital (1542–1620), *Book of Visions* (ספר החזיונות) 1:22; 1:24.
62. Genesis 22:2.
63. Esther 4:6–8; 4:13–16.
64. Isaiah 59:17; Psalm 93:1; 104:1; Job 40:10.
65. Hebrew: אלוהות.
66. For example, Mieke Bal, *Lethal Love: Feminist Literary Readings of Biblical Love Stories* (Bloomington: Indiana University Press, 1987); Bal, *Death and Dissymmetry: The Politics of Coherence in the Book of Judges* (Chicago: The University of Chicago Press, 1988); Bal, "Dealing/With/Women: Daughters in the Book of Judges," in *The Book and the Text: The Bible and Literary Theory*, ed. Regina M. Schwartz (Cambridge, MA: Basil Blackwell, 1990), 16–39; Elisabeth Schüssler Fiorenza, *Revelation: Vision of a Just World* (Minneapolis: Fortress Press, 1991); Schüssler

Fiorenza, *But She Said: Feminist Practices of Biblical Interpretation*
(Boston: Beacon Press, 1992); Schüssler Fiorenza, *Jesus: Miriam's Child,
Sophia's Prophet: Critical Issues in Feminist Christology* (New York:
Continuum, 1994); Laura E. Donaldson, "Cyborgs, Ciphers, and
Sexuality: Re-Theorizing Literary and Biblical Character," *Semeia* 63
(1993): 81–96; Yvonne Sherwood, *The Prostitute and the Prophet: Hosea's
Marriage in Literary-Theoretical Perspective* (Sheffield, UK: Sheffield
Academic Press, 1996); Silvia Schroer, *Wisdom Has Built Her House:
Studies on the Figure of Sophia in the Bible*, trans. Linda M. Maloney and
William McDonough (Collegeville, MN: Liturgical Press/Michael
Glazier, 2000; originally published in German, 1996).

67. Moses David Valle on Psalm 45:8 (45:9 MT).

68. Genesis 36:31–39. The broken vessels (מָאנִין תְּבִירִין) in Zohar II (בא) 42b
are traditionally understood as a reference to the role that the dead kings
of Edom play in the kabbalistic creation narrative. Elaborate expansions
of this interpretation appear throughout the Lurianic corpus—attributed
to Isaac Luria (1534–72), compiled and composed primarily by Hayyim
Vital (1542–1620)—especially in the *Tree of Life* (עץ חיים) and *Book of
Likkutim* (ספר הליקוטים).

69. Hebrew: אדם קדמון.

70. *Gate of Reincarnations* (שער הגלגולים) 7; 12; 15.

71. *b.Avodah Zarah* 5b; *Midrash Lekach Tov* (*Pesikta Zutarta*) on Genesis
3:12; Rashi on Genesis 3:12.

72. Aramaic: אתערותא דלתתא.

73. Genesis 2:6; Zohar I (בראשית) 35a.

74. Hebrew: נפש. Common transliteration: *nefesh*. In his English translation
of the *Book of Visions*, Morris Faierstein calls this part of the soul the
Animus. See *Jewish Mystical Autobiographies: Book of Visions and Book
of Secrets* (New York: Paulist Press, 1999).

75. Hebrew: רוח. Common transliteration: *ruach*.

76. Hebrew: נשמה. Common transliteration: *neshama*.

77. Hebrew: חיה ויחידה. Common transliterations: *chaya* and *yechida*.

78. For example, Joseph Gikatilla (1248–1305), *Gates of Light* (שערי אורה);
Abraham Cohen de Herrera (1570–1635), *Gate of Heaven* (*Puerta del
Cielo*) 1:12.

79. *Tree of Life* 6:1.

80. Genesis 1:5. In his commentary on Zohar III (אמור) 93a–b, Ashlag is
most explicit when discussing the evening and the morning as the female
and male aspects of the divinity (par. 95).

81. Bahya ben Asher (1255–1340) on Exodus 3:6.

82. *Tree of Life* 8:3.

83. *Tree of Life* 7:3.

84. Genesis 36:39.
85. Hebrew: מהיטבאל = זמן.
86. Hebrew: עקודים. Common transliteration: *Akudim*.
87. Hebrew: נקודים. Common transliteration: *Nekudim*.
88. Hebrew: ברודים. Common transliteration: *Brudim*.
89. Hebrew: ישראל סבא ותבונה.
90. *Tree of Life* 9:2.
91. Brueggemann, *Texts under Negotiation*, chap. 1.
92. Genesis 31:10–12.
93. Hebrew: לובן העליון.
94. *Tree of Life* 6:1.
95. Two additional spellings of the letters of the Tetragrammaton mark the lights that issue earlier from other openings in the primordial structure: seventy-two and sixty-three.
96. *Tree of Life* 9:7.
97. *Tree of Life* 9:3.
98. *m.Avot* 4:11.
99. Moses Cordovero (1522–70), *The Palm Tree of Deborah* (תומר דבורה), chap. 1, attribute 2.
100. Genesis 4:13.
101. Leviticus 16:21–22; Cordovero, *The Palm Tree of Deborah*, chap. 1, attribute 9.
102. Aramaic: סטרא אחרא. Zohar II (פקודי) 262a–b.
103. *b.Sanhedrin* 45b.
104. Daniel 2:31–45.
105. Zechariah 14; Zohar III (מצורע) 54a.
106. Cordovero, *The Palm Tree of Deborah*, chap. 1, attribute 9.
107. Isaiah 65:7.

CHAPTER 2

1. Luke 15:11–32.
2. Daniel 7:9–10.
3. Song of Songs 5:11.
4. Exodus 34:6–7.
5. Micah 7:18–20; Mordechai Sheinberger on *The Palm Tree of Deborah* (פירוש ויאמר משה) (Or Ganuz, Israel: Or Daat, 2003), 25–26 [Hebrew].
6. *b.Rosh Hashanah* 17b.
7. Joseph Gikatilla, *Gates of Light* (ca. 1293), chap. 10; Moses Cordovero, *The Palm Tree of Deborah*, chap. 1.
8. *Summa Theologiae*, second part of the second part, question 30, art. 4.
9. Zohar III (נשא) 129b (Idra Rabba).

10. Psalm 121:4.
11. Zohar III (נשא) 129a (Idra Rabba).
12. Psalm 33:18.
13. Zechariah 4:10.
14. Cordovero, *The Palm Tree of Deborah*, chap. 2, attribute 5.
15. Zohar III (נשא) 130a–b; 137b (Idra Rabba); Moses Cordovero, *Elimah Rabbati*, Crystal Spring (עין הבדולח) 3:21; 3:25.
16. Cordovero, *The Palm Tree of Deborah*, chap. 2, attribute 6.
17. Aramaic: רַעֲוָא דְּרַעֲוִין.
18. Zohar III (נשא) 129a; 136b (Idra Rabba).
19. Genesis 2:4–25 (יהוה אלהים).
20. Hebrew: הקדוש ברוך הוא.
21. Aramaic: קודשא בריך הוא.
22. Aramaic: מטרוניתא.
23. Genesis 1:26; Zohar III (בלק) 207b–208a.
24. Psalm 49:12 (49:13 MT) (וְאָדָם בִּיקָר בַּל יָלִין).
25. Psalm 8:4 (8:5 MT) (מָה אֱנוֹשׁ כִּי תִזְכְּרֶנּוּ וּבֶן אָדָם כִּי תִפְקְדֶנּוּ); 144:3 (מָה אָדָם וַתֵּדָעֵהוּ, בֶּן אֱנוֹשׁ וַתְּחַשְּׁבֵהוּ).
26. *Genesis Rabbah* 8:6.
27. *b.Shabbat* 88b.
28. *Genesis Rabbah* 8:4; 17:4; Zohar III (בלק) 208a.
29. Ashlag on Zohar I (הקדמת ספר הזוהר) 9b, par. 156; (בראשית) 23a, par. 178.
30. Hebrew: ביטול.
31. Zohar I (בראשית) 23a; New Tikkunei Zohar 115d–116a.
32. Genesis 6:2.
33. Zohar I (בראשית) 37a; III (בלק) 208a.
34. Genesis 6:4.
35. Hebrew: יצר הרע.
36. *Genesis Rabbah* 1:1.
37. Zohar I (בראשית) 22a; New Tikkunei Zohar 115b.
38. Carol Ochs, *Behind the Sex of God: Toward a New Consciousness Transcending Matriarchy and Patriarchy* (Boston: Beacon Press, 1977), 61.
39. Ashlag on Zohar I (בראשית) 22a, par. 160.
40. Genesis 1:26.
41. Hebrew: קבלה על מנת להשפיע. The cosmological and theological Kabbalah of Yehuda Leib Ashlag (1884–1954) can be found mainly in *Ten Luminous Emanations* (תלמוד עשר הספירות), *Preamble to the Wisdom of the Kabbalah* (פתיחה לחוכמת הקבלה), and throughout his commentary on the Zohar (פירוש הסולם). His social and psychological Kabbalah is to be found mainly in his collections of essays, especially in *A Gift of the Bible*

(מתן תורה). Notable scholarly approaches to Ashlagian Kabbalah include David Hansel, "The Origin in the Thought of Rabbi Yehuda Halevy Ashlag: *Ṣimṣum* of God or *Ṣimṣum* of the World?" *Kabbalah* 7 (2002): 37–46; Boaz Huss, "Altruistic Communism: The Modernist Kabbalah of Rabbi Ashlag" (קומוניזם אלטרואיסטי: הקבלה המודרניסטית של הרב אשלג), *Iyunim* 16 (2006): 109–30 [Hebrew]; Tony Lavi, *The Secret of Cosmogony: The Law of Divinity and the Essence of Mankind in the Studies of R. Yehuda Halevi Ashlag* (סוד הבריאה: תורת האלוהות ותכלית האדם בקבלת הרי"ל אשלג) (a possibly more accurate translation of the title: *The Essence of Creation: Theology and the Purpose of Humanity in the Kabbalah of Rabbi Yehuda Leib Ashlag*) (Jerusalem: Bialik Institute, 2007) [Hebrew]; Jonathan Garb, *Yearnings of the Soul: Psychological Thought in Modern Kabbalah* (Chicago: The University of Chicago Press, 2015), 104–11; Israel Koren, "The Transformation of the Kabbalistic Vessel in the Thought of Rabbi Yehuda Ashlag and Martin Buber" (הטרנספורמציה במושג הכלי הקבלי במחשבתם של הרב יהודה אשלג ושל מרטין בובר) [Hebrew] (unpublished, available on the author's personal website, https://independent.academia.edu/IsraelKoren). Notable contributors to the development of Ashlagian Kabbalah in the contemporary rabbinic world, particularly in modern Israel, include Yehuda Tzvi Brandwein, his most prominent pupil; Baruch Shalom Ashlag, his firstborn son; Mordechai Sheinberger, Brandwein's most prominent pupil; Adam Sinai, whose series of Hebrew audio and video lessons on the writings of Ashlag—especially *Ten Luminous Emanations* (תלמוד עשר הספירות), the *Preamble to the Wisdom of the Kabbalah*, and the commentary on the *Tree of Life* (פנים מאירות ופנים מסבירות), an early version of *Ten Luminous Emanations* originally published in the 1920s—are remarkably perceptive (https://www.hasulam.co.il); and Yaakov Elboim, whose series of Hebrew video lessons on the writings of Moses Hayyim Luzzatto (1707–46) are enhanced by an insightful synthesis of key elements from Ashlagian Kabbalah (nisimd.net).

42. Hebrew: מסך.
43. Hebrew: צמצום. Common transliterations: *tzimtzum, tsimtsum, zimzum, ṣimṣum.*
44. Hebrew: זיווג דהכאה.
45. Hebrew: ביטוש.
46. Hebrew: מלכות המזדווגת.
47. Hebrew: מלכות המסיימת.
48. Hebrew: פרצוף. Common transliteration: *partzuf* (plural: *partzufim*).
49. Hebrew: רשימו דהתלבשות.
50. Hebrew: רשימו דעוביות.

51. Zohar I (הקדמת ספר הזוהר) 2a (וְאִמָּא אוֹזִיפַת לִבְרַתָּא מָאנָהָא וְקַשִּׁיטָא לָה)
    (בְּקִישׁוּטָהָא).

52. *Preamble to the Wisdom of the Kabbalah*, pars. 57–60; Ashlag on Zohar
    I (הקדמת ספר הזוהר) 2a, pars. 16–17.

53. Ruth 3:3.

54. Song of Songs 2:2.

55. Ashlag on Zohar I (הקדמת ספר הזוהר) 1a, par. 1.

56. Hebrew: קטנות וגדלות.

57. *The Smiling Lieutenant*, dir. Ernst Lubitsch (Paramount Pictures, 1931).

58. Hebrew: השוואת הצורה ליוצרה.

59. David Steinberg, *The Foundation of Wisdom* (יסוד החוכמה) (Jerusalem:
    Otot, 2014), 90 [Hebrew].

60. For a comprehensive study of academic approaches to the
    Kabbalah, with a distinct focus on internal rivalries among
    twentieth-century scholars, see Moran Gam Hacohen, *Kabbalah
    Research in Israel: Historiography, Ideology, and the Struggle
    for Cultural Capital* (מחקר הקבלה בישראל: היסטוריוגרפיה,
    אידאולוגיה ומאבק על הון תרבותי) (Tel Aviv: Resling, 2016), esp. 79–221
    [Hebrew].

61. *b.Shabbat* 119b.

62. For an interesting discussion of theurgy in rabbinic and kabbalistic
    sources, see Moshe Idel, *Kabbalah: New Perspectives* (New Haven, CT:
    Yale University Press, 1988), 156–99.

63. Gil Anidjar, "Jewish Mysticism Alterable and Unalterable: On Orienting
    Kabbalah Studies and the Zohar of Christian Spain," *Jewish Social
    Studies* 3, no. 1 (1996): 89–157. While mysticism, myth, and symbol are
    the major concepts that Gershom Scholem and his disciples employ when
    discussing the Kabbalah, magic, ecstasy, and experience are the dominant
    terms adopted by the so-called younger generation of academic Kabbalah
    scholars, represented by Moshe Idel and Yehuda Liebes. Moran Gam
    Hacohen (*Kabbalah Research in Israel*) pays considerable attention to the
    differences between these approaches. Gil Anidjar, on the other hand,
    argues that there are no real differences between these sets of terms ("Jewish
    Mysticism," 103–4). Both, according to Anidjar, are equally useless. Both
    downplay the textual and cultural dimensions of kabbalistic literature.

64. For example, Peter Cole, *The Poetry of Kabbalah: Mystical Verse from the
    Jewish Tradition* (New Haven, CT: Yale University Press, 2012); Eitan P.
    Fishbane, *The Art of Mystical Narrative: A Poetics of the Zohar* (New York:
    Oxford University Press, 2018); Marvin A. Sweeney, *Jewish Mysticism:
    From Ancient Times through Today* (Grand Rapids, MI: William B.
    Eerdmans, 2020); Marla Segol, *Kabbalah and Sex Magic: A Mythical-
    Ritual Genealogy* (University Park: Pennsylvania University Press,
    2021). A notable exception: Boaz Huss, *Mystifying Kabbalah: Academic*

Scholarship, National Theology, and New Age Spirituality, trans. Elana
Lutsky (New York: Oxford University Press, 2020; originally published
in Hebrew, 2016).

65. Notable kabbalistic figures who advocate restrictions on Kabbalah study
include Shalom Sharabi (1720–77), who rejects all kabbalistic authors
except Isaac Luria and Hayyim Vital, and Shlomo Elyashiv (1841–1926),
who attacks Moses Hayyim Luzzatto for his innovative approach to
the Kabbalah and calls for a return to a plain, literal, so-called proper
reading of the Zohar and the Lurianic corpus. For recent summaries of
internal debates between kabbalistic writers who embrace metaphorical
expansions of earlier texts and those who oppose them, see Moshe Zuriel,
Treasures of the Luminaries of Israel (אוצרות גדולי ישראל) (Jerusalem: Yarid
Hasfarim, 2000), vol. 2 (on the Vilna Gaon and Moses Hayyim Luzzatto),
205–12 [Hebrew]; Alon Shalev, "Orthodox Theology in the Age of
the Search for Meaning: The Life and Works of Rabbi Isaac Hutner"
(תאולוגיה אורתודוקסית בעידן בקשת המשמעות: חייו והגותו של הרב יצחק הוטנר),
doctoral diss. (The Hebrew University of Jerusalem, 2020), 230–33
[Hebrew]; Bezalel Naor, "The *Leshem* and Luzzatto," in Abraham Isaac
Kook, *The Souls of the World of Chaos*, trans., introd., and notes Bezalel
Naor (New York: Orot/Kodesh, 2023), appendix G, 68–82.

66. Notable examples include *Barbarella*, dir. Roger Vadim (Paramount
Pictures, 1968); *Sleeper*, dir. Woody Allen (United Artists, 1973); *Death
Race 2000*, dir. Paul Bartel (New World Pictures, 1975); *Logan's Run*,
dir. Michael Anderson (Metro-Goldwyn-Mayer, 1976); *Blade Runner*,
dir. Ridley Scott (Warner Brothers, 1982); *Sleep Dealer*, dir. Alex Rivera
(Maya Entertainment, 2008).

67. Joseph Dan, *Jewish Mysticism and Jewish Ethics* (Seattle: University of
Washington Press, 1986), 98.

68. *m.Peah* 1:1; *Avot de-Rabbi Nathan* 4; *Gate of Reincarnations* (שער הגלגולים)
11.

69. Jean Baudrillard, *The Vital Illusion*, ed. Julia Witwer (New York:
Columbia University Press, 2000), 69–71.

70. Tikkunei Zohar 6:21b; 10:25a–b.

71. 1 Corinthians 13.

CHAPTER 3

1. Hebrew: *Migdal Oz* (מגדל עוז).

2. Fishel Lachower (1883–1947), *On the Border of Old and
New* (על גבול הישן והחדש) (Jerusalem: The Bialik Institute,
1951), 83 [Hebrew]. This posthumous collection includes two complementary essays on *Tower of Strength*, "At the Gate of the Tower"
(29–78) and "The Parable of the Tower" (79–84), in which Lachower

acknowledges the kabbalistic underpinnings of the play and attacks, quite convincingly, scholars who do not.

3. Zohar II (משפטים) 99a–b. Among these scholars are Jacob Fichman (1881–1958), Hayyim Schirmann (1904–81), and Yonah David (1919–2009). The latter, in his introduction to the 1972 edition of the play (Jerusalem: The Bialik Institute, 1972), provides a summary of modern Hebrew critical assessments, emphasizing those that, like his own, view the text as a direct descendant of secular Italian plays, most notably *The Faithful Shepherd* (*Il Pastor Fido*) by Giovanni Battista Guarini (1538–1612).

4. Hebrew: עיבור.

5. *Gate of Reincarnations* (שער הגלגולים) 5; *Book or Reincarnations* (ספר הגלגולים) 5.

6. Job 33:29; *b.Yoma* 86b.

7. Tikkunei Zohar 32:76b; 69:103a; *Gate of Reincarnations* 4; *Book of Reincarnations* 6.

8. *Gate of Reincarnations* 4.

9. Exodus 21:1–11; Zohar II (משפטים) 94a–109b.

10. Joshua 2:1–21; 3:17; 3:22–26; Judges 4:17–22; 5:24–27; *Mekhilta de-Rabbi Ishmael: Yitro* 1; *b.Zevachim* 116b; *b.Megilla* 14b; *Sifre* on Numbers 10:29; *Ruth Rabbah* 2:1; *Gate of Reincarnations* 36; *Book of Reincarnations* 46; *Likkutei Torah* (ליקוטי תורה): Joshua.

11. Obliquely, Hannah refers to Rahab when she says, "My mouth is wide open (רחב פי) against my enemies" (1 Samuel 2:1).

12. 1 Samuel 1:7–10.

13. 1 Samuel 1:15; *Gate of Reincarnations* 36; *Book of Reincarnations* 46.

14. *b.Nazir* 23b; *b.Yevamot* 103a.

15. 1 Samuel 1:21–28.

16. Hebrew: יחידה דחיה. *Preamble to the Wisdom of the Kabbalah*, pars. 69–72; Steinberg, *The Foundation of Wisdom*, 98 [Hebrew].

17. *Gate of Reincarnations* 4.

18. Hebrew: עם הארץ.

19. Numbers 16.

20. *b.Sanhedrin* 109b–110a; *Midrash Tanchuma*, Korah 10 (Buber Recension, Korah 24).

21. 1 Samuel 19:11–17; Menachem Azariah da Fano (1548–1620), *Reincarnations of Souls* 1.11.

22. *Yalkut ha-Machiri* on Psalm 118.

23. Menachem Azariah da Fano, *Reincarnations of Souls* 5.3 (par. 47).

24. Genesis 16:1–4.

25. Menachem Azariah da Fano, *Reincarnations of Souls* 16.6–7 (pars. 105–6).

26. *b.Shabbat* 87a.

27. *b.Ketubot* 61b–62b; *b.Eruvin* 22a.
28. *b.Ketubot* 62b.
29. *b.Temurah* 16a.
30. Joshua 15:16–19; Judges 1:12–15.
31. *b.Ketubot* 62b.
32. *b.Sanhedrin* 59b; *Avot de-Rabbi Nathan* 1:8; *Yalkut Shimoni* 15.
33. *b.Shabbat* 145b–146a; *b.Yevamot* 103b; *b.Avodah Zarah* 22b; *Pirkei de-Rabbi Eliezer* 21; Zohar I (בראשית) 28b; 35b; 36b; 37a; 54a; Zohar II (פקודי) 231a; Zohar III (אחרי מות) 76b; Tikkunei Zohar 69:99b; 113b; 117a; 118a–b; and elsewhere.
34. Genesis 5:3.
35. Genesis 1:26.
36. Zohar I (בראשית) 54b–55a: New Zohar on Genesis 5; omissions from Zohar I (בראשית: סתרי תורה) 55b (253b).
37. Zohar I (ויצא: סתרי תורה) 147b–148a.
38. *b.Eruvin* 18b; *Genesis Rabbah* 20:11; *Midrash Tanchuma*, Buber Recension, Bereshit 26; Zohar I (בראשית) 19b; 54b–55a; (וישלח) 169b; Zohar II (פקודי) 231b; Zohar III (תזריע) 48b; (אחרי מות) 76b.
39. *Genesis Rabbah* 20:11.
40. Elijah ben Solomon Abraham ha-Cohen (1659–1729), *Midrash Eliyahu* 90a (Czernowitz: 1864); Hayyim Yosef David Azulai (1724–1806), *Dvash Lefi* (דבש לפי) 1:3–4; 5:2; Tzvi Elimelech Spira of Dynów (1783–1841), *Bnei Yissaschar* (בני יששכר), Adar 7:7; 7:9–10; and others (who, following Elijah ha-Cohen, attribute this interpretation to Hayyim Vital).
41. Esther 2:7; 2:11.
42. Esther 4:16.
43. Aramaic: זיהרא עילאה. *Gates of Reincarnations* 6; 7; 29; 31; 32; and elsewhere in the Lurianic corpus.
44. *Gates of Reincarnations* 33; *Book of Likkutim* (ספר הליקוטים) on Genesis 5:21–22.
45. *Gate of Reincarnations* 33; Moses Hayyim Luzzatto (1707–46), *The Zeal of the Lord of Hosts* (קנאת ה' צבאות) 2:36; Abraham Isaac Kook (1865–1935), *Eight Collections* (שמונה קבצים) 8:157.
46. *Gate of Reincarnations* 36; *Book of Reincarnations* 72; *Book of Visions* (ספר החזיונות) 1:5; 1:9; 1:29; 3:3; 3:10; 3:14; 3:23; 3:29; 3:33; 4:16; 4:21–22; 4:25; 4:43; 4:48.
47. *Gate of the Spirit of Holiness* (שער רוח הקודש), Tikkun 27.
48. *Gate of Verses* (שער הפסוקים) on Exodus 1:8; *Gate of Intentions* (שער הכוונות), On the Passover (ענין הפסח) 1.
49. Hebrew: סיגים. Isaiah 1:22; Ezekiel 22:18–19; Proverbs 25:4; 26:23. In kabbalistic terms: קליפות. Common transliterations: *klippot, qlippoth*. Common literal translations: husks, shells, peels.
50. Hebrew: חיצונים.

51. Genesis 11:3; Exodus 1:14.
52. Exodus 1:22.
53. Biblical references to the Egyptian exile as an iron furnace include Deuteronomy 4:20; Jeremiah 11:4; 1 Kings 8:51.
54. *Gate of Intentions*, On Matters of the Night (ענין דרושי הלילה) 7; *Fruit of the Tree of Life* (פרי עץ חיים), Gate of the Bedtime "Hear O Israel" Prayer (שער קריאת שמע שעל המיטה) 5.
55. Aramaic: סטרא אחרא.
56. Hebrew: קריאת שמע שעל המיטה.
57. Deuteronomy 6:4.
58. Hebrew: יוד הי ויו הי.
59. Hebrew: פרח. Numbers 17:8 (17:23 MT) (וְהִנֵּה פָּרַח מַטֵּה אַהֲרֹן לְבֵית לֵוִי).
60. Hebrew: מרחפת. Genesis 1:2 (וְרוּחַ אֱלֹהִים מְרַחֶפֶת עַל פְּנֵי הַמָּיִם).
61. Psalm 149:5 (יְרַנְּנוּ עַל מִשְׁכְּבוֹתָם).
62. Psalm 149:6 (רוֹמְמוֹת אֵל בִּגְרוֹנָם וְחֶרֶב פִּיפִיּוֹת בְּיָדָם).
63. Zohar II (שמות) 7b.
64. *Four Hundred Shekels of Silver* (ארבע מאות שקל כסף), p. 241 in the Hebrew edition of the Lurianic corpus, ed. Yehuda Tzvi Brandwein; *Book of Reincarnations* 72.
65. Psalm 2:7.
66. Luke 1:26–38; John 1:1–5.
67. Matthew 3:16–17; Mark 1:9–11; Luke 3:21–22.
68. Exodus 24:18; 34:28; Deuteronomy 9:9; 9:18; 10:10.
69. *Book of Visions* 1:12; 1:26.
70. Zohar II (שמות) 8a.
71. Baruch Shalom Ashlag, quoting his father, appendix (ברכת שלום) to the Ladder commentary (הסולם) on Zohar II (שמות) 8a.
72. Yehuda Liebes, "New Directions in Kabbalah Research" (כיוונים חדשים בחקר הקבלה), *Pe'amim: Studies in Oriental Jewry* 50 (1992): 150–70, esp. 166–67 and n55 [Hebrew]; Liebes, "Two Young Roes of a Doe: The Secret Sermon of Isaac Luria before His Death" (תרין אורזילין דאיילתא: דרשתו הסודית של האר"י לפני מיתתו), *Jerusalem Studies in Jewish Thought* 10: *Proceedings of the Fourth International Conference on the History of Jewish Mysticism: Lurianic Kabbalah* (1992): 113–69, esp. 11–13 [Hebrew].
73. *Book of Reincarnations* 72; *Book of Visions* 1:9; 2:48; 3:14; 3:17; 5:17; Shmuel Vital, quoting his father, supplements (הגהות) to chap. 36 of *Gate of Reincarnations*.
74. *Book of Visions* 1:5; 1:6; 1:9; 1:14; 3:10; 3:20; 3:61.
75. Matthew 11:20–24; Luke 10:13–15.
76. *Book of Visions* 1:22; 1:23–24; 3:58–59.

77. Hebrew: עיבור, יניקה, מוחין. *Tree of Life* 22:1–2; *Gate of Verses* on 1 Samuel 2:19; *Gate of Reincarnations* 1.

78. Hebrew: מוחין דקטנות.

79. Hebrew: מוחין דגדלות.

80. Malachi 3:1; Matthew 24:43; Luke 12:39; 1 Thessalonians 5:2; 2 Peter 3:10; Revelation 3:3; 16:15.

81. Matthew 22:1–14; 25:1–13; 25:14–30; Luke 14:15–24; 19:11–27; *b.Shabbat* 153a.

82. *b.Sukkah* 52a–b; *Midrash Tanchuma*, Bereshit 1; *Genesis Rabbah* 75:6; *Book of Zerubbabel*; Zohar I (בראשית) 25b; 31b; Zohar II (רעיא מהימנא משפטים:) 119b–120; Zohar III (רעיא מהימנא בהעלותך:) 153b; (בלק) 203b; (רעיא מהימנא כי תצא:) 223a; 242b; 243b; 246b; 249b; 252a; (רעיא מהימנא פנחס:) 276b; 278b; 279a; *Book of Likkutim* on Genesis 17:15; on Ezekiel 37; *Book of Reincarnations* 72; Moses Hayyim Luzzatto, *515 Prayers* (תקט"ו תפילות) 31; 58; 184; 290; 327; 423; 434; 456; 460; 476; 494; 512; 515; Luzzatto, *New Tikkunim* (תיקונים חדשים) 1; 8; 14; 25; 30; 33; 43; 44; 53; Hillel Rivlin of Shklov (1757–1838), *Voice of the Turtledove* (קול התור); and elsewhere in midrashic texts, Zoharic literature, the Lurianic corpus, the writings of Moses Hayyim Luzzatto, and numerous other sources. For a comprehensive kabbalistic study of the two-messiah narrative, with special attention to the writings of Moses Hayyim Luzzatto and the Vilna Gaon, see Aryeh Shapira, *Great Salvations to His King* (מגדיל ישועות מלכו) (Jerusalem: self-published, 2018) [Hebrew]. For an academic treatment of the topic, see Martha Himmelfarb, *Jewish Messiahs in a Christian Empire: A History of the Book of Zerubbabel* (Cambridge, MA: Harvard University Press, 2017).

83. *b.Niddah* 61b (מצוות בטלות לעתיד לבוא); *Gate of Reincarnations* 1.

84. Shimon Agassi (1852–1914), *Sons of Aaron* (בני אהרון) on *Gate of Reincarnations* 1, sec. 9 [Hebrew]; Daniel Frisch (1935–2005) on *Gate of Reincarnations* 1 (מתוק מדבש) (Jerusalem: Daat Yosef Institute, 2006), 1:7 [Hebrew].

CHAPTER 4

1. Genesis 4:22; 6:1–2; Zohar I (הקדמת ספר הזוהר) 9b; (בראשית) 19b; 55a; III (אחרי מות) 76b–77a; Tikkunei Zohar 69:119a; New Zohar: Midrash Ruth 81a–b (other versions: 99a).

2. Zohar I (בראשית) 23a; 25a–b; 37a; 58a; (חיי שרה) 126a; III (בלק) 207b–208a; New Zohar: Midrash Ruth 81a–b (other versions: 99a).

3. Zohar I (הקדמת ספר הזוהר) 9b.

4. Ezekiel 1:10.

5. Isaiah 6:2.

6. *b.Pesachim* 94a.

7. Zohar III (כי תצא: רעיא מהימנא) 276a; Tikkunei Zohar 21:58a; *Tree of Life* 49:6.

8. Yehuda Fetaya, sometimes spelled Judah Fttaya (1859–1942), *The Offering of Judah* (מנחת יהודה). Originally published in Baghdad, 1933; reprinted several times in Jerusalem; alternative title: *The Spirits Speak* (רוחות מספרות). For a different English translation of the episodes discussed in this chapter, see Yehuda Fetaya, *Minhat Yehuda: The Offering of Judah*, trans. Avraham Leader, ed. Yehuda Herskowitz (Jerusalem: HaKtav Institute, 2010).

9. Fetaya, *Minhat Yehuda*, 287–303 (138–43 in the Hebrew edition of 1985). The senior rabbi of Baghdad is Yosef Hayyim (1835–1909), also known as the Ben Ish Hai (בן איש חי). His mentor, the Hebron-based rabbi, is Eliyahu Suleiman Mani (1818–99).

10. Yoram Bilu, while acknowledging some of the psychological dimensions in the writings of Yehuda Fetaya, sees him mostly as a mystical interpreter of dreams, while Mark Verman treats him primarily as an exorcist: Yoram Bilu, "Between Vienna and Baghdad: On a Mystical Tradition of 'Psychoanalytic' Dream Interpretations" (בין וינה לבגדאד: על מסורת קבלית של פירושי חלומות 'פסיכואנליטיים'), in *Fleeting Dreams and Possessive Dybbuks: On Dreams and Possession in Jewish and Other Cultures* (כחלום יעוף וכדיבוק יאחז: על חלומות ודיבוקים בישראל ובעמים), ed. Rachel Elior, Yoram Bilu, Avigdor Shinan, and Yair Zakovitch (Jerusalem: The Magnes Press at the Hebrew University, 2013), 165–88; Mark Verman, "R. Judah Ftayya: His Exploits as an Exorcist," *Australian Journal of Jewish Studies* 30 (2017): 199–232.

11. *Gate of Intentions* (שער הכוונות), On the New Year (ענין ראש השנה) 7–9.

12. Hebrew: כף הקלע. 1 Samuel 25:29; *Gate of Reincarnations* (שער הגלגולים) 22.

13. Ruth 1:17.

14. The other rabbi is Shimon Agassi (1852–1914), author of *Sons of Aaron* (בני אהרון), commonly considered the definitive commentary on *Gate of Reincarnations*.

15. Harold Bloom, *The Anxiety of Influence: A Theory of Poetry* (New York: Oxford University Press, 1973).

16. Job 31:2 (חֵלֶק אֱלוֹהַּ מִמָּעַל).

17. *b.Shabbat* 30a; *b.Niddah* 61b.

18. *Gate of Reincarnations* 22 (מתדבקים בו בהסתר גדול).

19. Fetaya, *Minhat Yehuda*, 307 (145 in the Hebrew edition of 1985).

20. *Book of Likkutim* on Jeremiah 8:13 (וְאֶתֵּן לָהֶם יַעַבְרוּם); Leviticus 25:49 (אוֹ דֹדוֹ אוֹ בֶן דֹּדוֹ יִגְאָלֶנּוּ).

21. Fetaya, *Minhat Yehuda*, 353–87 (164–76 in the Hebrew edition of 1985).

22. Fetaya, *Minhat Yehuda*, 374–75 (171–72 in the Hebrew edition of 1985).

23. *b.Megillah* 11a; *b.Shabbat* 30a; *y.Chagigah* 2:2; *Pesikta Rabbati* 28.

24. Jeremiah 29:21–23; *b.Sanhedrin* 93a; *Pirkei de-Rabbi Eliezer* 33; *Midrash Tanchuma*, Vayikra 6; *Pesikta de-Rav Kahana*, Buber Recension 25.

25. *Gate of the Spirit of Holiness* (שער רוח הקודש), Tikkun 20.

26. *The Unknown*, dir. Tod Browning (Metro-Goldwyn-Mayer, 1927).

27. *m.Sotah* 9:15.

28. Isaiah 33:14.

29. Isaiah 29:18.

30. For a different translation and discussion of this essay, see Kook, *The Souls of the World of Chaos* (trans., introd., and notes Bezalel Naor). For a discussion of Lurianic Kabbalah and Jungian psychology, see Sanford L. Drob, *Kabbalistic Visions: C. G. Jung and Jewish Mysticism*, 2nd ed. (London: Routledge, 2023).

31. Gertrude Stein, *Three Lives*, 1909; Rainer Maria Rilke, *The Notebooks of Malte Laurids Brigge*, 1910; Hermann Hesse, *Steppenwolf*, 1927; Djuna Barnes, *Nightwood*, 1936; Flannery O'Connor, *Wise Blood*, 1952.

32. Yehuda Leib Ashlag, "On Conclusion of the Zohar" (מאמר לסיום הזוהר), in *A Gift of the Bible*, trans. Samuel R. Anteby (Jerusalem: Research Centre of Kabbalah, 1984), 129–30.

33. Jude 1:8–16.

34. Fetaya, *Minhat Yehuda*, 358 (165 in the Hebrew edition of 1985).

35. Fetaya, *Minhat Yehuda*, 363–68 (167–69 in the Hebrew edition of 1985).

36. Zohar III (ויקרא) 15a.

37. *m.Avot* 4:11; Fetaya, *Minhat Yehuda*, 357–63 (165–67 in the Hebrew edition of 1985).

38. Some literary prototypes include stories about delinquent spirits that Hayyim Vital records in his *Book of Visions* and similar episodes in the various hagiographies of Isaac Luria, most notably the early seventeenth-century letters of Solomon Shlumil of Dreznitz (שבחי האר"י).

CHAPTER 5

1. Carl Gustav Jung, "The Role of the Unconscious," in *Civilization in Transition: The Collected Works of C. G. Jung*, vol. 10, trans. R. F. C. Hull, 2nd ed. (Stanford: Stanford University Press, 1970), pars. 17–19; Drob, *Kabbalistic Visions*, 142–43.

2. Zohar III (בהעלותך) 152a–b.

3. Hesiod, *Works and Days* 42–201.

4. John 1:1–5; Colossians 1:15–22.

5. David Andrews, "Of Love, Scorn, and Contradiction: An Interpretive Overview of Gilbert Sorrentino's *Imaginative Qualities of Actual Things,*" *The Review of Contemporary Fiction* 23, no. 1 (2003): 9–44, esp. 23–24.

6. Zohar II (משפטים) 99a–b.

7. Aramaic: רשימו.

8. *Tree of Life* 6:1–6.

9. Tikkunei Zohar 14a–b.

10. *Tree of Life* 7:1; *Gate of Introductions* (שער ההקדמות), Second Treatise on the World of *Akudim* (דרוש ב' בעולם העקודים).

11. *Tree of Life* 7:1–2; *Gate of Introductions*, First Treatise on Reaching and Reaching Not (דרוש בענין מטי ולא מטי).

12. *Tree of Life* 7:1; *Gate of Introductions*, Fifth Treatise on Reaching and Reaching Not (דרוש ה' בענין מטי ולא מטי).

13. Jeremiah 31:22 (31:21 MT).

14. Exodus 16:32–34; *Tree of Life* 7:3; Immanuel Hai Ricchi (1688–1743), *Mishnat Hasidim* 1.3.4 (סדר זרעים, מסכת אורות הטעמים, פרק ד').

15. Proverbs 12:4.

16. Aramaic: דלית לה מגרמה כלום.

17. Isaiah 30:26.

18. Zohar I (בראשית) 23b; Tikkunei Zohar 6:21a–22a.

19. Galatians 3:28–29.

20. Rabbi Aryeh Kaplan compiles and translates commentaries from several Hebrew sources in *The Lost Princess and Other Kabbalistic Tales by Rebbe Nachman of Breslov* (Jerusalem: Breslov Research Institute; Woodstock, VT: Jewish Lights, 2005), 25–51. The anonymous author of *The Chariots of the King* (מרכבות המלך) offers a vastly different commentary (Jerusalem: Beer Eliyahu, 2020), 109–58 [Hebrew].

21. 1 Kings 18.

22. Hebrew: רוח סערה, ענן גדול, אש מתלקחת, קליפת נוגה (Ezekiel 1:4). In this case, Rome, although it succeeded Greece, is the third rather than fourth *klippah*. This hermeneutical irregularity is based on the kabbalistic attempt to identify the twelve pirates with Esau and the eleven chiefs of Edom (Genesis 36:40–43). Edom has been traditionally regarded as synonymous with Rome.

23. Steinberg, *The Foundation of Wisdom*, 147–50 [Hebrew].

24. Hebrew: צמצום ב'.

25. Hebrew: את.

26. Yehuda Leib Ashlag, *Preamble to the Wisdom of the Kabbalah* (פתיחה לחוכמת הקבלה), par. 135; Steinberg, *The Foundation of Wisdom*, 152.

27. Zohar I (בראשית) 15a. Also, Tikkunei Zohar 5:19a; New Tikkunei Zohar 121d.

BIBLIOGRAPHY

Allen, Woody, dir. *Sleeper*. United Artists, 1973.

Anderson, Michael, dir. *Logan's Run*. Metro-Goldwyn-Mayer, 1976.

Andrews, David. "Of Love, Scorn, and Contradiction: An Interpretive Overview of Gilbert Sorrentino's *Imaginative Qualities of Actual Things*." *The Review of Contemporary Fiction* 23, no. 1 (2003): 9–44.

Anidjar, Gil. "Jewish Mysticism Alterable and Unalterable: On Orienting Kabbalah Studies and the Zohar of Christian Spain." *Jewish Social Studies* 3, no. 1 (1996): 89–157.

Ashlag, Yehuda. *A Gift of the Bible*, translated by Samuel R. Anteby. Jerusalem: Research Centre of Kabbalah, 1984.

Bal, Mieke. "Dealing/With/Women: Daughters in the Book of Judges." In *The Book and the Text: The Bible and Literary Theory*, edited by Regina M. Schwartz, 16–39. Cambridge, MA: Basil Blackwell, 1990.

———. *Death and Dissymmetry: The Politics of Coherence in the Book of Judges*. Chicago: The University of Chicago Press, 1988.

———. *Lethal Love: Feminist Literary Readings of Biblical Love Stories*. Bloomington: Indiana University Press, 1987.

Barnes, Djuna. *Nightwood*. London: Faber & Faber, 1936.

Bartel, Paul, dir. *Death Race 2000*. New World Pictures, 1975.

Baudrillard, Jean. *The Vital Illusion*, edited by Julia Witwer. New York: Columbia University Press, 2000.

Ben-Shlomo, Joseph. *The Mystical Theology of Moses Cordovero* [תורת האלוהות של ר' משה קורדובירו]. Jerusalem: The Bialik Institute, 1965.

Bilu, Yoram. "Between Vienna and Baghdad: On a Mystical Tradition of 'Psychoanalytic' Dream Interpretations" [בין וינה לבגדאד: על מסורת 'פסיכואנליטית' של פירושי חלומות]. In *Fleeting Dreams and Possessive Dybbuks: On Dreams and Possession in Jewish and Other Cultures* [כחלום יעוף וכדיבוק יאחז: על חלומות ודיבוקים בישראל ובעמים], edited by Rachel Elior, Yoram Bilu, Avigdor Shinan, and Yair Zakovitch, 165–88. Jerusalem: The Magnes Press at the Hebrew University, 2013.

Bloom, Harold. *The Anxiety of Influence: A Theory of Poetry*. New York: Oxford University Press, 1973.

Browning, Tod, dir. *The Unknown*. Metro-Goldwyn-Mayer, 1927.

Brueggemann, Walter. "Fidelity and the Seduction of Certitude." Lecture given at the University of Findlay. October 17, 2014. https://youtu.be/Cs2aHsbUBZw.

———. *Texts under Negotiation: The Bible and Postmodern Imagination.* Minneapolis: Fortress Press, 1993.

Cole, Peter. *The Poetry of Kabbalah: Mystical Verse from the Jewish Tradition.* New Haven, CT: Yale University Press, 2012.

Dan, Joseph. *Jewish Mysticism and Jewish Ethics.* Seattle: University of Washington Press, 1986.

Donaldson, Laura E. "Cyborgs, Ciphers, and Sexuality: Re-Theorizing Literary and Biblical Character." *Semeia* 63 (1993): 81–96.

Drob, Sanford L. *Kabbalistic Visions: C. G. Jung and Jewish Mysticism*, 2nd ed. London: Routledge, 2023.

Faierstein, Morris, trans. *Jewish Mystical Autobiographies: Book of Visions and Book of Secrets.* New York: Paulist Press, 1999.

Fetaya, Yehuda. *Minhat Yehuda: The Offering of Judah*, translated by Avraham Leader, edited by Yehuda Herskowitz. Jerusalem: HaKtav Institute, 2010. Originally published 1933.

Fishbane, Eitan P. *The Art of Mystical Narrative: A Poetics of the Zohar.* New York: Oxford University Press, 2018.

Gam Hacohen, Moran. *Kabbalah Research in Israel: Historiography, Ideology, and the Struggle for Cultural Capital* [מחקר הקבלה בישראל: היסטוריוגרפיה, אידאולוגיה ומאבק על הון תרבותי]. Tel Aviv: Resling, 2016.

Garb, Jonathan. *Yearnings of the Soul: Psychological Thought in Modern Kabbalah.* Chicago: The University of Chicago Press, 2015.

Hansel, David. "The Origin in the Thought of Rabbi Yehuda Halevy Ashlag: Ṣimṣum of God or Ṣimṣum of the World?" *Kabbalah* 7 (2002): 37–46.

Hesse, Hermann. *Steppenwolf*, translated by Basil Creighton. New York: Henry Holt & Co., 1929. Originally published 1927.

Himmelfarb, Martha. *Jewish Messiahs in a Christian Empire: A History of the Book of Zerubbabel.* Cambridge, MA: Harvard University Press, 2017.

Huss, Boaz. "Altruistic Communism: The Modernist Kabbalah of Rabbi Ashlag" [קומוניזם אלטרואיסטי: הקבלה המודרניסטית של הרב אשלג]. *Iyunim* 16 (2006): 109–30.

———. *Mystifying Kabbalah: Academic Scholarship, National Theology, and New Age Spirituality*, translated by Elana Lutsky. New York: Oxford University Press, 2020. Originally published 2016.

Idel, Moshe. *Kabbalah: New Perspectives.* New Haven, CT: Yale University Press, 1988.

Jellinek, Adolf. *Bet ha-Midrasch* [בית המדרש]. Jerusalem: Wahrmann Books, 1967. Originally published 1853.

Jung, Carl Gustav. "The Role of the Unconscious." In *Civilization in Transition: The Collected Works of C. G. Jung*, vol. 10, translated by R. F. C. Hull, 3–28. Stanford: Stanford University Press, 1970. Originally published 1918.

Kaplan, Aryeh, trans. *The Lost Princess and Other Kabbalistic Tales by Rebbe Nachman of Breslov*. Jerusalem: Breslov Research Institute; Woodstock, VT: Jewish Lights, 2005.

Kook, Abraham Isaac. *The Souls of the World of Chaos*, translated by Bezalel Naor. New York: Orot/Kodesh, 2023. Originally published 1913.

Koren, Israel. "The Transformation of the Kabbalistic Vessel in the Thought of Rabbi Yehuda Ashlag and Martin Buber" [הטרנספורמציה במושג הכלי הקבלי במחשבתם של הרב יהודה אשלג ושל מרטין בובר]. Unpublished article available on the author's personal website. https://independent. academia.edu/IsraelKoren.

Lachower, Fishel. *On the Border of Old and New* [על גבול הישן והחדש]. Jerusalem: The Bialik Institute, 1951.

Lavi, Tony. *The Secret of Cosmogony: The Law of Divinity and the Essence of Mankind in the Studies of R. Yehuda Halevi Ashlag* [סוד הבריאה: תורת האלוהות ותכלית האדם בקבלת הרי"ל אשלג]. A possibly more accurate translation of the title: *The Essence of Creation: Theology and the Purpose of Humanity in the Kabbalah of Rabbi Yehuda Leib Ashlag*. Jerusalem: Bialik Institute, 2007.

Liebes, Yehuda. "New Directions in Kabbalah Research" [כיוונים חדשים בחקר הקבלה]. *Pe'amim: Studies in Oriental Jewry* 50 (1992): 150–70.

———. "Two Young Roes of a Doe: The Secret Sermon of Isaac Luria before His Death" [תרין אורזילין דאיילתא: דרשתו הסודית של האר"י לפני מיתתו]. *Jerusalem Studies in Jewish Thought* 10: *Proceedings of the Fourth International Conference on the History of Jewish Mysticism: Lurianic Kabbalah* (1992): 113–69.

Lubitsch, Ernst, dir. *The Smiling Lieutenant*. Paramount Pictures, 1931.

Morrissey, Christopher S. "The Greek and Latin Dress of Judith: '*Ex Virtute Pendebat*'? (Idt 10:4 Vg)." Paper presented at the virtual Pacific Northwest regional conference of the American Academy of Religion and Society of Biblical Literature, May 14, 2022.

Ochs, Carol. *Behind the Sex of God: Toward a New Consciousness Transcending Matriarchy and Patriarchy*. Boston: Beacon Press, 1977.

O'Connor, Flannery. *Wise Blood*. New York: Harcourt, Brace & Co., 1952.

Raposa, Michael. "Some Applications of the Law of Mind." Paper presented at the 5th Biennial Philosophy of Communication Conference, June 7, 2022. Sponsored by the Department of Communication and Rhetorical Studies and the Communication Ethics Institute at Duquesne University.

Rilke, Rainer Maria. *The Notebooks of Malte Laurids Brigge*, translated by Burton Pike. Champaign, IL: Dalkey Archive Press, 2008. Originally published 1910.

Rivera, Alex, dir. *Sleep Dealer*. Maya Entertainment, 2008.

Sack, Bracha. *The Kabbalah of Rabbi Moshe Cordovero* [בשערי הקבלה של רבי משה קורדובירו]. Beersheba: Ben-Gurion University of the Negev Press, 1995.

Schroer, Silvia. *Wisdom Has Built Her House: Studies on the Figure of Sophia in the Bible*, translated by Linda M. Maloney and William McDonough. Collegeville, MN: Liturgical Press/Michael Glazier, 2000. Originally published 1996.

Schüssler Fiorenza, Elisabeth. *But She Said: Feminist Practices of Biblical Interpretation*. Boston: Beacon Press, 1992.

———. *Jesus: Miriam's Child, Sophia's Prophet: Critical Issues in Feminist Christology*. New York: Continuum, 1994.

———. *Revelation: Vision of a Just World*. Minneapolis: Fortress Press, 1991.

Scott, Ridley, dir. *Blade Runner*. Warner Brothers, 1982.

Segol, Marla. *Kabbalah and Sex Magic: A Mythical-Ritual Genealogy*. University Park: Pennsylvania University Press, 2021.

Shalev, Alon. "Orthodox Theology in the Age of the Search for Meaning: The Life and Works of Rabbi Isaac Hutner" [תאולוגיה אורתודוכסית בעידן בקשת המשמעות: חייו והגותו של הרב יצחק הוטנר]. Doctoral diss., The Hebrew University of Jerusalem, 2020.

Shapira, Aryeh. *Great Salvations to His King* [מגדיל ישועות מלכו]. Jerusalem: self-published, 2018.

Sheinberger, Mordechai. *At the King's Gate: Four-Layered Commentary and Essays on Esther* [בשער המלך: לקט פירושים וביאורים על מגילת אסתר בדרך הפרד"ס]. Or Ganuz, Israel: Or Daat, 2017. Originally published 2000.

Sherwood, Yvonne. *The Prostitute and the Prophet: Hosea's Marriage in Literary-Theoretical Perspective*. Sheffield, UK: Sheffield Academic Press, 1996.

Stein, Gertrude. *Three Lives*. New York: Dover, 1994. Originally published 1909.

Steinberg, David. *The Foundation of Wisdom* [יסוד החוכמה]. Jerusalem: Otot, 2014.

Sweeney, Marvin A. *Jewish Mysticism: From Ancient Times through Today*. Grand Rapids, MI: William B. Eerdmans, 2020.

Tishby, Isaiah. *Paths of Faith and Heresy: Essays on Kabbalah and Sabbateanism* [נתיבי אמונה ומינות: מסות ומחקרים בספרות הקבלה והשבתאות]. Jerusalem: The Magnes Press at the Hebrew University, 1964.

———. *Studies in Kabbalah and Its Branches* [מחקרים: חקרי קבלה ושלוחותיה ומקורות]. Jerusalem: The Magnes Press at the Hebrew University, 1982.

Vadim, Roger, dir. *Barbarella*. Paramount Pictures, 1968.

Verman, Mark. "R. Judah Ftayya: His Exploits as an Exorcist." *Australian Journal of Jewish Studies* 30 (2017): 199–232.

Zuriel, Moshe. *Treasures of the Luminaries of Israel* [אוצרות גדולי ישראל]. Jerusalem: Yarid Hasfarim, 2000.

INDEX